The Sweet Dell

The Sweet Dell

The True Story of
One Family's Fight to Save Jews
in Nazi-Occupied Holland

by

Nicholas John Briejer

PILGRIM SPIRIT COMMUNICATIONS

For my mother

Contents

viii

Author's Note

At times, the world of "nonfiction" and that of "truth" struggle to coexist. On rare occasions this involves an unscrupulous author, but mostly the tensions result from misunderstandings between reader and author that could have been easily resolved with an explicit qualification of the work.

The following is a true story—as true as the imperfect memories of those who inhabit its pages. As author, I remained faithful to the numerous interviews conducted and never altered any aspect of the stories provided me. Understandably, those I interviewed remembered some details differently. When this occurred, I worked to include the version that appeared the most likely, not the most dramatic.

At times, this book provides details that would seemingly not be available to an author dealing with events that occurred so long ago. In each case, these were built from letters or diaries written during or soon after the war.

Though I am not an historian or a journalist, I have labored continuously to provide a rendering of this story faithful to its origins.

On a lesser note, I have included the characters' names as written in Dutch. These largely translate phonetically, except for "Piet," which is pronounced the same as Pete in America. Similarly, "Iet" is pronounced as Eat. Lastly, in my childhood home, we always referred to my grandmother as Anne. Her given name is Annaatje.

Book One

Chapter 1

I'VE ALWAYS PICTURED this particular day as cold, clear and breezy: a brisk day when the sun warms your front side while the cool air blowing in off the North Sea freezes your back. But really, I have no way of knowing. What I do know, is that on this day, this fall day in 1943, my grandfather listened to the heavy iron doors of a basement cell in the Gestapo's Amsterdam headquarters close behind him. And I know that in those first seconds of his imprisonment, as he heard the cell door lock, he felt a great weight lift from his shoulders and he settled into a peaceful calm.

My grandfather's name was Pieter Schoorl. I like to think I look like him. I share his longish face, lanky frame and boyish dimples. And when we smile, the same wrinkle of crow's feet frames our eyes. But I never knew my grandfather. He was forty years old when the Germans arrested him, the same age I am now.

This is the story of my grandparents, Pieter and Anne Schoorl, and the story of my mother, Marianne, and her four siblings. It's a war story. And though the last bombs fell over six decades ago—this war lives on.

The story begins, as do most of my mom's family's memories, within the quiet of their beloved farm nestled in the outskirts of the Dutch town of Bennekom: a serene, rural village two hours southeast of Amsterdam by train. Holland had been under German occupation for three-and-a-half years. The German blitzkrieg had pummeled the Allies and Hitler ruled Western Europe with impunity. The world was not yet familiar with the names such as Auschwitz and Sobibor, but the wholesale slaughter of Europe's Jewish population was underway.

Despite the bloody war, mornings on my grandfather's farm began quietly with the same pastoral calm it had enjoyed for generations. The rooster's crow signaled the dawn, and a light dew glistened in the morning sun. My grandfather awoke that fateful morning, as he had for years, in the upstairs bedroom of his large farmhouse, an expansive residence surrounded by seven acres of pasture and trees. He left the warmth of his bed and walked across the cold wood floor to the bathroom. Piet enjoyed routine. He put on a dress shirt and slacks and then descended the broad staircase to eat breakfast with his family.

Before the war, the dining room's two large south-facing picture windows drew in that morning sun, and my grandfather could have looked out at the twisted trunks of the fruit trees or at the swallows darting in and out of the small hayloft. The Nazis had since ordered black paper over every window to muffle the village's evening light and complicate the navigation of Allied planes that flew overhead en route to German cities. The rising sun illumined the black paper gray, and Piet sipped his morning tea in the company of its somber light.

It had been over a year since Piet offered to hide 3-year-old Eline van Leeuwen, a blonde-haired, blue-eyed Jewish girl. Eline was almost exactly one year younger than my mother, Marianne, and the two girls had quickly become fast friends. They usually sat side-by-side at the long breakfast table.

Eline was only the first of many Jews to find refuge at the farm. She had arrived unannounced during the dark of a summer night in '42. Her mother and father, Leo and Pauline, would eventually join their daughter, followed by many others who were forced to flee and had heard rumors of an isolated farm in Bennekom that would provide refuge. Piet's farmhouse filled up first, and then Piet's second home—the one just a few blocks away that he had purchased to house his laboratory. Piet wasn't a farmer, but a food scientist. When the two homes filled, the Schoorls then searched for other hiding places.

The breakfast place settings were arranged with care, silverware on clean linen, and teaspoons next to teacups. A tea cozy was wrapped warm around a steaming porcelain pot. Marianne's legs dangled beneath one of the three thick wooden leaves her mother and the maid secured within the heavy table, which now stretched the length of the room with over a dozen chairs set closely together to accommodate the guests. Jams, jellies, and butter surrounded loaves of bread. My mother was five-and-a-half years old that autumn. Her shiny auburn hair shared the same regal tones as the room's hardwood trim. Piet and Anne thought the farm a perfect place to raise a family. They wanted their children to grow up close to the earth, in a place where they could roam free. The gentle farm and adjacent woods were near idyllic and had remained so until the spring invasion of 1940. Jews seeking the safety of the farm still arrived unannounced in the cover of night. My mom no longer asked who the strangers were at her table. She ate quietly. No one talked about the war.

Piet left that morning by bicycle. He opened and closed the farm's gate, turned right out of his driveway and pedaled down a side street. He rode past a neighborhood of newer single-story brick homes and turned right again onto the main avenue leading to Bennekom proper.

The village knew my grandfather as Dr. Pieter Schoorl. He passed near his lab, a tall, sturdy-looking stucco house just a few paces off the town's main street. Glass beakers and Bunsen burners rested on waist-high tables and rows of neatly organized chemicals lined the shelves of the first floor. Piet's three employees lived on the second floor and helped care for the Jews hiding in the spacious attic. The morning sun cast the building's shadow across the road.

Piet sat erect on his tall bike pedaling slowly. He wore a brown tweed coat with patches of tan leather sewn into the elbows. His tires bumped over the old cobblestones leading to the train station. The ride took no longer than ten minutes. He parked his bike and boarded the train bound for Amsterdam.

Though a successful businessman and owner of one of only two food science laboratories in Holland, Piet took a job in the city. He made the trip three times a week. And though I have never discovered proof of the fact, logic suggests the job provided my grandfather a cover story—a reason to travel back and forth between Bennekom and Amsterdam. For on his trips into the city he often smuggled falsified identification papers and stolen food-ration cards. On his way back, he smuggled Jewish children into the safer, rural countryside. The heavy passenger car vibrated rhythmically beneath him. Wet pastures, quintessential black-and-white cows, and trees turning fall-brown streaked past.

The train arrived at Amsterdam's cavernous Central Station. Piet stepped off, walked down the stairs and out from beneath the cover of the structure's immense roof. He passed over a small bridge spanning a canal and travelled the short distance toward the Swaab Cosmetic factory.

Before the war my grandfather's stride suggested levity. He ambled through the cindered trails of Bennekom with his children in tow, naming the flora and fauna and stopping habitually to converse with strangers. He had a habit of putting his hand on your shoulder when he spoke. But by 1943, his gait was pinched, and his lope weighted. The joy had drained from him.

Amsterdam's Jewish quarter was no longer Jewish. The Nazis had nearly completed their bloody work. Only a few stragglers remained, hidden behind false walls or—if their features allowed—assuming non-Jewish identities, and hidden in plain view. Piet tried to put out of his mind the things he had seen on those streets. He entered the factory, walked to his office, removed his coat and readied for work.

Less than one day earlier, while Piet slept, the Gestapo arrested a young Jewish woman named Hildegard Sara Wittner along with her fiancé. They found within the folds of the couple's clothes two falsified identification cards my grandfather had provided them. The Nazis interrogated Ms. Wittner. She told them that the man who gave her the identification had not revealed his name. She only knew where he worked.

The Germans approached the factory soon after my grandfather arrived. Somehow, Piet was alerted, and the fact provided Piet with what would prove to be a few terribly valuable minutes. Piet likely assumed the Germans were there for him, and he used those minutes to convince a co-worker to put on his brown tweed coat and casually leave the building. In the time it took the Gestapo to locate Piet, the co-worker and Piet's coat managed to slip out of the Swaab factory undetected. With the young Ms. Wittner likely present to identify the anonymous man who had tried to save her life, the Gestapo arrested Dr. Pieter Schoorl for the violation of Penal Code 74—providing false identity papers to a Jew. A conversation ensued regarding Piet's coat. The Germans didn't believe Piet when he said he often went to work without a coat. The Swaab employees assured the Nazis Piet was telling the truth. "He's a bit of an eccentric," said the owner of the factory. The Gestapo left the building, secured the still-anonymous prisoner in their vehicle and drove towards their headquarters.

THE ORNATE OAK STAIRCASE in my grandparents' home originally adorned a castle in France. It had been dismantled and shipped to Holland and reassembled in the stately farmhouse. The Schoorls' black phone hung in the hallway adjacent the stairs. The ring echoed up toward the second floor and also down the hall and into the living room and into the home's cramped kitchen.

I don't know who answered the phone that morning. But I do know that around that time of day my grandmother, Anne, always made the day's soup. In the late morning or early afternoon, she could be found standing in the long, narrow, and somewhat dark kitchen with a white apron wrapped around her solid frame, her strong fingers slicing fresh vegetables for her broth. And Anne could hear Pauline van Leeuwen's highheeled shoes clicking across the upstairs' wood floor. Though Pauline could never leave the confines of the home, she always brushed and styled her dark hair, put on her make-up, and picked out one of her fashionable dresses before descending the staircase.

The home almost always appeared a tranquil place, one wrapped in the gentle domestic rhythms that accompany most households. The birds did not notice the war. There was no blood spilled, and one had to look closely to see the thin margins separating survival from death.

By the time I knew my grandmother, she appeared a tough, hard woman. I remember her wide hands. I remember watching her cart raw wool, and then spin it into yarn on an antique spinning wheel in the living room of my childhood home in America. She pursed her lips as she spun, emanating a half-whistling, half-wheezing sound that felt peacefully meditative. These are perhaps the most gentle memories I have of her. Otherwise, Anne was coldly stoic. It's hard for me to envision Anne as a young woman answering that phone. It's hard to see her panic or shed tears.

Someone from the underground in Amsterdam was on the other end of the line—Piet had been arrested. The Gestapo could arrive at the farm any minute.

If my grandmother grieved outright, it was brief. The war years had already proven her an effective and decisive force. Though it was Piet who masterminded their role in the Dutch underground, it was Anne whose sturdy nature and resourcefulness kept their guests fed and safe, her role similar to a veteran sergeant whose boots on the ground made plans possible. Anne remained on the phone dialing numbers. She needed a new hiding place for all of the Jews . . . both homes. And she needed to hide her own children too. The Nazis had made it very clear—if you hide a Jew you will be treated like a Jew. No one was safe. And it all had to be done in the light of day . . . they needed a car. Anne continued on the phone while bags were hastily packed. Pauline dressed her daughter for the cold.

Minutes later, Anne called outside to Gerard, the farm's handyman. She gave him careful instructions as to where each of her five children needed to be hidden. Gerard mounted his bicycle and turned down the gently curving driveway. The frenzy within the home disappeared behind him. He passed beyond the farm's gate and turned right following the same path Piet had travelled earlier that morning, next to the truck-sized hedge that obscured the farm from view on two sides, then near the lab and onto the stone road leading into the heart of the village. He continued beyond the high steeples of the town's two churches and next to the rows of shops, the bakery and green grocer, and turned again, into a cramped side-street toward my mom's school. He waited outside until the classes ended and my mother walked out of the building.

"It's not safe for you to go home," Gerard said. "Your mom has made arrangements." Marianne didn't ask any questions. The kindergartner quietly climbed on the back of Gerard's bike. As was usual, my mother was told nothing. No one ever explained the war to her using particulars. No one explained exactly why her family hid the Jews. Hitler was never explained, nor the fact that his armies now ruled nearly all of Europe. But Marianne understood the war in other ways. She had learned about the war the way children learn most things, not by what they're told but by what they witness. Marianne was educated by the eyes of the Jewish parents who sat across from her at breakfast silently anguishing over the safety of their own children. She learned about war as she watched the weight of it press down upon her own father, as that light that used to animate him slowly dimmed. She understood the glare of the professional soldiers stationed on the intersections. As her small body and mind grew toward the light like the bright green leaves of the fruit trees on her farm, the echoes of war that met her daily braided their darker strands inside her. She knew what "not safe" meant. The rows of neat brick homes blurred past as Gerard pedaled toward the residence of a family friend.

DUTCH CITIZENS regularly gathered outside the gates of the Nazis' Amsterdam headquarters hoping to hear the news of a loved one locked inside. The Dutch had named the building Euterpe Street, after the road that skirted the compound. Thick ivy crawled up sections of the structure's three brick stories: a pleasant green accenting the redbrick walls and elegant white window detail. Blood stains turned rusty brown on the cold cement floor of the building's prison cells. Throughout Holland, the name Euterpe Street was synonymous with death. The vehicle carrying Piet entered the gate. The Germans' newest prisoner remained silent during the drive and throughout his processing.

When the little Jewish girl first arrived in Piet's home, it felt good to be doing something to help. He had made each of his four older children recite the names of their siblings in order of their birth, adding Eline's name second-to-the-last: "Hans, Iet, Ruud, Marianne, Eline, Helene." He had them repeat the names over and over again to prepare them if anyone ever asked about Eline. At first, Piet enjoyed the cat-and-mouse.

Piet faced the Germans as they asked their questions. He remained mute. It wasn't his life he had worried about. The responsibilities that had hung on Piet during the last year were ones that shouldn't hang on any man, and the weight had pushed too hard. But without his coat, the Germans didn't have Piet's ID, or his address. And now his war diluted into one sublimely simple task—to remain silent. A part of him couldn't help but revel in the simplicity of it.

Within hours the farm and the lab were emptied. Members of the Dutch underground helped Anne. She removed the dining room table's three extra leaves and dismantled the extra beds. Every cupboard and drawer of the large home had to be cleaned of evidence. No one knew how much time they had. When the job was done, the farm was nearly deserted. The swallows still darted under the small hayloft and the fruit trees continued to drop their autumn leaves, but they did so in relative obscurity. Only Anne and the maid remained, waiting.

It was only a matter of time before the Germans found the farm. They would come to the closed gate, their vehicle idling as they read the words "de Soetendael" carved into the top rail.

All of Piet's aged children still refer to the farm by this name, de Soetendael—the Sweet Dell.

The present-day gate leading to the farm

Chapter 2

THREE DECADES AFTER Piet's arrest, I tapped a small egg-eating spoon on the top of my soft-boiled egg, peeled off a few bits of cracked shell and placed them in the bottom of the egg-holder. "Weren't you scared during the war?" I asked my mom. The subject came up every now and again. Shaky images of black-and-white war footage filled my young head.

Mom sat at one end of our long dining-room table. Homemade jams and jellies, and a cardboard carton filled with Dutch chocolate sprinkles, surrounded a loaf of fresh bread. A quaint tea cozy was wrapped around a steaming porcelain pot. Mom carved off a slice of Dutch cheese, made an open-faced sandwich and ate it with a fork and knife. "The war never affected us children," she said between bites. "We were too young; we didn't know any different." Her jaw made a popping sound when she chewed.

In his dress shirt, slacks and a tie, Dad sat across from Mom, his beard trimmed tight. The same age as Mom, he grew up during the same war; he rarely commented. I scraped out the last bite of my egg. My sister asked to be excused from the table.

I had no reason to question Mom's assertions. I was in my first years of grade school, that innocent time when I still depended on my mother and father to supply my truths. When Mom told me the war didn't affect her, her eyes held steady with the strength of her conviction, and I believed every syllable.

I already knew that several Jewish families had hidden from the Nazis in my mom's childhood home. When the war ended, the Schoorl family did their best to forget those dark years. They had kept a few anecdotal tales alive, which became a sort of family folklore. I remember one story about my grandmother helping Dutch commandos stop a Nazi train in the night so they could liberate a prisoner, and another about how my grandmother stole her own bike back from the Germans after they took it from her. I never imagined that my grandmother was having anything less than an adventurously good time.

"It's just how the life was," Mom said. "One day you would come home and the home wouldn't be there anymore, and then the family just had to find another place to live." I remember her smiling when she said it.

I would become a grown man and a father before I began to understand our family's delusion. But in a way, deep inside, I think I always knew the truth. I am also fashioned by this tale.

Piet, Anne, and Hanneke

Chapter 3

I HAVE A FADED PHOTOGRAPH of Piet and Anne shot around 1935, five years before the German invasion. Piet sits grinning on his Douglas motorcycle. Anne is seated behind him with their eldest daughter Hanneke squeezed between them. Piet's loose-fitting, off-white suit hangs stylishly from his lanky frame. His goggles rest on his forehead. Hanneke looks to be around four, with a large bow in her hair, wearing white shorts and a blouse. Anne is also dressed in light colors, a skirt and sweater with a fashionable hat pulled over her ears. Her shiny white shoes rest on the motorcycle's rear foot pegs.

Piet's smile fills the picture. With his family seated behind him and the road twisting off into the flat Dutch horizon, Piet looks contented, in charge, and enjoying life. Anne's demeanor, however, looks strained and her face suggests discomfort. Maybe the small seat was too hard, or the dusty road too dusty. In some ways the photograph captures the early character of their marriage, for it was Anne who left her world for his. And no matter the fact that she loved her new life, she wore it awkwardly.

* * *

THE TWO HAD MET five years earlier at Anne's childhood home, a small dairy farm just outside of the rural town of Alkmaar in the province of Northern Holland. Anne was just emerging into womanhood. Piet was a visiting graduate student placed on the farm to study animal husbandry. The scene was a particularly Dutch one. Distant windmills waited for a breeze. Their broad sails caught the wind and turned a shaft that pumped water from the grid of drainage ditches cutting across the farm. The water emptied into elevated canals where it then flowed slowly back to the tireless sea from whence it came.

Anne was born and raised on that farm. The first of Jan and Greet Borst's nine children—seven daughters and two sons—her father removed her from school in the fourth grade to work on the farm full-time. For over a decade, Anne rose every morning at 4:00 a.m., dressed for the cold, and walked out into the dark and often rainy pastures. Along with her brothers and sisters, she corralled the cows into the barn.

The routine was painfully predictable. Anne tied a cow's rear feet together and, sitting on a small milking stool, she moved her hands from tit to tit, squeezing the milk into a pail, her head ducking the inevitable swat of the cow's hard tail. Seven-days-a-week, twice-a-day, Anne filled pail after pail with milk. She hated it.

Pieter Schoorl was a fit 24-year-old when he arrived at the Borsts' home. Already a bit of a ladies man, and I can only imagine his reaction after his first day at the farm, when he sat down to share dinner with the family, and watched as Jan's seven daughters slowly arrived at the table.

That first meal he shared with Anne's family was a far stretch from those Piet was used to receiving with his own. Piet's mother would lay out fine china for each meal, the silverware resting on bars of crystal. The Schoorl family ate properly and quietly, the sounds of fork and knife scraping against plates accompanied the occasional restrained conversation. The Borsts, on the other hand were carnival-loud, a constant din of voices, laughing and poking fun at each other. Before the end of Piet's first night, he had been affectionately nicknamed Proffie.

It's easy to picture Piet enjoying the company of Jan's daughters with a smooth ease. As a child, Piet made friends easily. He led his buddies into various forms of mischief and excelled in anything athletic. He played tennis, joined the rowing team, and learned to box.

Jan's daughters were smitten with Piet's charm. How the romance unfolded between Piet and Anne is as suspect as all of the particulars of this story. One version has it that Piet had eyes for one of Anne's younger sisters, and she certainly for him. But somehow, as was her nature, Anne bent circumstances in her favor, and somewhere amongst the milk cows and the damp green pastures, possibly in the small orchard, or in a cozy corner of the home itself, Piet and Anne became lovers. The two left the farm together; despite the protests of their parents the couple married and welcomed their first child, Hanneke, into the world nine months later on Sept. 2, 1930. Piet was twenty-six, his new wife, twenty-two.

Twelve days after Hanneke's birth, the economically depressed Germany held a Parliamentary election. The fiery political upstart, Adolf Hitler, and his National Socialist Labor Party, vowed to make Germany strong again. They promised to end government corruption, to refuse to pay more reparations for World War One, and to rid the country of parasitic capitalists—especially if they were Jews. All true Germans would have a job and a meal. To everyone's surprise—even his own—Hitler's party received 6,409,600 votes, gaining seventy seats in the Parliament and making the Nazis the second largest political party in Germany. Within a little more than two years, Hitler would be handed the chancellorship, and the Nazification of Germany would begin.

Newlyweds

Pre-war Bennekom

Chapter 4

MY MOTHER REMAINED faithful to her declaration that "the war never affected us" throughout my entire childhood. It wasn't until all of her four children were grown and gone and Mom moved out of the home she had raised us in that things began to change. Mom was now in her fifties, and if you asked her, she would remember this period as the hardest of her life. Despite their seven gently sloping acres and the wild salal and rhododendrons skirting the paths that ambled through their property and their regal view of the Olympic Mountains, Mom found little peace in her new setting. After Dad left for work, the solitude and silences closed in upon her. But it was never like my mom to ignore a problem once it had reared its head. Like her own mother, she always marched forward.

On the morning of her appointment, Mom worked to keep herself busy until midmorning, then started her sky blue Subaru and drove down her gravel driveway. She turned right onto Stavis Bay Road and passed the rotted black pilings of an old marina. The road continued next to the calm waters of the Hood Canal. An hour later she parked in front of a small office building next to a busy freeway.

"Tell me about your childhood," the therapist said to her. It wasn't the first time my mom had heard this clichéd line. She had seen several therapists in the last ten years, and they had all started like this, and when the subject of the war was breached Mom always answered the same.

"The war didn't affect me," she said earnestly. "War was all we knew; that's just the way life was." Mom's once-thick auburn hair had thinned and streaked gray.

Maybe she didn't deliver the line with the same blank-faced certainty she had with the previous therapists. Or maybe this therapist was simply better than the rest.

"That's not possible," the man said. "These were your formative years." Mom said nothing. She raised her hands, shrugged her shoulders, then dropped both and sat slumped on her chair looking down. "I remember nothing. I was only two when the war began."

The therapist looked into Mom's eyes and quietly said, "You can remember if you want to remember, Marianne. Take a few seconds . . . relax and breathe. Picture yourself as a child."

Mom left the air-conditioned building and walked across the hot blacktop and toward her car. "Go home and start writing," the therapist had said, "just one sentence at a time. It will start coming back to you."

I don't know if Mom believed him, or if she had any inclination to return home and put words to paper. For fifty years Mom's mind had kept her safe from her own memories; I imagine it was reluctant to drop its guard.

Mom started her car. She drove down a side street and onto the freeway onramp toward home. A nearby truck backfired, and the small explosion pulled her backward in time. For an instant her senses became young again. She smelled the burn of sulfur and heard the dull drone of bombers in the distant sky. She could no longer feel the steering wheel or see the pavement in front of her. She lost control of the vehicle and it turned into a ditch on the side of the road.

Chapter 5

O N AN EVENING in December 1939, a heavy snow fell on the village of Bennekom. The wide road that curved through the village was covered several feet deep, and benches and garbage cans disappeared under gentle rolling mounds of white. The large flakes accumulated on the two church steeples. The snow grew heavy and the white blankets slid off the roofs and into the drifts below. As the sun rose, the town remained silent. The train would not arrive on time, nor would the butcher open his store. Even the chronically punctual fires in the baker's brick ovens remained unlit and cold.

My mom and her siblings awoke to this new white world. Piet and Anne now had four children. Hanneke was nine, her younger sister, Iet, eight. The Schoorls' first boy, Ruud, had recently turned six, and my mother, Marianne, would be two in the coming month. The holly bushes bent low under the weight of the flakes, and most of the farm's greenery had simply vanished. Even the rooster's morning cry fell muted in the winter storm.

The three eldest children hurried through breakfast. They put on their coats, knit-wool gloves, and hats and slid the heavy garage door open just enough to squeeze their bundled bodies outside. The snowdrift angled steep in front of them, so steep the children couldn't manage more than a half step forward. They quickly realized that the entire household was imprisoned by white. And this is the first memory that any of the Schoorl children have of the war. For though the fighting had yet to begin, two dozen Dutch soldiers were stationed at the Schoorls' farm as part of a strategic troop dispersal.

The children returned inside. They walked past the young soldiers sleeping on temporary bunks in the old animal stalls of what used to be the home's attached barn since transformed into the garage.

Later that morning the soldiers took turns digging a pathway through the Soetendael's gravel drive. Hanneke, Iet and Ruud walked down the narrow trail. With the shovel-loads of snow piled high on each side, the path felt more like a tunnel to the children and they followed it past the open gate.

Piet and Anne had leased the large house because they thought it would provide a pleasant place to raise a family. The area was rural, but only a short walk or bike-ride to town and close enough to the major cities of Holland for Piet to maintain his work as a business consultant. After completing his PhD in 1936, Dr. Schoorl had started his own consulting company, providing scientific studies to large food manufacturers. Business was good, and Piet had since bought another home a few blocks away that housed his laboratory. The life he and Anne had created seemed, in most ways, nearly idyllic, and (barring a freak snowstorm) the days unfolded with a gentle, predictable rhythm. The maid usually helped Anne cook breakfast while the nanny roused the older three kids from their beds. Washed and dressed, the family ate together; then Piet walked to work at his lab, and Hans, Iet and Ruud rode their bikes to school—the girls often arguing over who would steer their tandem. The greengrocer delivered Anne's produce and picked up her list for the next delivery. The baker dropped off bread and milk. After everyone had left for the day, Anne would relax in her garden, or tend her beehives, or sometimes shop in town. Marianne was cared for by her nanny. At noon, the entire family returned to the farm for lunch. At 1:00 pm. Piet turned on the radio and everyone listened to the news. After the news the family returned to work and school. Dinners were served promptly at 6:00 p.m., tuck-ins at 7:30 p.m.

As the snowy morning gave way to afternoon, the children wandered out beyond the hedge and onto the road. Other villagers also trickled out from their warm homes.

As usual, the kids explored wherever they pleased. To the north and east the hedge enclosed their property. To the south and west the pastures of the Soetendael met the pastures of the two neighboring farms. The kids could be gone for hours. Neither Piet nor Anne would worry. They wanted their children outdoors in nature. Piet, in particular, made efforts to introduce the children to the woods beyond the farm. It was some of his favorite time. His children still remember the outings fondly.

On one particular day earlier that year, Iet had followed her father through the honeycomb of footpaths meandering across the wooded countryside in search of bugs. Piet loved the outdoors. The two walked under the canopy of oak and beech trees and near an ancient road built by the Romans until they came to a meadow.

Iet sat down in the summer sun. Thistles stretched toward the light, their pink blossoms open. She remained still and waited. Thistles attract all sorts of insects, and bugs lit upon the thorny weeds. Iet removed a cork from a test tube with an ether-soaked cotton ball placed in the bottom, and she slowly guided the tube over an interesting bug. The fumes of ether killed the insect, and Iet carefully placed it inside the glass.

The two walked back into the woods and toward Piet's lab. During the week, Piet worked hard. He put in long hours at the lab and traveled regularly to visit his customers throughout Holland. But he always found time for walks with his children. When Iet and Piet met fellow villagers during their outings, Piet would always stop to talk.

When they returned to the lab Piet inspected the insects. He placed the interesting specimens inside one of his many drawers filled with similarly entombed invertebrates.

Iet also remembers hunting for salamanders, and how, as the two walked through the woods, her father would suddenly stop and crouch down and then spring forward through the air—completely outstretched above the ground—and drop, with his hands cupped over a salamander. Piet collected the little lizards in a large terrarium he had built against the outside south-facing wall of the farm's garage.

The snow had produced a postcard picture of the Soetendael that winter day. The gathered flakes hung in a thick tuft from the home's thatched roof above the garage, and the shuttered windows of the attic and the three large, black garage doors accented the billowy snow. The children's large timber swing set, visible in the distance, was also capped with pillows of white.

In the previous century the farm's backyard had been the front. The structure used to be much smaller—the humble residence of a working farmer and a classic example of farms typical of the era, with the cows living under the same roof as the farmer and both man and beast helping to warm the often frigid air. The farm's land used to stretch out in all directions. But in the early 20th century, the land toward the front and one side had been sold and subdivided and new neighborhoods built. And now, one had to enter the property from the rear of the house via a hard-to-locate gravel drive. The small front door opened toward the back of the property, which now faced a nearly impenetrable hedge.

Standing beside the garage and next to Piet's terrarium one could see the swing's two ropes disappearing beneath the snow, the wooden seat lost underneath the flakes. Anne's vegetable garden was also covered thick, and the trunks of the fruit and nut trees appeared diminished. There was no livestock on the Soetendael. Besides the trees, the vegetable garden, and Anne's beehives, the farm had been relegated to the children's plaything. The separate hayloft remained empty and the grass in the fields grew long. When the children enjoyed their swing, they did so in near obscurity. Only Mr. van de Brink, the farmer next door, and his few cows could look on. Were it not for this distinct topography, this would be a far different story.

The record snows soon melted into the pastures, and the boy-faced Dutch soldiers who had played in the snow with the Schoorl kids were reassigned. The Nazis seemed content with their conquest of Poland and the Schoorl family settled back into their daily routine.

* * *

THE CALENDAR TURNED to a new year—1940. While Anne prepared for the celebration of my mother's second birthday, Hitler prepared for the invasion of Holland. One of his underlings, Major Helmut Reinburger, a Luftwaffe staff officer, carried copies of Hitler's detailed plans in his attaché case. Reinburger boarded a small aircraft on an airfield in Muenster and ascended into the sky in route to Cologne. Flying with classified documents was forbidden by the German military, but the major had been up late drinking with the airfield's Commandant. He was tired and the roads were icy and the Commandant had offered the use of one of his planes.

En route, the aircraft encountered weather. The pilot lost his bearing in the clouds above Belgium and was forced to land. The major quickly deplaned and headed for some nearby bushes. As Belgian soldiers neared the downed plane, they saw smoke from a small fire. Major Reinburger was burning maps detailing the impending invasion. The soldiers hurried to put out the flames with their boots and took the major and the partially burned papers to their military quarters.

The event transpired only twelve days before my mother's second birthday and the celebration planned to mark the event. Marianne had come into this world on a cold winter evening. Her brother and sisters had waited patiently at the bottom of the stairs for news of the birth. Eventually their father appeared. He descended the stairs with his newest daughter bundled tightly in his arms. Piet's face seemed to glow. He had always wanted a lot of children.

Major Reinburger watched the Belgian soldiers organize the partially burnt documents on a table in their quarters. He waited for an opportune moment, then snatched up the papers and threw them in the room's lit stove. A Belgian officer quickly rescued what he could. Later, when Reinburger contacted the Luftwaffe through his embassy in Brussels, he assured them the papers had been adequately destroyed. But Hitler had no way to be absolutely certain his plans hadn't been discovered. He postponed the invasion and my mother's birthday passed without event.

WITH MARCH AND APRIL came warmer temperatures. The famed bulbs of Holland pushed their shoots sunward. The oaks shadowing the Soetendael were heavy in bud, and the birds were busy nesting in their branches. Renegades inside Hitler's government had warned their Dutch and Belgian counterparts on several occasions that an invasion was imminent. No one was sure exactly what to expect.

One afternoon, while riding together on a bike path beside a main avenue leading out of Bennekom, Anne and her son, Ruud, spotted a group of Dutch soldiers ahead in the distance. The soldiers gathered around one of the tall beech trees lining the road. As Ruud pedaled closer he could see one of the men fastening a leather belt around the thick trunk. "What are they doing?" he asked his mother. Spools of wire and tools rested on the ground at the soldier's feet.

"They are attaching explosive charges," said Anne. "If the Germans try to drive down this road, the soldiers will blow up the trees to block their way."

Another World War seemed inevitable, but like the last one, the Dutch hoped they could remain neutral. The mother and son looked at the long row of trees shadowing the road in front of them. Each had a similarly attached charge strapped to its trunk, standing like doomed sentries waiting for war.

Chapter 6

THE ENGINE OF Mom's Subaru clunked dead, the car's front wheels stuck in the grassy ditch. The jolt brought Mom back to that sunny afternoon. She could again hear the freeway traffic and feel the car's steering wheel beneath her calloused hands. She pushed the stick shift into reverse, and all four wheels turned in unison as the vehicle crawled out of the ditch.

Mom exited the freeway and turned onto the backroads that cut through thickly forested ravines. Towering cedar trees cast dark shadows. Mom felt increasingly anxious; the random shot from the truck's tail pipe still echoed. She knew it was absurd, but as she crested a hill, or came to a bend in the road she worried another piece of the war would be waiting for her.

In the weeks to come, remembering or not remembering her childhood was no longer a conscious choice for my mother. The years between May 1940 and May 1945 emerged, seemingly of their own volition. A week after her session with the therapist, while sorting through bolts of fabric at a store, Mom suddenly burst into tears. She had no idea what had triggered the emotions. Certain smells and sounds pulled her back into those war years. She followed the advice of the therapist and began writing down everything.

There is a certain irony that the only child of the Schoorl family to leave Holland for good would be the first one willing to put those broken years back together. Mom and Dad had immigrated to California in 1960, and our family soon moved to Washington state. I never felt like I had a past beyond our home in Maple Valley. It was as though Mom and Dad and all four of us kids had been spawned from that same place: our one acre of land in the wet foothills of the Cascade Mountains with our two fat dogs, a horse, and a chicken coop, and the long rows of Mom's and Dad's vegetable garden. I knew I had grandparents the same way I knew that the earth spun on its axis. But they didn't feel real.

Most of the citizens of Holland did their best to forget the war years. The Schoorl family had done the same. They didn't talk about the war during the war, and they rarely talked about it after.

The front of the farmhouse, facing the impenetrable hedge

The rear of the home

Chapter 7

THE MORNING OF the Nazi invasion on May 10, 1940 began in splendor. The night's dew trickled down the broad roof of the Soetendael catching the sun's early light as the drops fell to the earth. Anne was up before the children. Piet was away on business. Anne wandered down a grassy path next to the row of carefully pruned alder trees and toward her vegetable garden. Each year the branches of the alders had been cut back, and now the old limbs had formed large burl-like knots from which the season's new shoots sprang forth. I imagine Anne was enjoying the sweet quiet of the farm at dawn, her hands darkened by the soil.

Hanneke awoke in her upstairs room. She had been up late the night before performing a piano recital. Iet and Ruud still slept soundly in the bed they shared on the other side of the room. Hanneke quietly slipped out. Her hand glided down the rail of the staircase as her small feet navigated the treads. By the time she reached the lower floor, her mind had shaken off the last bits of slumber and Hanneke noticed an odd sound building in the distance. She walked down the hallway next to the kitchen and out the side door onto the patio, squinting against the glare of the morning light, looking up toward the sound.

The first wave of German transport planes split the air above her, several hundred Junker Ju 52s, flying in formation, the dull drone of their BMW Hornet engines buzzing in concert. Hanneke looked across the lawn toward her mother's voice. "It's war," said Anne, standing motionless, her solid frame partially shaded by the blossoming apple trees. Muffled blasts of Dutch anti-aircraft guns sounded beyond the trees, three or four reports at a time in quick succession. The two watched and listened as what had loomed as a dark rumor now breached the boundaries of their quiet life with concrete certainty. The bursts of hot shrapnel cutting through the morning sky sounded against the constant chop of the Nazi propellers grabbing at the Dutch air. The early sun punctuated the scene above— flashes of light reflected off the aircraft, and the puffs of smoke from the Dutch shells illuminated white, till they dissipated into swirling wisps.

Hitler had committed his 18th Army to cut its way through the center of Holland. Commando teams had infiltrated the borders as early as May 8. While Anne still slept that morning, a squadron of German planes had flown out over the North Sea feigning an invasion of England, then turned eastward, crossed over the sandy dunes of Holland and attacked the Dutch airfields, destroying many of the Dutch planes while they sat idle on the tarmac.

Hanneke and her mother continued to stare at the scene unfolding before them. The Dutch guns had little effect on the German planes, and the sounds of the aircraft continued unabated until the dark swarms disappeared into the northwestern horizon.

Anne walked inside and began preparing breakfast.

* * *

WHILE THE SCHOORLS ate their breakfast, German paratroopers dropped from the Ju 52s above The Hague. They planned to capture Holland's Queen. The three older Schoorl children sat silently at the table wishing their father were home. After breakfast, Anne told Iet to listen to the radio while Anne and Hanneke packed suitcases. Iet remained in the corner of the living room; the news of the battle filled the airwaves.

Since the 17th century the Dutch depended on a somewhat natural military defense called the Water Line to defend their country, a geographic line which ran from the southern tip of a large bay named the IJsselmeer to the south of Holland just east of Amsterdam. The line combined easily flooded land with strategically placed gun towers and pillboxes. The Dutch planned to flood the countryside east of the fortifications. Only a few feet deep, the flooded area would be too shallow for the Germans to cross by boats, and the loamy soil would create a quagmire impossible for their soldiers to walk through, or would slow them enough for the Dutch guns to cut them down.

The news commentator's voice crackled into the living room. Iet's skinny butt sat on the rough-hewn oriental mat. Both were east of the Water Line—on the wrong side of the planned defenses.

New swarms of planes continued overhead. German Stuka dive-bombers had now joined the Ju 52 transports. The Schoorls' maid and nanny left the farm to be with their families, and Anne and the children waited for Piet who was struggling to return to the farm.

The Dutch armed forces had taken control of the trains. Piet quickly abandoned any hope of boarding one and instead rented a bike and pedaled toward home. German tanks and aircraft continued to pour across the Dutch borders. Piet arrived at the Soetendael at dusk. The farm grew quiet as the sun dropped and the Schoorl children greeted the first night of war within the warmth of their own beds.

By dawn of the following morning, Piet and Anne had made their decision. The family couldn't stay in Bennekom nor could they head toward Amsterdam. The chance of getting caught in the planned flood, or between the two colliding armies, was too great. To the southwest were the rivers and the bridges that both the Germans and the Dutch would be fighting to occupy. The family's only evacuation option lay eastward, directly into the arms of the German forces.

The children followed Piet and Anne down the Soetendael's driveway. The parents balanced suitcases on their bikes. Iet, Hans, and Ruud took turns pushing Marianne in her stroller. The morning air blew cool, as the family walked towards downtown Bennekom. They planned to head south, temporarily, to the town of Wageningen, then east toward Arnhem.

Along the way the family met Aster van de Sleezen, a friend of Anne's. Aster's husband, a Dutch officer, had left his wife and their 2-year-old daughter to fight the Germans. Aster's's two sisters accompanied her and the families merged. With the two toddlers and the burden of their suitcases, the group moved slowly. The road inclined into a gentle hill. They passed the last few homes on the outskirts of Bennekom and then entered the forest.

"Auntie Pau' was the 80-year-war as bad as this one?" Iet asked, referencing a war that had ended nearly three centuries earlier. On both sides of the road the forest floor disappeared into a shadowy darkness.

A group of soldiers appeared on the horizon. One of them carried a long pole. Hanneke noticed the uniforms. They weren't the green that she had seen the soldiers wearing during the snowstorm at the farm. These were grayish. The man with the pole raised it up to the phone lines and clipped the wire. As they neared, the soldiers smiled at the children. They offered candy. Piet bristled. He addressed the Germans curtly and told the children to keep walking. One of the soldiers snapped a picture of the kids as the two groups passed.

The families kept on, and another group of German soldiers again appeared on foot. One of the men carried a spool of wire on his back and was trailing it behind him. An officer approached Piet and Anne. "You had better get your children off this road," he said in German. "The Luftwaffe will be overhead soon and there's a good chance there will be a battle. It's not safe out in the open."

The families stepped off the road and into the thick forest of pine trees. A soft carpet of needles covered the ground. The group walked until they came to a small depression in the otherwise flat landscape. Anne took Marianne from the baby carriage and held her close. Everyone lay down on their bellies. Broken rays of afternoon light flickered through the pine boughs.

MY MOTHER DID NOT remember those first few days of the invasion in any conscious way. She could not have told you how she had looked up at the clear blue sky as her brother and sisters pushed her stroller along the road eastward, or how she smelled the pine trees as she lay next to her mother on the forest floor. But it was part of the whole that pushed against her mind, snapshot moments that became more animated as Mom let them loose inside her.

Mom lifted Dad's old IBM typewriter out of the closet. She pecked at the keys. The more her fingers moved, the more the memories came.

"I need some time alone," Mom said to me. "It's not just you I'm calling, but everyone. I need some time without distractions. I'm asking that no one call me or come over for a while." Mom was not only making a peace with the silence and solitude of her new home, but was now embracing it and turning deeper inward. More similar to her own mother than she would ever feel comfortable admitting, Marianne shared some of Anne's unflinching and hasty courage. Mom journeyed alone, back into the war.

A FEW HOURS passed before Piet decided to move on. There was no battle in the spring sky. The day was quickly passing and the families needed to find shelter. The children brushed off the pine needles and walked back out onto the open road. Their shadows stretched in front of them.

Columns of German soldiers and their gray uniforms continued to appear from the east. The cloudless sky turned cold, and the families moved slower than either Piet or Anne had anticipated; the sun disappeared behind the woods. The families eventually came upon a sole home by the side of the road and stopped and asked if they could sleep there for the evening.

The Schoorls did their best to get comfortable in the little house. The children didn't ask many questions, and neither parent did much to explain the circumstances. The kids drifted to sleep, each alone with the images of German bombers and gray uniforms and the Soetendael left empty behind them.

The next day the group set off for Arnhem, to the home of friends of Auntie Pau'. Hanneke, Iet, and Ruud again took turns pushing Marianne's stroller. German soldiers passed the families with growing frequency. Soon the troops filled the streets and German trucks rumbled past. The two-day journey had covered less than ten miles.

Throughout Holland, skirmishes between the Germans and Dutch soldiers continued into the night. Auntie Pau's friends owned a large stately home. The families were welcomed inside. The children's footsteps echoed in the cavernous rooms. They could hear the occasional muffled blast of artillery.

Three days after the invasion, the Germans had successfully penetrated the Netherlands, but they had yet to occupy any of the key cities. The stubborn, yet pitifully armed and equipped Dutch army—they had one tank, which they bought used— stood their ground and the fighting bogged down. Hitler feared the English would come to Holland's defense if he didn't crush the Dutch army quickly. If the English secured a beachhead on the Dutch coast, they could spoil his entire plan. Hitler ordered detachments from the 6th Army's Air Force to abandon the fighting in Belgium and be readied for use on the Netherlands.

On May 14, the fifth day of the invasion, while Hanneke, Iet, and Ruud sat down to their lunch, over a hundred German bombers flew west towards the port city of Rotterdam. Hitler needed a swift victory. His methods were simple, crude, and militarily unprecedented. His bombers would level the city and murder the citizenry of Rotterdam—men, women, and children—if the Dutch didn't surrender.

The German commander contacted the Dutch commander and offered the Dutch a chance to lay down their arms. With almost no planes with which to defend their city, the Dutch generals had few choices. They surrendered their nation to the Nazis that afternoon. What followed is still hidden within the fog of war.

Half of the German bombers turned back to Germany. Fifty-seven of them continued toward the city. The bombs ripped through houses and leveled buildings. Fires stormed through the neighborhoods. Hundreds perished. Seventy thousand became instantly homeless. Queen Wilhelmina fled to England, and as dusk fell, Dutch soldiers throughout Holland were ordered to cease fighting. The nation fell to one man's ruthlessness.

The following day—the first of Nazi occupation—the Schoorls returned to their small farm to find several Germans inside their home. The Germans quickly apologized for their presence then left. The children found broken eggshells partially ground into the dirt of the chicken coop where some of the soldiers had pilfered eggs and then attempted to hide the evidence.

Columns of German soldiers now goose-stepped through the streets of Bennekom, their boots dropping in unison against the old brick pavers. The children slept in their own beds. But for them it was the beginning of a different world. The Germans had invaded their happy childhoods and the sounds and smells of the first days of war followed them to sleep.

FOR NEARLY THREE MONTHS, Mom lived alone with her memories. She filled twenty-three single-spaced pages with her words, then returned the typewriter to the same dark corner from which it came, placed the pages in her file cabinet, and returned to the business of her life.

I read Mom's story shortly after she finished writing it. But I wasn't able to replace this newer, bloodier version of Mom's war with the one she had indoctrinated me with as a child. It was too sudden, and, in truth, I just wasn't that interested. It wouldn't be until nearly ten years later, after I had used up most of my thirties and my life had slowed, that I became reflective enough to consider my past and wonder about my ancestors. I picked up Mom's story for a second time. And still it took a while for me to begin to understand.

I remember sitting in my office and rereading those pages. It was fall, and I'd pause now and again and look up from the story and out my window and into the Puyallup Valley. Orange pumpkins filled the farmers' fields. Birds rested on my feeders. I'd watch while I tried to add flesh to Mom's words.

"I am fashioned by this tale," I wrote on my laptop on one of those fall mornings. "When my bones were still soft and my mother held me in her arms she was telling me this story—not with her words, but with her being. Her breath had always held the fragrance of war; it was wound in her gait and it hid in her silence." I looked at the words on the screen. They looked true.

The moment marked the beginning of my own journey back to the Second World War, to the nation of my ancestors, to the quiet streets of Bennekom, and the little farm where my Mom was born. I did not yet understand the war that still trembled inside my mother, nor did I understand its legacy. But I wanted to understand.

Chapter 8

THE BOEING 757 reached altitude and I reclined my seat. I looked down at the rugged peaks of the North Cascades as the jet headed toward that imaginary line separating the U.S. from Canada. It's a ten-hour flight to Amsterdam. My mom's two oldest sisters were expecting me.

Earlier that summer I had sat with Mom in her sewing room. It was one of those days when the lush and the wet of the Pacific Northwest mingled with the warm sunlight. I placed my new mini tape recorder on Mom's round antique table. We were both unusually quiet. I set my stack of interview questions next to the recorder and worked to peel the cellophane wrappers off of the new cassettes.

At sixty-five, my mom was shorter than she used to be. Her hair was now white. We sat across from each other, my back toward the large picture window, which looked out on Mom's pampered garden. Quilts Mom had made lay draped over the end of the room's bed. Her dolls, the fancy ones she never had as a child, sat peacefully on the shelves. I fidgeted with the recorder, placing it more directly between us, and pushed the start button. "Do you remember anything

about the war before Eline came to live with you?" I
began.

"Really . . . really nothing, uh uh," Mom said as she
moved her head slowly side-to-side gesturing no. Her
eyes looked distant as though she were scanning some
dim lit horizon.

"What do you remember about the Soetendael?
Can you describe it?"

"Well of course. It's still there, so I know what it
looks like," she said slowly.

The Englishman sitting next to me on the plane ordered another drink. "Nothing to do but get bombed,"
he said with a smile. I smiled back and resumed looking out the oval window, down at the seemingly endless
lakes of Northern Saskatchewan and Manitoba. I was
flying with the Dutch airline, KLM, the same carrier
my mom used on her first trip to the U.S. when she immigrated to America at the young age of twenty-two. It
was a spring day in early April 1960. She stepped out of
the plane and down a portable steel stairway and onto
the New York City tarmac, then took her first step in
the country she would call home for the rest of her life.
She wore a white bonnet and knitted white gloves and
a white overcoat on top of her dark calf-length dress. A
dark canvas travel bag dangled from her arm. Her thick
hair was trimmed short and accentuated the long pleasant lines of her neck. My mother has a beautiful smile.

During the five-day train ride to Los Angeles, where
my father anxiously waited for her arrival, Mom ate
only one apple. She was too afraid to ask for food and
equally unnerved by an advertisement she saw for hot
dogs. Mom had never eaten dog. Four days after arriving in L.A., she and dad were married. Carla Polak—
a young Jewish woman who had been saved from the

Nazis by my grandmother—witnessed the wedding along with her husband.

As the jet moved closer to the icy expanses of Greenland, I felt as though I was journeying into another time, as though I was reversing Mom's trip to America. For nearly a year, I had been puzzling together the broken bits and pieces of the lives the war had shattered. I had tried to make a proper time-line, tried to organize all of the principal characters. But more often than not, I lost myself in the details. Who was Carla again? I'd think as I sat at my desk. Wait . . . oh . . . yes, I remember. And I would lean forward, place my elbows on each side of my laptop and rest my head between my hands as I tried to add flesh to Carla's name. I'd picture my grandmother sitting next to Carla in the living room of the Soetendael; I'd envision the large south-facing picture windows taking in the afternoon light. I would try to look out and see the fruit trees and the hayloft.

I interviewed my mother for nine hours over two days. Whenever she struggled to answer a question, Mom looked away from me and slightly upward, and another time and place poured through her fixed gaze, and she pulled that world into the room, and it surrounded us and permeated us. The world outside the sewing-room window, the bees and the blossoms and the leaves in the sunlight seemed distant. Together we traveled the stone roads of Bennekom.

By the end of the second day, whenever Mom couldn't remember a fact or detail or reconcile the chronology of events she repeatedly said, "You should ask Iet or Hans, they would know. They were so much older than me." Hanneke was eight years older than my mom, Iet, seven. Neither had ever talked about the war to anyone—ever. Not even to each other.

The last week before my flight I exchanged a flurry of emails with my aunts and the days of the interviews were set. My cousin, Bram, Iet's youngest son, agreed to meet me at the airport.

The jet passed beyond Greenland. I had been to Holland before, three times. I had met relatives, seen tulips, canals, and windmills, and biked with my dad through the dunes by the North Sea. But this time, as the jet completed the last of its arc toward Amsterdam, I descended into a different Holland—the one I had discovered on the pages of Mom's story—the place of her birth, to a sleepy farm named the Soetendael. With each step I took closer to the past, the more it consumed me, and the more time I spent imagining the events of those years. I was in search of my 40-year -old grandfather, Piet Schoorl and his headstrong wife, Anne, and all five of their children who lived during the war. I watched the flat landscape blur past me as the 757 set up for its landing. The jet, flying opposite our spinning globe, had taken off in the early afternoon, consumed a whole day, and it was now morning again. Bram met me at the terminal. We took a train to his apartment in Amsterdam.

"Just remember, if you need to find my flat, take the #17 tram and get off at the stop after the Anne Frank House," Bram said in his British-sounding accent. Behind us, the ornate dome of Amsterdam's Central Train Station rose up toward the morning sky. Tram #17 lunged forward, and I grabbed the stainless steel handrail.

We travelled down a northwesterly corridor of one of Amsterdam's main four-lane streets. The almost exclusively brick buildings lined the street, one built against the side of the next, each capped with an ornate façade representing different eras of architecture—all centuries old. Bram and I had met a couple of years back, when he was in Seattle on business. He had called me while I was at work. I had no idea he was in town. "This is your cousin Bram," the voice on the phone had said. The statement failed to resonate. I don't have any cousins, I thought. There was a moment of awkward silence as my mind scrambled for context. I did, in fact, have cousins. And I had a faint memory of that name. I recovered my poise, much as I would on a business call, and we made plans to meet that afternoon at a restaurant above Snoqualmie Falls.

As odd as it might seem to people who have grown up close to their cousins, it wasn't until well after lunch, as we walked down a slick muddy trail to the misty base of the falls, that it dawned on me that Bram and I shared the same grandparents. The fact struck me rather forcibly. I was standing next to a near stranger, and we shared not only a common history but were fashioned of the same blood.

My parents had not only worked to forget a war, they had followed it up by moving to the other side of the world, as if to complete the job. I was standing next to another grandson of Pieter and Anne Schoorl. Like so much of this story, it took time for the simple fact of it to settle in.

"Next stop Anne Frank house," the conductor called out in English. A load of tourists poured out of the tram and into a brick-paved square. They joined the long line of people waiting to walk through the claustrophobic hallways of the Frank family's wartime home. I looked through the glass, watching the tourists as the tram pulled away. My journey intersected Anne Frank's in more ways than the obvious. When the Nazis finally discovered the Frank and van Daan families and old Mr. Dussel living behind their fake bookcase, they brought them to the same Euterpe Street headquarters as they had my grandfather—to the same cold cells beneath the Nazis' headquarters.

"This used to be the Jewish section of town," my cousin Bram said. I was immediately enamored with the old city. Placid canals bordered nearly every road, and narrow avenues led to quaint pubs and restaurants where patrons sipped small cups of strong coffee while watching boats slowly motor by. Bram and I got off at the next stop and stepped onto stone pavers worn smooth by generations of traffic. Growing up on the west coast, mine was a world of strip malls, big-box stores, and acres of newly laid asphalt. I wasn't used to walking on history older than the nation in which I lived.

We ascended the steep corkscrew staircase to Bram's fourth-story flat. It occupied the top two floors of another old brick building that overlooked the main avenue travelled by Tram #17. Bram brewed some coffee, and we could hear the sounds of Amsterdam below: the ding of the tram, an occasional car horn, and the whine of one of the many gas-powered scooters darting through traffic.

Bram and I don't look very similar. He's maybe six feet to my six-three and more slender. Years of working construction have weathered my skin and added some bulk to my frame. Bram's nearly unblemished features account for more than the ten years separating us in age. He looks and acts finishing-school-refined: well-groomed but casually so and every part the international businessman that he is. "I didn't think this was any big deal," Bram said sitting across the table from me. "I thought there was just this Jewish girl living in their house. I didn't think it came to much."

The words could have been my own only one year earlier. The this he referred to was the reason for my trip: the story, my mother's story, his mother's story. I set my coffee cup on the table. Those last months I spent sifting through the details of the war, the weight of the few memories I had already collected, and the hours I spent trying to place the war in real context—adding back the flesh, and working to see the events as plainly as I could see my own three children—had prompted in me something similar to the evangelical fire smoldering inside the newly saved. The conversation with Bram no longer felt casual. I moved closer to the table. I asked him if he knew what happened to his grandfather. But I already knew he knew. I knew all of the information that had been passed to him because they were the exact same details that had been told to me. And I knew they had been told to him with the same duplicitous smile and the same casual dismissal they had been told to me, and that somehow even the simplest of horrible facts had been tailored to rest comfortably on Bram's young pallet just as they had my own, where they still rested, inoffensively.

The war that revisited my mom, the one that smelled of sulfur, where parents mourned their dead children, and children mourned their murdered mothers and fathers, had by now taken hold of me. I could feel its grip tightening and the sounds of Amsterdam trickling through Bram's window fell silent in my head. I don't remember the exact words that came out of my mouth when I leaned over and stared into Bram's eyes. But the voice came from deep in me, from a genuine place. Bram looked back at me and then turned to one side. A silent tear dropped down his cheek.

The Soetendael

Chapter 9

TWO YEARS HAD PASSED since those first German bombers invaded that sunny spring morning at the Soetendael. The farm still enjoyed its solitude—the rooster continued to signal the cold hours of dawn, and the dusk settled quietly over the Schoorls' farmhouse. But despite the outward calm, the war was real, and it colored the lives of all of the citizens of Bennekom. Gray-uniformed German soldiers were now stationed on the village's main intersections. Yellow German road signs were placed next to the Dutch ones, and imported items such as chocolate and oranges had disappeared from store shelves. Along with the black paper that the Nazis ordered placed over the windows came ration coupons, now necessary to purchase anything, from a new pair of shoes to flour for Anne's pancakes. The Nazis touched every part of the Schoorl family's routine, and the war the Germans started invaded the children's young lives—often with the ominous features of a dark dream.

On one particular evening, Iet lay awake in her bed. She could hear the occasional creak of the old house, and the rise and fall of her sibling's slumbering breath, and then a foreign sound: a low hum building in the distance to a dull groan. The groan grew louder, and Iet sunk down into her bed and pulled the covers over her head; she knew what was to come. The sound slowly built until it became the only single discernable noise. The groan transformed into a roaring wave as hundreds of British long-range bombers navigated the skies directly above the Soetendael. Blasts of nearby German anti-aircraft guns joined in, shaking the night air. Iet endured the first moments alone, then flipped back her sheets, darted out of bed, and scampered across the cold hallway floor toward her parents' bedroom. She walked to her father's side of the bed and bumped her hips against the mattress. Piet took his daughter in his arms as the sky ignited above them.

The blast of the German guns and the muffled bursts of exploding flack and the whine of the bomber's Rolls Royce engines continued as one sound. Hot flack tore through the thin metal skins of the English planes. Iet could recognize the sound of a mortally wounded aircraft: as the planes fell, the propellers bit madly into the dark night, spinning the craft's engines into a shrill shriek—the scream then silenced by the soft Dutch soil and ending as just another of the long procession of explosions.

Iet held tight to her father. And the sounds soon left just as ethereally as they began, drifting eastward toward the industrial centers of Germany. The quiet of the farm resumed, yet Iet remained in bed pressed against her father's chest. Though the sounds of war had left, the images remained alive in her young mind. She pictured the crew of the bombers struck by German flack. She imagined the faces of these men who were trying to rescue her nation, who risked their lives to save her. She wondered if the men escaped from their bomber before it slammed into the ground. She wondered if they survived, if they were hurt, where they might be at that very moment.

Anne's three words—"It is war"—were truer than she could have ever imagined. The Nazi Blitzkrieg had rolled through all of Western Europe, and the whole of it was firmly in Hitler's grip. Hitler appointed the Austrian Nazi, Arthur Seyss-Inquart, as Reich Commissar of the occupied Netherlands. Though the Dutch civil administration was left mostly intact, Seyss-Inquart ruled Holland, and had organized the fanatical, fascist—and anti-Semitic—Dutch called the NSB into a separate paramilitary force to help the SS police the country. The morning the Germans stormed into Holland had shocked the nation, but those dramatic first days slid into weeks, then months. If the invasion had been a jarring blow to the nation's skull, the occupation was a slow-eating cancer.

At first, the family's day-to-day life changed little. The Nazis had yet to openly persecute the Jews in Holland, nor had any sort of Dutch resistance formed. Piet still left for work after breakfast, and the children still walked to school. But simple things, like the smell of the synthetic leather, which had replaced the real leather that used to cover the children's schoolbooks, or the fact that they were no longer allowed to mention the Dutch Queen, served as daily reminders of the war. And each month, as trainloads of Dutch products traveled east into Germany, Anne worked harder to find the foods the family was used to eating. In time, she needed a coupon to buy pretty much anything, and instead of shopping in Bennekom while the nanny and maid kept the household, Anne visited the local farms and bought extra food directly from the farmers in the emerging black market. And she now had one added mouth to feed. On April 26, 1941, Anne had given birth to her fifth child, another girl she named Helene.

Iet eventually left her parents' room and walked back over the cold wood floor and into her own. Her bed had cooled, and she bundled the covers around her.

The next morning, the farm woke before the family. Spring was in the air, and the swallows had returned to the hayloft. Iet opened her eyes to the dawn light; she walked down the hall, descended the stairs, and joined her brother and sisters at the breakfast table. On the other side of the dining room's blacked-out windows, the rising sun could have played on the dew-filled blossoms of the fruit trees or burned away a fog that had settle over the pasture. But there was no way for the family to tell. Iet ate quietly. She didn't talk about the bombers, nor did anyone else.

MY FIRST CONVERSATION with Bram about the war had ended before we finished our coffee. Later that evening we met some of his friends at a restaurant just below his flat. The establishment was—again—European-old, time not counted in decades but centuries. We ate tapas and drank for hours before the jet lag caught up with me. I woke early, gathered my bags and took Tram #17 back to the Central Station. I walked over the same canals as had my grandfather on the day of his arrest, and through the same cavernous train station, and then followed the same tracks he had navigated back-and-forth between Amsterdam and Bennekom. Bram's mother, my aunt Iet, picked me up at the train station. She lived alone in one-half of a mansion-size Victorian-style home looking directly down on one of Wageningen's many busy brick courtyards just a few miles from Bennekom. Her long gray hair was pinned behind her head.

The following morning, we sat together in her living room. "Shall we get started?" I asked. Iet smiled behind her glasses and nodded yes. The second-story windows, stretching from the floor to a few feet short of the room's high ceilings, lit the room. "I'd like to know what your life was like before the war," I began. It was a logical placed to start. But looking back, I remember the moment as almost irreverent—too quick of a jump into a thing that had remained unspoken for so long, as though something more should have been said or done. But even now, I am not sure what that would be, so I just started. "Do you have very many memories?"

Iet paused and seemed to stare out into that same void that my mother had gazed into, her head looking slightly up toward the corner of her spacious living room. "Not many memories," she said. "But I think I was just a happy child. There was this big house, this farm—the Soetendael. There were fruit trees and a large swing. I played with flowers and sand and pebbles, simple things," she said, smiling. She remembered playing with her brother, Ruud, but not so much with her older sister Hanneke. "She was bossy; Ruud was more my mate," she said with a grin, her melodic voice revealing remnants of the many adult years Iet had lived in Australia.

When Iet remembered her early childhood, she continued to smile. And it was easy to look inside that smile and see pieces of the happy carefree life she described. A bit of a tomboy, Iet liked to climb to the top of the tall swing set in her backyard and adventure alone into woods surrounding Bennekom. She described her walks with her father in search of bugs and lizards and how she loved that time. We continued to journey through those early years together until we had filled two one-hour tapes and begun a third. We then arrived at the day when Piet and Anne welcomed their first Jewish "guest" into hiding.

"Do you remember when Eline first came to the house?" I asked.

"Yes, yes, I remember." Iet paused and said nothing more.

"What do you remember?" I asked after a long silence.

IT WAS THE THIRD summer of the Nazi occupation. Early in the day, Iet—along with Hanneke, Ruud, and their parents—rode her bike to the Bennekom train station. The five boarded the train to Amsterdam. The farmlands of Bennekom disappeared behind them as they rumbled westward toward the old city. The small houses that dotted the green landscape soon gave way to the brick and steel of Amsterdam's ports, and the train eventually slowed to a stop inside the city's central station. The family stepped onto the terminal floor only long enough to transfer trains, and then headed north, through the old neighborhoods of Amsterdam, past the city's outskirts, and towards Alkmaar and Anne's childhood home. The day was July 16, 1942, the birthday of Anne's father, Jan Borst.

My mother, now four years old, stayed behind at the Soetendael with baby Helene. Two of Anne's sisters, Auntie Toe and Auntie Ety, who both lived at the lab and worked as Piet's assistants, had come to the Soetendael that evening to care for the children. The summer-evening sun had yet to completely fall when Toe and Ety tucked the girls into their upstairs beds.

The windows still reflected the day's light. My mother fell to sleep.

When the sun did finally drop beyond the North Sea and darkness enfolded the farm, a woman and a child rode together on one bike as they passed the Schoorls' hedge. Wearing a blue dress and a matching cape, the small girl held tight to the woman's hips as her cape fluttered behind her. The woman turned left at the side street leading toward the farm, then left again and onto the dirt and gravel drive until she came to the gate. The two got off the bike. The woman carried a suitcase. She unlatched the Soetendael's gate and guided the little girl through, and they walked together, hand-in-hand, toward the large farmhouse.

Anne's sisters heard the knock at the front door. They weren't expecting company. Those familiar with the Soetendael rarely walked all the way around the house and to the front porch, and it was rather late for a social call. Nonetheless, they opened the door to see the two strangers, the woman and child, standing in front of them. The woman didn't offer any salutations. She didn't introduce herself or the child. "The time has come," she said, nothing more, and handed the small suitcase to the two sisters. The child stood silently next to the woman's leg. Three-year-old Eline van Leeuwen was instructed to enter the home. Obediently, she stepped across the threshold; tears dripped off her cheeks. And as quickly and quietly as the stranger arrived, she left.

Piet and Anne and the older children returned to the farm late that evening. Anne's sister had tucked Eline in the same bed as Marianne. The tears had continued to stream down Eline's face until she fell to sleep. Anne's sisters explained the evening's cryptic events.

Anne and Piet walked up the stairs and into Marianne's room. They stood side-by-side looking at the fair-skinned, blonde-haired girl sleeping next to their daughter. Anne looked questioningly at her husband. He had not discussed hiding the Jewish girl with Anne. "It's all right," Piet said. He had been expecting the child. Piet left the room and Anne remained, standing over the bed and watching Eline sleep. She could see the streaks the drying tears had left on the child's rosy cheeks. She watched Eline's small chest rise and drop with each little breath. In the silence of that darkened room, Anne stood alone, watching. The quiet scene provides a window into the complex nature of my grandmother.

Marianne, playing in the fields of the Soetendael

Those who remember Anne as gruff, hasty, and opinionated would not be in error. Nor would those who sometimes questioned Anne's often-dismissive attitude to the more subtle needs of her own children. But they would be in error if they mistook Anne's nature as selfish; she had her blind spots, but Anne's strengths and weaknesses were both fed from the same fire that glowed in her. As she watched Eline, Anne did so with a tender, open, and particularly able heart, a heart that could travel further than most. She stood there imagining the child's mother—picturing how she must have felt while dressing her daughter in that blue dress and cape, how she hugged her goodbye, and then endured those moments as Eline disappeared on the back of a bicycle and into the darkness. The images echoed in Anne, and they carved deeper that space in my grandmother that led her forward. Her compassion smoldered as part of a fire that inhabited Anne, and she lived subordinate to it.

My grandmother remained standing and watching the daughter of Pauline and Leo van Leeuwen. Anne knew Pauline must be somewhere close and she imagined how the mother was at that very moment, alone, anguishing. Anne didn't commit herself to the care of Eline in any outward, formal manner. Unlike her husband, she had never agreed to become responsible for the child's survival. However, now the little girl was in her care, and it was Anne's constitution that made the choice for her. She would defend Eline's life as if the child were her own, no matter the cost. And it was on that evening of July 16, 1942 that the Dutch resistance received one more anonymous member to their numbers. If something captured Anne's heart, she gave herself to it completely.

Eline awoke the next morning alongside my mother and began the first day of her new life at the farm. After breakfast, Anne sat down with Eline. "Your new name is Eline Bruijn," she said, underlying the significance of that last name. "You're the daughter of my sister, Aaf." The particulars of the story could prove deathly important. "If any strange men question you, this is what you tell them," Anne continued.

After Anne felt Eline understood, she left the girl alone. But before she had walked out of the room Eline called out to her. "If any strange ladies question me do I say the same thing?" she asked earnestly. The van Leeuwens had raised an outspoken—if not precocious—3-year-old.

Anne invested a similar amount of time drilling her own children. She made them repeat the names of the six children in order of their age, as though Eline had been a fixture at the farm for years. "Hans, Iet, Ruud, Marianne, Eline, Helene," the Schoorl children repeated over and over again, until the list had written itself permanently in their minds.

IET'S TALL WINDOWS were slightly ajar, and we could hear the constant din of pedestrians and bicyclists crossing the square. "I was told that if I was ever asked who she was, to say that she was my cousin." Iet paused again as if she were watching a movie and needed to let a few more frames pass before she could describe them.

"She was a tiny little girl, smaller than Marianne. She was younger of course . . . she was a stranger in the house. We were asked to get used to her and to see her as our sister."

"Was it explained to you that she was Jewish?" I asked.

"No," Iet quickly answered. "No. I'm sure that word was never used."

But even though it was never discussed, the children knew. Or, at the very least, they knew they were hiding Eline, and that the stakes involved were grave. The same month Eline arrived at the Soetendael, the Nazis began removing the Jews from Holland, transporting them to the death camps of Auschwitz and Sobibor.

My mini-recorder continued to turn atop Iet's antique living room table, a piece of furniture that continually grabbed my attention. It was not the type of antique one usually pictures with dainty carvings and intricate wood inlays. Iet collected a different type of antique—hers were of a more personable, working-class ilk. They had survived generations of hard use and were completely covered with scars, cracks and crevices that blended into a rich patina and were now buffed to a sheen. Iet continued: "I think I must have been aware of the Jews. I remember people walking with this star. I just accepted it, just like all the other things that slowly got worse . . . each day . . . each week. Bad things happened and that was part of it. I think I rather liked Eline after a while. I always think of her along with Marianne. They played a lot together."

Iet would sometimes mumble a phrase, as if thinking out loud. "Marianne did her best to be her friend . . . Eline was more outgoing. They played with dolls . . . in the big living room . . . in the corner by the heater, I think." I watched as she resurrected images not visited for six decades.

As the tape continued to record, the stories darkened. Iet's smile left her. She was remembering the war at my request. I don't know for sure why she had agreed to do it. I had asked my mom if her older sisters would be willing to let me interview them. Mom had asked them. They both said yes, and I quickly bought my plane ticket to Holland. It all happened very fast.

My recorder came to the end of its tape and snapped off. I looked at Iet. "How are you doing?"

"I think I'm done for the day," she said, sounding tired. I labeled both sides of the tape and put it on top of the other two stacked neatly by my notes. A heaviness pressed against the room. "I think I'm a bit hungry," Iet said.

We descended to the first floor. Iet's pottery studio occupied one half of the lower level. The room's windows faced the public square. Shelves filled with her work surrounded her pottery wheel. Growing up, I drank tea from cups Iet made. In the twilight of her career, Iet had become an artist of some repute in Holland, and her plates are now too valuable to find their way underneath a slice of bread. When I was young, I visited Iet's home, which was then located in Bennekom. She had a pottery studio there as well, a barn-like structure in the forest behind her home. Pots and plants and bags of clay littered the large building. Earthen vases overflowed with wood potting utensils and sponges, and, despite the mess, the whole of it had a sort of unified organic feel, a chaotic symmetry, as though each half-built pot or raked pile of dried leaves needed to be exactly where it was. When I think of Iet's hand molding clay, I think of my mother's hand. A day hardly passed during my childhood without Mom's fingers touching fresh soil. Her hands were always warm when she rubbed my back. Both Iet and my mother got their hands from Anne—calloused, able, and sensitive—the hands of an artist.

I pumped up the tire of Bram's old bike and joined Iet out in the warm summer evening air. We rode past the front of her shop. A large, feminine-looking statue of the Buddha stared at us from behind her studio glass.

I followed the slow rhythms of Iet's pedals through Wageningen, past a delicatessen and a cheese store, and the many rows of old shops that filled the city's narrow corridors. The Dutch grew up on bikes and despite sometimes walking with a cane, Iet had no problems pedaling through the twisting streets. The bumpy road opened to another courtyard, a larger one, built around a towering Catholic church. Restaurants lined one side of the square. We parked the bikes next to a pub and sat down at a table under the building's awning.

I watched a farmer in the courtyard pack waxy cardboard boxes into his Mercedes cargo truck and pick up wilted leaves of lettuce. He was the last vendor from the day's market. The diesel engines of a large street sweeper hummed as it drove back and forth across the brick pavers. Young men and women at the tables next to us laughed between sips of beer and drags from their cigarettes. Neither Iet nor I felt talkative. It seemed as though we both still had pieces of her story working out their details inside us.

"How old is that church?" I asked. It looked as though it had lorded over this part of the city for centuries.

"Not very old really," Iet said. "It was blown up twice during the war, and the Dutch rebuilt it twice."

A record-setting heat wave had broken only a few days before my arrival in Holland, and as we sipped our drinks a hard rain started to fall. Children came from the apartments above the shops and restaurants and ran through the square, chasing each other and jumping off the steps of the church and into the fresh puddles.

The awning keeping me dry seemed to increase the distance between the children and me. I watched the raindrops bounce on the red glassy sheen of the courtyard. The children's singsong voices and the new rain trickled together into a joyful sound. The melancholy didn't lift as much as it settled, and my mind wandered between two worlds.

LEO VAN LEEUWEN HAD met Piet at the tennis club in the adjacent town of Ede. Places like the club, where Piet had long been a member, were still relatively undisturbed by the Germans. Hitler tried not to disrupt the fabric of upper-class Holland because when the war ended, he needed educated men like Dr. Schoorl to keep the Reich strong. Hitler hoped to simply assimilate the Dutch into his Aryan dream, and hence Piet could enjoy a weekend afternoon on the groomed grass courts. The Schoorl children often accompanied their father through the cindered bike trails to the adjacent town, following the handle of Piet's racket that stuck out of his bag as he pedaled. The kids chased errant balls and watched their father. Piet, always competitive, played to win, and it was here, probably in the spring of '42, amongst the pressed tennis whites and knitted sweaters, that my grandfather met Leo van Leeuwen.

Unlike Piet, whose lean body suited the game of tennis, Leo was stocky. His solid frame would have served him better had the pair engaged in a heated game of rugby. However Leo did possess the most important physical features that allowed him to dart across the cut spring grass—the same bright blue eyes and sandy blonde hair he had given his daughter.

* * *

TWO YEARS EARLIER, on the fifth day of the war, Leo, his wife Pauline, and their two children had been underneath the bombs that fell on Rotterdam. When the fighting first turned fierce, they had left their downtown home to stay with a friend who lived in the outskirts of the city. Eline was only a year old, and Pauline placed her daughter on a bed of straw in a cast-iron tub in the home's cellar. The bomb's concussions rolled through the city, and Rotterdam erupted in flames. Eline's older brother, Carel, was three.

After the surrender, the van Leeuwens were able to return to their own residence. By chance, it had escaped the fires.

The family first came to Bennekom in 1940 as tourists. They had rented a house in the quiet village and enjoyed the trails and fields and the sunshine. They also found the place idyllic. Eline turned two in January of '41, and that following summer she had made friends with Bennekom's milkman. He took the small girl on short rides atop his horse-drawn milk cart. The family had other Jewish friends in the area and they entertained in their home.

Leo and Pauline had met in Rotterdam in 1930 through the Jewish youth movement. Though barely twenty, they were both mature and firmly entrenched in adult life. Leo had learned the commodities trade from his father and earned a good living buying and selling grain. After finding her father dead of natural causes in the bathroom when she was only eighteen, Pauline was forced to run the family business—a cinema in Rotterdam that also produced a variety show before each film. Pauline booked performers of all sorts, from acrobats to musicians. The couple married early. They lived well and enjoyed the upper reaches of Rotterdam's social order, attending late-night dinner parties and evenings at the theaters. Leo's wife had long dark hair and brown eyes. Despite bearing two children her imported dresses still fell fashionably from her petite frame. She was beautiful and looked distinctly Jewish.

By the end of '41, Leo sensed his family was no longer safe in Rotterdam. People had a bad habit of underestimating Adolph Hitler. It was a mistake Leo would never make. When the Nazis demanded all Jews register their presence with the newly-formed Jewish council, Leo knew better. He moved his wife and two children to Bennekom permanently and planned to remain in the sleepy village until the war came to an end. It would soon prove that even more radical measures were necessary.

WHILE LEO AND PIET played tennis, Pauline remained home in the relative safety of their little rental. The tennis club was as much a social gathering point as an athletic one. And Leo not only looked the part of a non-Jew, but added to his appearance a calm and confident swagger. Leo chased balls across the cut grass seemingly oblivious of the war, and could ease into the couch inside the tennis club lounge as though the place had been built especially for him.

Just as Eline resembled her father, Carel looked like his mother, and both remained behind the drawn shades of their home. Living confined within the walls of their modest rental didn't suit Pauline's energetic and outgoing nature; however, the family weathered 1941 with relative ease. But by '42, rumors of the Nazi death camps trickled into Bennekom. The Germans were forcibly removing families from the Jewish neighborhoods in the larger Dutch cities at night, and shipping them to the transit camp Westerbork, a concentration camp located on the eastern edge of Holland. Cattle cars departed the railroad at Westerbork for Poland at regularly scheduled intervals, filled to standing-room-only with the families who had, only weeks earlier, lived as discreetly and hopefully as Pauline and Leo and their two young children. Soon the Nazis would be finished with the cities and could then focus on the few remaining stragglers who had fled to the country. Over 140,000 Jews populated Holland before the Nazis invaded. Fewer than 10,000 would survive within its borders by the war's end.

Pauline and Leo regularly pleaded with their three living parents to join them in Bennekom. Each refused. They didn't believe the stories about the death camps, and as required by the Nazis, they registered with the Jewish council. When they received news that they all needed to take the train to Westerbork, they arrived at the station together, and early, in order to buy first-class tickets. They also brought a deck of cards with them to play on the train. All three would perish.

Leo eventually concluded that his family couldn't survive without help. In time, someone would wonder who lived beyond the drawn shades of his little house.

When Leo van Leeuwen stood on those courts and asked if he could rely on Piet to help his family if their situation worsened, he received an answer immediately. It wasn't a decision Piet pondered. Leo asked if Piet could care for his daughter, Eline. I picture Piet holding Leo's hand and placing the other on Leo's shoulder as they spoke. Neither man knew for sure if, or when, the agreement would be necessary. Leo was taking precautions, putting in place a plan if one was ever needed. Leo's foresight would—again—prove invaluable.

Leo had forged several important friendships in Bennekom, and on one of those bright summer days, someone alerted him that the family needed to go underground immediately. Leo and Pauline had prepared for this moment. They would divide the family. Their son and daughter would hide separately, and Leo and Pauline would remain together. It was the safest option. And though the bags were packed and the children's destinations carefully chosen, Pauline struggled to endure the evening. Pauline was a typical doting, devoted mother. In peacetime, she often organized her children's social calendar from hour-to-hour. She had chronicled their lives in detailed albums, identifying each lost tooth, the date it was tugged out, and its previous location in the mouths of her son or daughter. There was no way for her to internally prepare for what was to come. Leo had told her about the Schoorls' farm and their five young children. Eline would be happy there, he assured her. And Leo had found a good hiding place for Carel. He could stay with a woman named Frau Broekman, the widow of Bennekom's late piano teacher, who had a daughter. The couple packed their children's suitcases. Pauline gave Eline a hug and a kiss before wrapping her in the girl's blue cape. A close friend of the family, a Dutch nurse named van Bockelen who had assisted at Eline's birth, arrived from Rotterdam. She placed the van Leeuwens' daughter behind her, and pedaled into the night. Pauline repeated the ordeal with her son. The couple then packed their own belongings and removed any evidence of their lives from the rental home. Together they fled to a third residence, that of the Troostenburg de Bruin family, where Pauline would now be forced to live in the confines of a single room. Dividing the children made cold statistical sense. If one was found, the other might survive. The family would now endure as *onderduikers*—"under-divers"—hiding beneath the veneer of visible society.

Carel, Eline, and Marianne

ON THE WARMER DAYS of their first summer together Eline and Marianne often played in the shadow of the hayloft, arranging their dolls in beds of grass. Eline missed her mother and father, but soon settled into the rhythms of the Soetendael. When a doll became sick, it was pampered with medicines the girls made with summer wildflowers.

Despite my mom's large family, she was born during one of those unkind intervals: too young to play with her older siblings and too old to play with the youngest. But that wasn't the only reason she was a loner; she seemed to have been born that way. Since her birth, she had had little tolerance for older brother and sisters. Baby Marianne screamed if they touched her; she screamed if they touched her toys. Up until the time Eline arrived, Marianne was content to live alone in her own imaginary world with her nanny by her side. Leo and Pauline's daughter would become my mother's closest, and perhaps only, childhood friend. The two wandered together nearly every day amongst the swing set and the flower gardens. Because of her fair skin, Eline didn't live like most hidden Jews. She was now Anne Schoorl's niece, a talkative and outgoing little girl, able to come and go from the farm just like all of Piet and Anne's children.

THE BATTLES IN THE SKIES over Bennekom continued into the fall, and Iet continued to find safety in the arms of her father. When the leaves turned, school began. Together as usual, Eline and Marianne prepared for their first day of classes. After breakfast they left the Soetendael, following a narrow footpath through a small hole in the thick hedge. Walking hand-in-hand, they continued through the adjacent field and onto the road and to their Montessori school. To the east, Hitler's armies battled the Russians in the rubble of Stalingrad. In Poland, the Nazis commenced with their final solution.

Chapter 10

PIET AND ANNE'S first months as newly forged members of the resistance passed without incident. The pages of the calendar turned, and the cold winter winds blew through the Soetendael turning the branches frosty white; the pastures hardened and the canals froze thick. If it didn't snow, the air cut crisp. Soon the family began to prepare for a day in Holland known as "Sinterklaas." As a child, I called it Dutch Christmas.

When I was growing up, December 25 was always overshadowed by December 5. By the third grade I knew Santa Claus wasn't real. We discussed this fact across our desks at school. But I always inserted what had, by then, become obvious to me—Saint Nick and Black Pieter were real. "They come every year on a ship from Spain," I told my classmates. "If you're good, Saint Nick puts a gift in your wooden shoe at night; if you're bad, Black Pieter will put you in his bag and take you back to Spain, and you'll have to work for him for the whole year." The haunting truth of it sparkled in my eyes with such clarity my friends could do nothing but believe it themselves.

While the rest of our neighborhood quietly endured another rainy Pacific Northwest evening, our home bustled with anticipation as we readied for the arrival of the Saint and his mischievous assistant. Mom made traditional Dutch desserts, dropping dollops of apple-filled batter into a pan of sizzling oil. Our fireplace crackled, and we kids scurried through our home preparing gifts for one another.

Mom worked for weeks preparing for the night. Christmas never had a chance. When the sun finally set and night descended on our dead-end road, we opened our windows and sang Dutch songs until Black Pieter heard us. He threw candy through the breezy holes, and our singing stopped mid-breath as we dove for the treats, the rough carpet scraping hot against our little knees. Eventually, Black Piet would bang on our front door. By the time we opened it, he would be gone, leaving piles of manila-wrapped packages in his place. The festivities wandered into the late-night hours.

ON DECEMBER 5, 1942, Anne made soup inside her warm kitchen. Unlike the spacious dining and living rooms, the kitchen hardly allowed room for the maid to pass behind her. It had a cave-like feel with only one small window, opening to the darker north side of the home. Anne always finished making dinner early on the day of Sinterklaas so she had the rest of the afternoon to finish wrapping the children's gifts. Despite the war, Anne would make sure that both St. Nick and Black Pieter managed the journey to her little farm.

When the dark of night descended on the farm, Anne peeled back the black paper covering the windows and opened the glass panes. The five older kids gathered excitedly around the piano. Anne's fingers danced on the keys as she sang with the children. Handfuls of candy flew through the breezy holes and bounced off the wood floors. The kids squealed and raced for the treats. Piet Schoorl worked behind the scenes.

After a few songs, the doorbell rang and the kids hurried to the front door and pulled it open. Standing in the night, beside the family's large wicker laundry basket filled with gifts, stood Black Pieter and Saint Nicholas. The children stared, wide-eyed. Nicholas had a long white beard, and his assistant had a large smile. The children looked at the two with part reverence, part fear, and squirming with excitement. They led the holy man to the living room and offered him a seat on the large leather recliner. Black Pieter's face glistened dark as he handed gifts to the children. The basket overflowed with even more packages than usual. Discarded wrapping paper soon piled up between the children's seats.

After the flurry of gift opening calmed, Black Pieter invited little Eline up on his lap. Ruud and Hanneke both watched as tears filled the corners of Black Pieter's eyes. The drops grabbed the light as they trickled down his dark face. Leo watched his wife's arms wrap around his daughter. Pauline's thin body trembled.

Protected by black face paint and a saint's clothes, Leo and Pauline eventually departed back into the night. As they walked down the Soetendael's curving gravel drive, the dim lights of the home disappeared behind them. The last seconds with their daughter had surprised them both. Neither Leo nor Pauline had divulged their true identity to Eline. But as they bid the children farewell, Eline looked up at her mom. "Goodbye Momma," she said with a smile.

Leo and Pauline continued through the dark avenues of Bennekom. There were perhaps hundreds of couples dressed as they were, all visiting the children of Holland. They soon arrived back at the Troostenburg de Bruin home. It wasn't a welcome sight. Leo and Tinus Troostenburg de Bruin had recently shared harsh words. Tinus suffered from some sort of mental disability, and whenever he felt bothered by Leo or Pauline, he threatened to turn them both over to the Germans. Soon after the New Year, Tynus had become so unstable it was evident that Leo and Pauline were no longer safe.

IT TOOK THREE DAYS in Iet's living room to fill ten hours of interview tape. The voices of pedestrians and the occasional ring of a bike's bell continued to rise up from the town square beneath her open window. The number of commuters swelled at rush hour and flowed to a trickle during those lazy afternoon hours. "Do you know what that building is?" Iet asked, pointing out her window and across the square. Opposite her home, and no taller, stood the Hotel de Wereld, the words painted an ivory that matched the red brick building's elegant portico. "That's where the peace was signed," she said, answering her own question.

On May 5, 1945, after almost exactly five years, the war formally ended across the street from Iet's home with the swipe of a pen. The sun's slanted light filled the square with shadows and lit up one side of Iet's face as she looked out the west-facing window. I watched a motherly-looking woman ride her bike across the pavers while holding the leash of her large black dog.

The corners of Iet's living room darkened in the twilight. The deep gouges in her worn antique table turned black. The names and faces of the world my aunt resurrected seemed to linger in the shadows, and I lingered

with them. I was born under the bright lights of a hospital room in Mountain View, California, but this is
where I came from—nobody I'm related to was ever
buried in America. I was trying to place the pieces of
my past—my family's fractured legacy—back into order, to follow the story to its end: an ending that, in a
way, marked my beginning.

The next morning, I rode Bram's old bike past the
Hotel de Wereld and the delicatessen and disappeared
around the same corner as the woman and her black
dog. I rode through the heart of Wageningen, by the
twice-blown-up church, past the ruined Roman walls
that once defended the city, and over the arch of a wide
brick bridge. The pavers turned to an asphalt bike path
as I left Wageningen and pedaled under a row of old
oaks towards my mother's hometown of Bennekom,
my mind drifting between the sights and scents of 20th
century Holland and those my aunt had brought to life.

When Piet first accepted the van Leeuwens' daughter into his home, he had felt uneasy. He worried about
the possible outcomes of harboring Eline. Piet was a
man of science, a thinker. Bent over the wide tables of
his laboratory, he would distill customer's products into
their essential elements. He had surely done the same
when contemplating the possible outcomes of harboring a Jew. But as his first months as an enemy of the
Nazis passed, something changed.

Piet had always felt obligated to right society's
wrongs. Piet's socially progressive father—a university
professor—had nurtured his conscience. As a college
student, Piet had joined the Social Democrats, an ardent group of idealists whose sensibilities and values
are perhaps best described as a mix between Marx's
communism and the American hippie movement of

the sixties, minus the drugs. Neither Piet nor Anne drank alcohol—they believed it the cause of many of society's struggles. When living in Bennekom, Piet and Anne were always quick to help their poor neighbors. They had organized community day-hikes through the woods of Bennekom and gathered with close friends in their parlor at night, discussing the ills of capitalism and their hopes for a future that took better care of the common man. But war added something new in the mix for Piet. There was more at work than just his political or moral sensibilities. Hiding Eline had tickled the same part of him that loved throwing his Douglas motorcycle into a tight turn and that relished a hard game of soccer. Piet grew partly fond of the intrigue, of the game of cat-and-mouse he now played with the Germans. He liked to win. He hated losing.

The bike path continued beneath the shade of a forest and toward the heart of Bennekom. I had only begun to grasp the story of my grandparents. I had yet to patch all the disparate memories together. But I understood enough to recognize 1943 as the year that Piet and Anne had been picked up in a whirlwind.

The tires of Bram's bike bounced over a split in the asphalt where a root had rippled the black surface. I passed the road where, five years after the war had ended, my mother and father first met. I passed the rows of stores that my grandmother had once shopped and then the two church steeples that still competed for Bennekom's skyline. I passed the baker and the greengrocer and glided toward the Soetendael.

I don't think either of my grandparents could have ever closed their door on a person in need, especially someone in mortal danger. Piet and Anne were both uncommonly giving people. But for both of them, and especially Anne, helping the Jews touched a more base part of their nature, a place beneath their beliefs and ideals—that seemingly complex, shadowy place where most forge their decisions and unconsciously choose their lives.

For my grandmother, it seems the war gave her a place in this world. Always conscious of her humble beginnings as an uneducated farmer's daughter, Anne had struggled to feel a part of Piet's life outside their daily routines. When the couple entertained guests from Piet's days as a student or Piet's business associates, Anne's sixth-grade education stood out in the company of Ph.D.s. And the fact made her feel painfully awkward. But it was never in Anne's nature to simply put up her arms in frustration; Anne read voraciously, especially on subjects involving any one of the many scientific projects Piet might have been working on at the time. However, the fact was that no matter how hard she railed against it, Anne gave up her life on her father's farm for that of a housewife, and the role didn't particularly suit her. From childhood, Anne was driven by a nameless ambition. She seemed born with a passion and a hunger for some way to express a latent potential she felt inside, for a challenge, a fight: a good fight, something to test her mettle and prove what deep down, beyond that place formed of words, Anne probably knew to be true—that she was an abnormally capable woman, capable of the extraordinary.

Hiding Jews was to become the first enterprise in which the couple engaged as equals. And when Leo and Pauline asked if they could join their daughter and hide at the farm, Piet and Anne did not refuse—nor would they refuse anyone, ever. And the requests for sanctuary continued with predictable results. Before the apple blossoms of '43 blew across the Soetendael's vegetable garden, the family's farm and Piet's laboratory would fill with Jews.

A blue Opel was parked in the driveway of the laboratory. I braked in front of the home and leaned the bike to one side resting my foot on the pavement. The creamy white stucco house sat back no more than two car-lengths from the avenue. I looked inside the arched picture window. I imagined Piet standing behind the glass panes wearing his white lab coat and scribbling sums in his notebook with the twist and curls of slender glass tubes bubbling under the blue heat of a Bunsen burner flame. He stood just a few inches shorter than me. Pauline van Leeuwen's little sister, Adele, and her husband, Simon, were the first Jews Piet hid inside his place of business. Their arrival mimicked that of Leo and Pauline in many regards. The family had followed Leo and Pauline to Bennekom and had rented a house in the same neighborhood. Faced with the same predicament as Leo and Pauline, they also decided to go into hiding. They also had two children, a boy and a girl, and before they found refuge in the attic of Piet's lab they had also surrendered their children to a stranger. That day proved no less harrowing.

The couple had driven toward the adjacent town of Renkum with Ruth and Ruben. The car turned into a wooded estate. "You're going to stay with a nice auntie," Adele said to her 6-year-old daughter. But something didn't seem right to young Ruth.

"How come I've never met this auntie?" Ruth asked. Similar to her cousin Eline, she was also a precocious and strong-willed child. Large hardwood trees shaded the road and soon the estate's immense white mansion came into view. "Is this where we're going?"

The car passed the mansion and turned right on the road to the caretaker's house, a small dwelling hidden in the woods of the estate. Simon took his daughter and his 2-year-old son into the home of Ms. Bos. Ruth screamed in protest. The girl was used to getting her way. Her parents had never treated her so forcibly in the past. Something was desperately wrong and Ruth knew it.

That the family was even in Europe was something of a mistake, and unfortunately a horrible one. In 1939, unaware of the storm of violent anti-Semitism brewing in Germany, the couple had decided to travel from Palestine to Holland so Simon could take a six-month course in car mechanics in the Dutch town of Driebergen, and they could also visit their relatives in Rotterdam. The threat of war never crossed their minds. No one suggested the family not come. After the couple and their daughter Ruth arrived in Holland, the borders closed, and they couldn't return home.

Adele, more an intellectual than her fashionable sister and not as becoming, had been a practicing lawyer in Palestine. Simon had played the violin in the Palestinian philharmonic orchestra and was also an accomplished painter and photographer. Trapped in the Netherlands, the family eventually moved to Rotterdam to be close to Leo and Pauline. The couple's baby boy, Ruben, was born only a few months before the Nazis' bombs rained down on the city. Simon had also placed his children in an iron bathtub as the explosions rolled through their neighborhood.

Ms. Bos held blonde-haired Ruben in her arms. Simon paid the widow—Ms. Bos charged by the head— and Simon then hurried out her front door.

I looked up at the burgundy tile that skirted the roof's flat top. The attic wasn't small. A slender dormer with a sizable window opened toward the street. Piet had a secret button installed in the first-story laboratory that triggered an attic alarm to signal if strangers were downstairs.

"My dad wanted to have a lot of children so they could help change the world," Iet had told me a day earlier, "to make it a better place."

"He said that to you?"

"Yes, he did . . . I remember it."

"He told you this when you were a child?"

"Yes." Iet smiled.

Piet didn't believe in a God. But he did have a sense of the good in the world. And he firmly believed he had a responsibility to serve that good and help it grow. The lab could hide several families and I worked to remember each.

Simon and Adele were soon joined by another Jewish couple, Kurt and Lisel Dannenbaum, and then by a single young Dutchman, who called himself Bart Bes. Kurt and Lisel were German Jews. They had fled their homeland to Amsterdam. When the Nazi blitzkrieg followed them to the old Dutch city, they again fled, this time to the countryside, to a small town close to Bennekom named Heelsum. Kurt was a dentist, and during the calm of 1941, he set up a practice in the village. When it became obvious the couple couldn't survive in the open, Mr. Hartman, Bennekom's butcher—who also operated independently as a member of the resistance—directed the Dannenbaums to Piet and Anne. Thankfully, the Dannenbaums had already sent their teenage son to live in England.

Bart Bes was a more shadowy, enigmatic figure. Short and thickly built, the Dutchman's history wasn't clear to anyone except Piet, who had known the quiet and unassuming man when Bart was still known by his real name, Jan Slof. Piet had met the young biological scientist at the University in Wageningen. By 1943, Jan was on the Germans' list of "wanted men." No one knew exactly why. No one asked.

I looked up at the black railing of the second story balcony. I felt the breeze of a car passing on the road behind me. Dr. Gorter, Piet's assistant, and Anne's two sisters had lived in that second story. All three helped care for Adele and the Dannenbaums, and the five guests lived comfortably. The Dannenbaums and Adele looked Jewish and they would rarely leave the attic. Simon, a tall, broad and fair-skinned man, also with blue eyes, came and went as he pleased.

The thorny bright-green husks of yet-to-drop chestnuts hung from the trees above my head. I thought about knocking on the front door and asking the owners if they knew the unique history of their home. But I had only stopped to take a quick look on my way to the farm.

The little orange, blue, and green plastic balls that Bram had fastened to the spokes of his bicycle when he was young bounced melodically against the rims as I pushed the bike off the sidewalk and crossed the road. The Soetendael was only a few blocks west. I left the main avenue and pedaled down a side road toward the farm. I could see the Soetendael's immense hedge from two blocks away. I rode around it on a side road and toward the back of the house. In 1943, if I were on foot, I could have exited the road about halfway between the lab and the farm and walked on a narrow trail across a small field and then through a hole in the hedge, arriving at the farm's front door. Adele made the journey at night, once a week on Sunday nights. It was bath night for the Soetendael's children and Adele helped wash them, first the older three—Hans, Iet and Ruud, and then the younger three—Marianne, Eline, and Helene. The precious moments out of the lab's attic, and the company of the children, helped Adele remain sane.

Even today the farm is difficult to locate. The driveway leading to the Soetendael branches off of the neighbor's. If you hope to find it, you need directions. I pedaled past the open gate; the words "de Soetendael" were painted white across the gate's top board. I steered the bike into a patch of grass next to the driveway, dropped the kickstand and removed my camera from the saddlebags. Two sisters, granddaughters of the man who had leased the farm to Piet and Anne, lived at the farm.

The large imposing garage doors had been painted a glossy black. The broad brick walls of the building's first story angled halfway up the second-story gable and were met by the straw hip of the carefully thatched roof.

After Leo and Pauline's arrival, Anne unhinged the latch underneath her dining-room table and pulled it open on its tracks, placing a leaf within the space. By the time summer arrived she had repeated the task two more times, installing all three of the table's extra leaves.

I walked toward the garage. I had been told about the awkward way the house sat on its own property, how the front door was facing the rear of the farm, but it wasn't until that moment that I felt the uncomfortable choice upon me. I looked behind the house. The oaks shadowed the grass. There was no obvious path. I decided to walk around the building's front, past the large living-room windows. I felt like I was trespassing.

By midsummer, the farm's reputation as a safe hiding place had made its way through the underground. On one evening, a priest knocked on the farm's door. He had a young Jewish woman with him who had escaped from the Germans and tried to hide inside his church. The Schoorls had never met the priest. He didn't say who had guided him to the Soetendael.

The Dutch resistance around Bennekom didn't form any type of single group. It was instead more like a web, each person forming an intersection of trust connecting one member to another. An individual may have only been connected to one or two others, and each person in turn trusted another. Jews were passed through these lines of trusts. No one shared where he or she had come from, or who had passed from whom. The less any single person knew the better.

Chel van Dijk, the young woman in the priest's care, had endured some type of trauma at the hands of the Nazis. To Anne, she looked confused. Whatever the Germans had done to her, it had affected her mind. Anne took Chel into the home and she became another of the Soetendael's long-term guests. Her mind never healed. Sometimes the children would see Chel wandering naked through the house. As with so many of the events at the Soetendael, Anne didn't bother to explain anything to the kids. When Chel suddenly appeared in the nude, Anne would just get up and take her back into her room and help her put her clothes on. The children called Chel "funny auntie." I knocked on the same front door as the priest had on that evening.

A slender woman greeted me. She held the leash of a large German Shepherd. "My name's Nick Briejer," I said. "My grandparents lived here during the war. Did you get the letter I sent you?" I had written a letter stating my interest in the farm. The well-behaved dog nudged his dark muzzle forward.

"Is there a chance I could look inside? It would mean a lot to me."

"I was just going to take my dog for a walk," she said, not looking particularly inviting. However, it wasn't an option to leave. I needed to be inside the home. It was as much of the reason I had travelled to Holland as interviewing my aunts. The Soetendael lived so vividly in everyone's memories it was as though the farm was animated—a living benefactor—and I had resolved to summon my grandmother's legendary stubbornness to gain entrance if necessary. I'd already run through scenarios in my head, but they weren't necessary.

"I can wait," I quickly replied, and asked if I could look around the property. She obliged, and I was alone, standing on the soil of my ancestors for the first time in my life.

I walked across the lawn where the swing set used to be, and by the brittle branches of the unpruned fruit trees and toward the hayloft. The loft still stood. The four posts had weathered a light gray and the cracked and twisting grain spun to a dull point high above the roof's peak. I looked at the thick rusting hardware that fastened the roof to posts. Holes had been bored into each post at forearm-length intervals so the hardware could be raised or lowered. I doubt the roof had moved from its present position during my lifetime, but the relic still held strong.

Ollie van Dyk, another young Jewish woman, also came to the Soetendael that summer. She had been hiding in a small room above the Post Office in the town of Harderwijk. The cramped quarters were driving her mad. She became my mom's second nanny, after Mom's first had left the farm because her family thought it was too dangerous. I walked past the hayloft and toward the pasture. I could see the abandoned one-room farmhouse where the Schoorls' neighbors, the van de Brinks, used to live.

Leo and Pauline and their daughter Eline, and Ollie van Dyk and "funny auntie" were not the farm's only guests. During the summer of '43 there was a constant stream of Jewish refugees trickling into the Soetendael. The farm and the lab quickly filled and Piet and Anne continually searched for new places to hide the Jews, new "addresses" as they called them.

The Soetendael had remained almost unchanged since the war. I walked the pastures in near isolation, surrounded by nothing but the birds and the trees. I remembered a story I had been told by Iet. It was one of the ones I had remembered being told as a child.

"I know someone who can help you find a place to hide Jews," a trusted friend once said to Piet, and he directed Piet to this mystery person. Piet met the man, but he wasn't the one who actually knew about this safe hiding place, but he knew someone who knew. Piet went from person to person following the leads. As was the rule, Piet didn't ask anybody's name, and no one ever asked for his. Eventually, Piet met the man who actually knew the location of the hiding place. "The man you're looking for is named Pieter Schoorl," the stranger said. "He has a small farm in Bennekom." The exact same thing also once happened to Anne.

I remembered my mother telling me this story. The funny stories survived the war and had traveled with Mom across the Atlantic. I snapped pictures of the farmhouse and the hayloft and berry bushes climbing over a barbed wire fence. I wandered until the Soetend-ael's owner and her dog returned and then stepped over the threshold and into my mother's childhood home.

I walked through the narrow hallway, past the study and the cramped kitchen. "This is the living room," the woman said in exacting English. "My grandfather was an officer in Indonesia, and he filled the home with items he imported from around the world." She gestured toward the ornate tiles skirting the fireplace mantel. The sun was unobstructed in the cloudless sky and beams of light shone through the window, cutting a line down the middle of the room and illuminating those usually invisible bits of dust that hung, seemingly motionless, in the air.

The Schoorls' piano used to be in this room. Anne would play at night, accompanying the voices of the families as everyone in the home gathered together and sang songs. Twelve-year-old Hanneke had her mother's singing voice and she treasured those nights by the piano. The families always finished with the same song, Ha Tikvah—The Hope: the Jewish national anthem. "In the Jewish heart, a Jewish spirit still sings" the song begins.

I looked over at where the Schoorls' large dining-room table once sat, and could see the hayloft through the two picture windows. The sweet aroma of Anne's Dutch pancakes, thin crepe-like creations with the edges slightly browned by sizzling butter, had filled this room. Bart Bes often joined the family for breakfast along with Dr. Gorter. The children always noticed the curious lunchbox-size apparatus Bart concealed beneath his heavy shirts. No one ever told the children to not ask questions, but they had somehow learned not to.

The Schoorl kids didn't mind the strangers who appeared regularly at the table, nor the fact that they

never knew whether or not their beds would be needed for one of the Soetendael's more temporary guests.
For the children, the extra company brought additional warmth and coziness to the home, particularly
the presence of the affectionate and elegant Pauline
van Leeuwen. Anne—never inclined to fawn over her
children to begin with—grew increasingly busy as the
war progressed, searching for extra food and providing for the needs of the guests. Pauline brushed the
girls' hair and talked with them about their dreams for
the future. She was affectionate and attentive in ways
Anne had never been, and all of the children luxuriated in her care. In many ways, Pauline was Anne's
opposite: slender, educated, and fashionable, and she
rarely stepped outside of the safety of the farmhouse.
The flow of her fine dresses became an ever-present
fixture in the children's lives. Even when kids from the
Montessori school gathered on the Soetendael's front
lawn on a sunny summer afternoon to celebrate Eline's
fourth birthday, Ruud could see Pauline's head peeking
down from the second-story deck as she watched her
daughter open birthday gifts. The Schoorl children had
learned to call all of their parents' friends Auntie and
Uncle, but within only a few months, Leo and Pauline
had truly become a part of the children's family.

The interconnected living room and dining room
aren't large by today's standards, but in its day the room
seemed expansive. "It's just me and my sister," the
woman said. "We do our best to keep things up." My
eyes darted from corner to corner, trying to refashion
the memories swelling in my head.

Hanneke and Iet used to help their mom set up card
tables on the weekends. All of the guests from the lab,
and some from other close-by hiding places, snuck to

the Soetendael under the cover of a moonless night for an evening of bridge. Anne worked hard not only to feed all of the guests, but also to keep them busy. She brought Kurt Dannenbaum one of her spinning wheels and taught him to spin wool. Kurt's fingers, disciplined from years of dentistry, could twist a thin thread. His wife, Lisel, knit the new yarn into shawls. Anne encouraged Hans and Iet to visit the lab and spend time with the couple.

This room was the heart of the home. The slants of sunlight drew lines on the dark mahogany trim. One evening several members of the Dutch resistance gathered at the dining room table along with Piet and Anne and Anne's sister, Toe. The Gestapo had captured a fellow member of the resistance. The children listened as the group discussed their plan to free the man. He was injured and the Germans had put him in the local hospital where Anne's sister, Toe, worked as a nurse. The Dutch policeman guarding the injured man had agreed to help with the escape plan. Toe smuggled a revolver into the hospital and gave it to the unarmed policeman. The policeman let the prisoner free and shot himself in the leg to make it appear as though he had struggled.

I looked at the far window. There were so many stories. The old memories I had captured on tape were like images seen through a narrow tube, isolated moments. But I knew the moments had unfolded in the complete spectrums of the world in which I now stood. I tried to bring the two together, the patches of history with the smell of the room, the dim memories with the sunlight.

On one of those summer days of '43, after their home was already filled with Jews, Piet and Anne stood next to the small window in the kitchen, looking toward the bend in the gravel drive leading to the farm's gate. They had heard that a *razzia*—a systematic German raid—had been ordered in the village and the Germans were moving from house to house, searching for Jews. Up to that point, the farm had proven safe enough and isolated enough. A false wall had been constructed in the third-story bedroom precisely for this type of event, and after gathering up all evidence of the large number of people who lived in the home, the guests squeezed behind the false wall and labored to remain silent. But just before the Germans closed in on the farm, on the other side of the property, a Jewish family—a husband and wife and two young boys—pushed their way through the hedge and into the Soetendael's pasture. They were fleeing from another location and must have known about the farm. They ran toward the house. Piet and Anne knew they only had a few spare minutes, and they hurried the family into the attached barn and hid them in the loft.

The day's sun had reached its zenith. The lit dust hung motionless. Out the picture window I could see the black and white of the neighbor's cows. My grandparents wrapped their arms around each other and continued staring out that window, waiting. They both doubted the soldiers would fail to find the four new Jews. If they marched down the driveway, it would be over. I heard the rhythmical click of the German Shepherd's claws as he walked down the hallway behind me.

An official warning, signed by Bennekom's physician, had been attached to the Soetendael's closed gate earlier that summer when my mother got sick, cautioning the public against a possible case of diphtheria at the farm. For obvious reasons, Piet had left the sign up. The soldiers finally came into view and turned into the Soetendael's driveway. They came to the gate, and Piet could see one of the men read the warning. Perhaps a more clever soldier might have understood the sign as the device that it was, or maybe this soldier was both clever and kind. No one can know for sure what went through his mind, but he read the warning closely and then decided not to search the farm. Piet and Anne continued to hold each other as they watched the Germans pause, then turn away. It's likely the shock took time to drain from them, and whatever illusions the couple had, whatever cavalier ideas that may have lived in them, whatever denial of the danger they had put their family in, also likely died within that moment by the window. As they stood there, looking through the panes, I expect they both understood the thin margins separating survival from death.

After the soldiers left their neighborhood, Piet sent Ruud upstairs to tell the Jews it was safe to come out. Anne invited their four newest guests into the living room. She served tea. The couple introduced themselves as Paul and Greet Wagenaar. They had two kindergarten-age boys, Ben and Joost. The boys looked dazed, their bushy black hair disheveled. It appeared as though their parents had just grabbed them from some other hiding place before racing to the Soetendael. The large living room seemed to swallow them both.

I stood quietly in that same space. The images in my head felt like those manifold bits of suspended dust that played in the sunlight, pieces of the past lacking an orbit, history fractured. Only a single day had passed since I first heard of the Wagenaars' two children.

"I see those two boys, Ben and Joost, in the middle of the room ... frightened," Iet had told me. "They were very scared." Iet had paused, staring hard against the wall of her own home and then repeated herself. "I see them in the middle of the room—I still see them." The images had remained in her, and unspoken, for longer that I had been alive, but the decades separating the old woman in front of me from that tomboy she had described didn't seem to slow the wash of memories. "Perhaps it's because I learned afterwards that they were sent to Westerbork."

The Wagenaars had stayed at the farm until the Schoorls could find a new hiding place for the family. Paul had also been a dentist. They were a well-educated and quiet couple. An address was found. But for reasons no one remembers, Paul and Greet didn't feel safe there. They left the new hiding place and, again, split the family up, hiding the two boys separate from themselves. The parents soon learned that Ben and Joost were both found by the Nazis. After Westerbork, the children were transported east to Auschwitz and murdered.

My fingers traced a path down the smooth railing as I descended the Soetendael's wood staircase. I had wandered through every part of the farmhouse. I saw the large upstairs room Piet had built for the children before the war. I saw the room where my mom slept, and the steep ladder-like stairs that led to the home's attic where the maid and the nanny lived and where the Schoorls created the false wall. There were too many rooms to remember them all. I stepped down onto the stairs' middle landing and gripped the railing as I turned right. The dark patina of the wood underhand shone with generations of use. The home's owner invited me to share tea on the front lawn. Her dog panted in the heat.

My mom was five years old in '43. Fall came. The leaves of the oak trees again turned brown and fell on the farm's gravel drive. School resumed. After sharing breakfast, the kids left for their classes. And as had been the ritual for years, they all returned at noon for lunch at the farm.

Mom now walked the mile home from her kindergarten class alone. Eline no longer joined her. The family had decided it was too dangerous. Though most of Bennekom's villagers were sympathetic to the Jews, several families had joined the NSB—the Dutch arm of the Nazi party—and though vehemently despised by their fellow citizens, these few enjoyed new power and prestige in their community. And since long familiar with the village and its people, they were also more capable of smelling out a charade such as Eline's. Mom wore a dress to school, and on colder days, wool stockings underneath. Her silky hair was pulled into two pony tails, tied with ribbons matching the color of her clothes. It always took a good amount of time for Marianne's short legs to travel the distance home. But as the school year progressed, she arrived later and later for lunch. The family became concerned.

Eventually Anne asked one of the children to find out what was taking Marianne so long. The reason, they discovered, was as simple as it was peculiar. As soon as Marianne left the school, she began to scan the street, looking carefully at the entrance of each home she encountered between her school and the Soetendael. If any of the residence's gates were open, the 5-year-old stopped, walked over to it, closed the gate and secured the latch. The job took time.

Marianne was not the only member of the family whose life developed idiosyncratic tendencies. There was something insidious about the way the war lived on the edges of the Schoorl home. The bombers appeared in the night sky like bad dreams and left with the same abruptness of a nightmare's specter. The numerous guests arriving under the cover of night entered and departed the farm with calm civility. They drank tea and played cards and did their best to talk of anything but their terrible fears. The war didn't drop its blood on the floor of the home, or explode in the farm's fertile soil. But it was there, haunting everyone. Iet, if she could survive the night in her own room, regularly slept at the foot of her bed, balled up beneath the covers. Every couple of weeks, Leo was bedridden with a mysterious ailment. Pauline would nurse him until the fit passed. Adele had not seen Ruth or Ruben for more than a year, and her mind suffered through each day wondering and worrying.

The families still did their best to introduce levity into their routine. They still gathered at night to sing, or sometimes they put out all of the lights in the house and played hide-and-seek; Hanneke still removed the blue and white china from the cabinet and made place settings on the family's fine linens for dinner. But the shadows—the ones no one would talk about, the ones that remained dormant for so many years until they descended on my adult mom as she drove her blue Subaru home on that fine summer day—continued to darken. The war pressed down on everyone's soul, and Dr. Pieter Schoorl suffered under the heaviest load.

I thanked the Soetendael's owner and pedaled down the farm's driveway. I turned past the hedge and toward the lab. My mind drifted between generations as the sun began its decline. I was traveling the exact road my grandfather had traveled on the day of his arrest. The bike's tire bumped over cobblestone.

Three times a week, Piet rode to Bennekom's station and boarded the train to Amsterdam. On his train ride to the city, Piet often carried falsified identification cards and food ration coupons. Piet had stolen the ID cards. He took them from anyone. His friends' IDs regularly turned up missing. During the summer, Piet and Anne went on a vacation to a sailing school by the IJsselmeer. They stole IDs from their fellow sailing students. With the careful hands of an artist, Simon de Leeuwe used peroxide to scrape off the names of the original owners, and refashion the cards in the manner needed.

On Piet's return trips back from Amsterdam he smuggled Jewish children out of the city. I don't know who, or how many. Some of them he brought to the home of Ms. Bos, the widow who lived in the woods of Renkum. There could have been others. Most of what Piet did occurred beyond the eyes and hence the memories of his children.

I passed near the lab. The blue Opel was still parked in the driveway.

Piet had established a routine upon returning to the Soetendael at night after his trips to Amsterdam. It reminded me of my mother's gate closing, though not as benign. He would walk through the door of his home, set down his coat and briefcase and immediately begin cleaning and picking up toys left out by any of the six children, and while he cleaned he'd berate Anne, blaming her for the mess. He grew increasingly aggressive, despite the fact that the home wasn't particularly messy. It was simply bursting at the seams with people.

One evening, in an attempt to calm her husband, Anne with the help of Pauline, Hans, and Iet cleaned the home spotless. Every child's toy, or piece of sewing, or teacup that had been set down and forgotten was put away, and when Piet arrived not a single item in the home was out of place. Piet noticed the clean home immediately. He didn't say a word. He set down his effects and looked around. Anne watched his eyes nervously scan the room. Piet then walked to one of the home's many drawers, pulled it open and began anxiously rearranging the contents.

It's impossible to say what exactly took place inside Piet. The details of his trips to Amsterdam remain a mystery. Piet never told anyone anything unless they absolutely needed to know, not even his wife. I knew Piet worked independently. This, he had stated clearly. Somehow he had connected with elements of the resistance in Amsterdam, probably through his work. But it's all conjecture.

I glided through downtown Bennekom, over the curving main avenue where the train used to run and passed the same rows of three-story buildings that greeted Piet on his trips. I wondered how the last hours of the day unfolded for Piet before returning to the farm from Amsterdam—not the simple logistics, the where and the who—but the subtler details. I wondered if he sat close to the children in his care, if he rested his hand on the child's shoulder, if he comforted them. I wondered if my grandfather felt any warmth in his belly at all, or if the stress had drained him so cold that he wouldn't allow himself to contemplate the future of the child by his side, if he felt so strained that he counted the minutes for the train ride to end. His war had escalated slowly. One simple choice in the name of "good" and "right" had led to another. By the fall of '43, the choices had consumed his life, and he had risked the lives of everyone he loved.

Weeks later, when I returned home from Holland, I took a bath with my youngest son, 18-month-old Adam.

My family's war was still fresh in me, and I had spent months trying to understand the truth about what my family and their guests had endured. As I lathered my boy's head, feeling the ridges of soft growing skull underneath his thin skin, I continued the work of imagining war. The water and soap fell down the shiny ripple of his small vertebrae. As Adam's short hair turned dark in the water, I thought of Ben and Joost, and the boy's parents. I thought of Westerbork and Auschwitz. It's hard to do but I also couldn't help it. Adam turned around. He bit into a red plastic ball and looked at me. His new eyes, long wet lashes and the smooth skin of his face looked unblemished—perfect. He stared into my eyes and grinned. I thought of dressing him in his favorite denim overalls, combing his wet hair, choosing what to pack in his suitcase, remembering his favorite blanket that Grammy gave him. I pictured saying good-bye and placing him in the arms of a stranger. I pictured hiding in a small attic and looking at the walls remembering his tiny fingernails on the evening of his birth, or the look in his eyes when he used to hit his head against our iron coffee table or tripped on the feet of his own pajamas and would look at me questioningly—as though I let it happen. I pictured the moment I learn he's been found and will die. I pictured hoping he still has his favorite pacifier, and I get a sense of what unbearable means.

Despite his deterioration, Piet continued to push himself. Ms. Bos eventually had over a dozen children hiding in her attic. Piet continued to make the trips, and the sun dropping in the western horizon continued to stretch the evening shadows as he and his smuggled cargo rolled along the tracks.

Iet, Marianne, Piet, Hanneke, and Ruud

Book Two

Chapter 11

THE HUSBANDS AND WIVES, mothers and fathers of those imprisoned within the Gestapo's Euterpe Street headquarters still remained just beyond the guards and gate, waiting for any news. A black flag with the two white thunderbolts of the SS insignia hung from a pole in the courtyard. The structure's clock tower loomed above, and ivy fell from the thick brick walls of what had once been a girls' school. Piet sat across from his interrogators. The Nazis had learned his name, but that was all they had. Piet refused to answer any of their questions. To the best of my knowledge, the Germans remained civil. The arrest of this coatless Dutchman was probably routine, and when it became evident Piet wouldn't cooperate, they led him down a flight of stairs and into the guts of the building.

The autumn sun did little to warm the cold earth. The concrete hallway underneath Euterpe Street still held the night's chill. The rows of narrow cells were menacing more by notoriety than simple appearance. For some, the walls of the shadowy underbelly of the SS headquarters would be the last they ever saw. The Nazis regularly tortured their prisoners till death; the process was systematic and effective, and evidence of it still stained the floor Piet walked upon.

The heavy hinged door of a prison cell closed behind Piet. He heard the bolt of the door latch shut, and stood alone in the cold. The sudden silence and solitude caught him off guard, so much so that for a moment he considered himself from a distance, as he would a puzzling chemical reaction. It was as though all of the events of the last year had continued to build in both tempo and volume until they had reached a final crescendo in the last twelve hours, and then it was as if all of a sudden the maddening music stopped, and all of the players simply disappeared. And his next moments also proved equally counter-intuitive. Piet's shoulders dropped. He relaxed, and a wave of relief warmed his body. Still analyzing his reactions, he recognized the feeling as oddly reminiscent of gentler times before the war, before the bombers and the soldiers and the Jews who would push through the hole in his farm's hedge or knock on his door at night and yoke him with the responsibility for their survival. One day earlier, his every moment had been carefully calculated. He fashioned each of his days as demanded by the chaos of war. If idle, he worried over the endless scenarios that could go terribly wrong. Each time he turned a corner, he had no idea what lurked beyond it—whether friend or enemy—everyone took a piece of him. The cell's silence and the solitude reminded him, in fact, of a particular moment before the invasion, during his former life, when, after scurrying to put his lab's business in order, he left on vacation with his wife. It was that same feeling he enjoyed when he first walked into a resort, when the burdens of the outside world melted behind him and he could luxuriate in the peace of each moment. Piet's eyes scanned the four walls of the cell. He noted the irony. The cold room felt warm.

Piet's war had now ended. He had done all he could. His work was complete. Eventually the Germans would find out where he lived, but by then it was possible that Piet's able wife and committed friends would be ready.

THE PASTORAL QUIET of the farm, the rustling of the wind through the trees and long pasture grass made the ominous sounds of German boots on wood floors even more menacing as they searched the home. More than twenty-four hours had passed since Piet's arrest, and when the gravel on the Soetendael's driveway popped underneath the tires of the Nazis' vehicle as it rounded the bend and stopped in front of the large garage, Anne was indeed waiting and ready. The soldiers opened and closed drawers and cupboards, sorting through contents. Anne could hear them tread from room to room. They searched everywhere, but with no results. There was nothing in the home for them to find. The Soetendael had been so completely cleaned and organized and so thoroughly sanitized of anything incriminating that the house itself seemed to sit awkwardly on its own foundations, like a child dressed in a starched suit and awaiting a photographer. Anne had even picked the hair from each brush.

The maid was the only one to remain in the home with Anne, and the young woman watched as a soldier found a coin with the outlawed face of the Dutch Queen Wilhelmina. He threw it on the floor and stepped on it with the heel of his boot.

The Nazis asked Anne about Piet's coat and his missing identification papers. Anne knew nothing about either. And if she had, she would have looked directly into the uniformed soldiers' eyes and boldly denied it. There was little fear in my grandmother. She wasn't easily intimidated, and she was a convincing liar.

The soldiers left the home without incident. They turned their vehicle back down the driveway, rounded the hedge and drove toward Piet's second home. On the bottom floor they found Dr. Schoorl's business along with his employees. The rest of the building was also empty and as completely devoid of life as the farm. The Germans had no idea what exactly it was they were looking for. The search, like Piet's arrest and his imprisonment, was simple routine.

MARIANNE NEVER ASKED anyone what exactly happened on the day her father was arrested. "It's not safe for you to go home," was all Gerard had said to my mother before he helped her on the back of his bicycle. The two had navigated the cozy streets of downtown Bennekom and then turned onto a wide thoroughfare and toward Wageningen, to the home of a family friend. The 5-year-old knew what "not safe" meant, but not in its particulars.

As a child my mother had learned never to ask about the war. And if she had decided to ask questions, the family she hid with probably knew nothing. No one ever directly explained the war to my mother, but like all children, she learned from the world around her— "not safe" was a German soldier, a midnight bombing raid, an unsympathetic classmate. "Not safe" was the looming threat of Westerbork, the Star of David, the trains heading east. "Not safe" was in the eyes of the guests at the breakfast table. And because it was never explained, the particulars of the war lived in the same blurry world that hid monsters under children's beds.

After the Nazis searched the Soetendael, my mother and her siblings returned to the farm, dropped off at various times by the various friends of Anne and Piet who had helped hide their children. The home felt eerily quiet. The maid told Hanneke about the soldier who found the Dutch coin. However, none of the children remember their mother telling them what happened to their father. Surely she told them that he had been arrested. But Anne was vague. She wasn't one to languish in her own emotions, and she didn't invite them in others. It wouldn't be until decades later, after my mother steered her blue Subaru into the ditch that Marianne would even know exactly why the Gestapo had arrested her father. No one had ever told her about the fake IDs. But when the children heard the name "Euterpe Street" they knew the implications. Every child in Holland knew that name.

The antiseptic home felt unkind. The patina of the children's recent weeks and months of life had been wiped clean, and the cleanliness punctuated the fact that their father was no longer with them. Despite an often-clear picture of those first few days back at the farm, none of the children remember Anne's grief. As was her way, she kept herself busy. As soon as she learned Piet was in a cell underneath the Gestapo's Amsterdam headquarters, she left for the city and joined those gathered outside the gate. And for the first time in years, the children occupied the farm without the comforting presence of an adult. For the kids, the farm now felt dreadfully empty. Though Piet was often away for the day or longer on business, their mother anchored the home and was almost always present to cook and enjoy the three punctually served meals. Leo would also come and go, but the children had enjoyed his company daily, and Pauline had remained in the home and with the children for nearly every minute of every day as had Eline. And then there was Marianne's Jewish nanny, crazy auntie Chiel, and whoever else happened to be hiding at the farm during that last morning the kids left for school. Even with their mother close, the Soetendael felt hauntingly empty—empty with only the seven of them. Those first days moved slowly.

Anne continued to travel to Euterpe Street with her usual dogged determination until her efforts bore fruit. Somehow she managed to get word to Piet that everyone was safe. The Nazis had interrogated Piet a dozen times. He adamantly denied involvement with any resistance group. They didn't believe him. But they also had no proof he had done anything more than help two Jews obtain fake IDs. They had searched both of his homes and found nothing incriminating.

The first weeks without their father were the hardest for the children. Even though he had struggled in the recent months, Piet had still read the children stories at night. Piet still supplied hugs and smiles. On more rare occasions the children could persuade their father to become an ape. Piet had mastered the role, lengthening his jaw, raising up his shoulders, and scraping his knuckles on the floor as he swayed back and forth while grunting and howling. His children's faces always lit up with glee.

Piet had been arrested on the morning of October 6, 1943, and it was within only a few weeks of that date that the van Leeuwen family returned to the farm. There was no safe place for a Jew in Holland. There were only less-dangerous places. And wherever the family escaped to on that fateful fall day, they didn't consider it less dangerous than the Schoorls' farm, even so shortly after Piet's arrest. Simon and Adele also soon returned to the lab along with the Dannenbaums. Before the calendar turned to November the only person missing from the farm and lab was their owner.

More than anyone, the children's father had been the author of their lives, guiding them forward as he thought best. It seemed that even the home mourned the loss of its patriarch. The children now lay under their covers at night missing their dad, and Iet endured the bombers alone. Every morning, when Piet's kids opened their eyes, their stomachs told them something was dreadfully wrong before their minds filled in the details.

No one had heard anything about Piet for nearly one month when an official-looking envelope arrived from Euterpe Street. The children watched as Anne and Leo opened it at the dining room table. Their father had been transferred to the concentration camp Herzogenbusch, across the Rhine, next to the Dutch town of Vught. And just as the Dutch referred to the Gestapo headquarters by the name of the adjacent street, they referred to Camp Herzogenbusch simply as "Vught"—it was the only concentration camp the Nazis had built in Northwestern Europe. Piet's transfer wasn't necessarily good news, but at least it was news. And the concentration camp allowed care packages. The family set to work immediately.

A row of freshly made jams cooled on the small kitchen table. In the company of the tart aroma, Anne hunched over a piece of paper writing a letter in tiny script. After the jars reached room temperature, Anne poured hot paraffin wax over the jam to seal it shut. When finished with the letter, she popped the round cardboard insert out of one jar's lid and fit the paper between it and the metal. She screwed the lid tight and placed the jars in a small box next to a wedge of cheese, some sausage, and vitamins from Piet's own laboratory. The cheese and sausage were both hard-to-find delicacies, but Anne had a knack for locating items no one else in Bennekom could. When finished with the package, Anne combed Marianne's hair, tied two ribbons in her daughter's ponytails, and had her put on a warm coat. The two left for the train station together.

My grandmother was 36 years old when she traveled that morning to Vught. I am told Anne was pretty as a young woman, and when I look at photos of her in her early twenties, they understandably resemble my mother at the same age. Both had thick auburn hair, slender necks and the voluptuous curves the Greeks carved into their statues. But Mom had more of a chin than Anne, straighter teeth, and a narrower nose. It's always been hard for me to picture Anne as attractive. By age 36, her body had sacrificed most of its beauty to the births of her five children. She never recovered her figure and had put on some weight. But the main reason I have trouble seeing Anne in any sort of tender or forgiving light is that I still harbor vivid memories of Anne as my grandmother.

Already tightly wound, my mom was even more tense when Anne traveled across the Atlantic to visit our family. I remember my grandmother in grey sweaters and wool skirts. Mom and Dad and Anne spoke Dutch at the dinner table. Anne had thick, coarse hair and heavy jowls, and the bad habit of eating the fat we kids had carved off our steaks. She was opinionated, outspoken, and gruff. In neither her appearance nor countenance did Anne seem to make any efforts toward grace. Despite this, there was a warmth to my grandmother, but it wasn't the kind that was going to invite you into her lap.

In the evenings, next to the fire in our living room, I would watch Anne as she carded raw sheep's wool then spun it on the antique spinning wheel she had brought with her from Holland. With her right foot rising and falling on the wheel's pedal, her thick fingers guided the fresh wool into the small hole of the spindle. Anne hummed while she spun, and she radiated a peace, and looking back I sense something tender in those moments. But as a child, I experienced Anne's warmth much like the fire crackling next to me. I could see it, and it drew me close, but I dared not get too close. In many ways, my grandmother scared me. I think my parents had much the same experience. Anne could be loving, but also predictably critical. And those who knew her, knew better than to lock horns with Anne. Anne decided what was right or wrong, and she made it so with the force of her will. And her will was stronger than yours, much stronger.

Dad usually counted the days until his mother-in-law boarded a plane back to Holland. As soon as Anne did leave, Mom often broke out in shingles.

The Anne I discovered during my journey into those war years reminds me of the surly, battle-hardened drill sergeant written into many a Hollywood script—both feared and respected by his troops. But by the movie's end, we see the sergeant place his own life in harm's way to save that of some young soldier, and we glimpse a soulful tenderness.

Anne's stubbornness and exceptional will might have been within her from the moment she was born— a character of her spirit, perhaps—for it appears she arrived in this world with both qualities firmly established. And if one might enjoy the idea of a benevolent creator, the idea that Anne was armed thusly makes a sort of cosmic sense, for she was born to a stubborn bully of a father. Though Jan Borst had his jovial moments, he lorded over his children with a stern hand, and he and his eldest daughter's wills clashed near immediately. No matter how one imagines the origins of Anne's character, it is simple fact that Jan Borst was the anvil that had made Anne's steel hard. Jan Borst liked his life and his family a certain way—Jan's way—and the battle lines were drawn from the outset.

When she was a young schoolgirl, Anne was required to attend classes wearing the modest clothes Jan had chosen for her. And though Anne had wanted to wear a more fashionable dress, there were no opposing Jan's decisions—at least not directly. But even though Anne was still counting her years in single digits, she was already hip-deep in subterfuge.

As Anne left the farm for school each morning, she could see the elevated railroad tracks ahead and the small trestle that carried the train over the road on which she walked. Days earlier, Anne had convinced her grandfather to help her with her plan. The two spent a good amount of time together; Anne would often slice his apples into thin slivers so her toothless grandfather could eat them, and she presented her plan to him carefully and solicited his help. Grandfather Borst appreciated Anne's spunk, and he decided to indulge his granddaughter's scheme.

Underneath the bridge, Anne opened the packet that her grandfather had delivered for her the night before. She shivered against the morning air as she changed into her new dress and completed the ensemble with a colorful ribbon laced through her hair and then proceeded to school. Grandfather Borst continued the routine, replacing the clothes when necessary. Jan never knew. It was a rare win for Anne.

When Anne was still in middle school, Jan forced her to abandon her education She would never forgive him for it, and the two would continue to lock horns.

The final battle between father and daughter occurred during Anne's eighteenth year when she decided to cut her hair. Not a significant event in most households, but in the Borst home it was an act akin to mutiny. A large photo of Jan's seven daughters, all dressed to his liking, their long hair falling over their small shoulders, sat proudly on the mantle in his parlor. I doubt Anne even flinched when her father banished her from the home. She packed her belongings and took the train to Arnhem where she became a live-in maid. She eventually lived with the family of a well-known publisher in the city of Deventer. Anne loved the city and she loved her freedom, and it was with some reticence, after half a year away, that she returned home when her father invited her back to live at the farm.

Even after Anne was married and left home, she still battled Jan. Anne would regularly place herself between Jan and Anne's younger siblings. One of the reasons Anne's two sisters worked at the lab was that Anne had liberated them from Jan's farm. Despite my earliest memories of Anne, she was kind and caring and in many ways selfless. For her, love was freedom. And though she was abrasive and often blind to the more subtle needs of her own children and those close to her, she was also, in her own way, their most fierce advocate.

* * *

THE TRAIN CARRYING Anne and Marianne crossed the Rhine and soon stopped in the actual town of Vught. Anne carried the care package under one arm, and mother and daughter departed the station. Soon the concentration camp came into view. The two rows of electric wire fencing supported by concrete posts that bent inward at the top were separated by a moat. Slender guard towers, positioned at 100-yard intervals, loomed over the grounds. Anne continued with her daughter in hand. The letters she had hidden in her jams were written in a nuanced code in case they were discovered. Sometimes Anne hid the letters in a meatball, other times in a cake. As they approached the concentration camp post office, Anne picked Marianne up in her arms. The quiet 5-year-old had large hazel eyes—pretty, but with a hint of sadness. Anne held Marianne as she conversed with the officials at the concentration camp's post office. She kept her daughter close and visible. Marianne's presence was a necessary piece of Anne's plan, her staging choreographed—a calculated prop meant to persuade. For the camp only allowed one package every two weeks per prisoner. Anne had already sent the first by mail. But she figured if the rules stated two packages a month, she could manage four. For my grandmother, rules had always been (and would always be) for all of the other people—and as usual, her efforts proved successful.

Every other week, Anne made the trip south across the Rhine to Vught. She took either my mother or Mom's little sister Helene with her. She would leave the packages at the prison's post office and then turn and begin her trip back to the Soetendael. The wire fence and moat and looming guard towers grew distant; inside its walls, Piet struggled to survive.

* * *

THE DULL GRAY SKIES above Vught threatened rain. I walked underneath the gabled entrance with Iet. "No, I want to go," she had said the previous evening when I offered to take a bus there on my own. "I've been meaning to go."

Chalky lichen shaded the red north-facing roof tiles a light green. The buildings look benign, almost friendly. The oaks in the courtyard had grown tall. A tour guide narrated Vught's history. We walked the camp's perimeter, next to the two rows of fencing. The wires stretching between thin concrete posts rose up just above my reach and, without the lethal electrical current running through them, they would be easily scalable. The moat was dry, and the guard towers looked as though they had been built recently, and I suspected they had. The camp had two gallows built of thick timber.

Iet walked with a cane that folded into a seat, and we would stop intermittently so she could sit and rest. In the short time I had been with my aunt she was nearly always smiling. But now, with her old body propped up by the cane, her face held stern, and her eyes seemed to lose themselves in the distant woods.

I walked toward the crematorium's single square smokestack alone. Vught wasn't constructed with wholesale murder in mind. By the time my grandfather arrived nearly all of the camp's Jews had been transported east and only Dutch "political" prisoners remained. I followed the pavers toward the entry. A breeze stirring through the grass announced the coming rain, and a few rays of sun shone through the heavy clouds.

I stepped over the threshold and into the building and stopped so my eyes could adjust to the lack of light. As my pupils dilated a stone autopsy table in the middle of the room came into focus. The smooth surface had a precise lip machined along the table's perimeter to contain the body's juices and two thin channels cut in a large X from corner to corner to direct the flow toward the black shadow of another precisely cut drainhole in the table's center. The table's length was shorter than the average man. The stiff calves and feet would have hung over the edge. I felt the blood drain from my head, and the air around me seemed to thicken. I quickly made my way through the room and out the other side only to arrive in the crematorium. I could see the sunlight shining through a doorway at the opposite end of the room. My head swirled as I passed the black iron doors of the long ovens. I didn't slow my pace until I made it back outside.

The grass and the trees and the swirling wind settled my stomach. I had snapped two pictures of the autopsy table. Later I would download them to my laptop. But they felt like a stain on the circuitry and I would eventually delete them; however, it didn't matter. The images remained vivid. And they weren't the only ones Vught seared into my mind.

The Dutch built a new visitor center next to the crematorium. It was filled with images of the holocaust. I'd seen many of them before. But one particular photo, a shot of a tall metal warehouse with bales of human hair stacked 30 feet high and many more deep juxtaposed in my mind next to the story Iet had told me only a few days about the two Wagenaar boys, Ben and Joost. I couldn't help contemplate the possibility that the hair belonging to those two scared boys who had sat awkwardly in the farmhouse I had visited only a few days earlier was somewhere within those bales. The story within that photo—the magnitude of the life lost—felt too immense to contemplate. And though

I would work to put it out of my mind, just like the photo of that autopsy table, it would remain.

I continued to wade through the pieces of the Nazis' legacy hanging from the walls until I found Iet sitting next to a large window looking out into the parking lot. "I am ready to go," she said.

As Iet turned her van north, the rain that had threatened finally fell, and like the same drops that splashed in the courtyard when Iet and I ate dinner near her home, it felt soothing.

PIET HAD ARRIVED at Vught on October 29, 1943. He was assigned prisoner number 1103, and housed in barracks number 13. The concentration camp loosely resembles Auschwitz. The Dutch building's brick is a touch redder, and the entrance isn't arched like the Polish camps, nor is the Dutch camp as large, but the similarities remain obvious. Diagonal brick pavers formed pathways through the main courtyard lined with newly planted oak trees. The white-painted windows and heavy gables gave the camp a gentle Bavarian feel.

Though tiny compared to camps in Poland, Vught was still vast. Each barracks stretched the length of several rail cars: squat buildings made of the same brick and tile as the courtyard and built close together in long rows. The prisoners slept on three-tiered bunk beds, two deep. Before Piet arrived, hundreds of prisoners had died from lack of food, infection, and overcrowding. The Germans issued Piet prison clothes and two left wooden shoes. Coincidentally, Piet arrived at the camp at about the same time as that of Vught's new commander, officer Adam Grunewald. Both men were forty years old. The first commandant was now on trial, charged with stealing supplies meant to sustain the prisoners. After issuing Piet his clothes, the Germans shaved his head.

Each day, Piet woke early and marched to his work detail at the new Philips plant, a large factory built within the camp, where he assembled radio components.

Piet believed in the goodness of man. He had believed that justice in this world was only a matter of time, and he saw himself as an agent of change. But this was before the war and before Vught. Life inside the concentration camp soon began to corrode his sensibilities.

Commander Grunewald had put Vught back into order. Commodities such as food and medicine meant for the camp were no longer sold for a profit, but used, as they were initially intended. But despite the improvement of day-to-day conditions, Grunewald was a sadist, and his character annulled whatever immediate benefits the camp enjoyed. When prisoners lined up in the courtyard Grunewald let his young son toy with them. "Jump up, sit down, pull down your pants," the child ordered. Guards with dogs watched the humiliation.

On January 16, two-and-a-half months after Piet's arrival, a woman from barracks 23B was placed in a cell in the camp's small prison. Her fellow female inmates, who believed she was unjustly treated, protested. Incensed, Grunewald ordered all of the protesters—seventy-four women—be packed into that same small cell. After the guards pushed the iron door closed, the room fell dark, and waves of hysteria swelled as the bodies turned the air hot. There was so little space in that cell that when a woman lost consciousness and went limp, she remained upright. Some screamed. Some prayed. All fought for oxygen. The rest of the camp listened all night to the horror. The next day, when the doors swung open, ten of the women had died. And these weren't the only deaths at Vught. Members of the Dutch resistance were regularly marched through the adjacent woods and executed by a firing squad.

Ten days after the murder of the women, Piet's appendix burst. Luckily, the Philips company—a Dutch company—had negotiated the construction of a state-of-the-art hospital for the prisoners when planning to build their factory on the grounds of the camp. Piet's surgery went without complication. Nineteen days later he re-entered the prison population.

Piet was allowed to write to his wife. In his letters to Anne, Piet thanked her for the meatballs. He also joked about his two left shoes.

WINTER DESCENDED on the Soetendael for the fourth time during the occupation, this time without Piet. The ground again turned hard and frost covered the lazy pastures. The children had no choice but to get used to a life without a father, and the family fell back into their routines.

On one of those winter days, little Eline lay in bed recovering from a fever. Her father had left the farm on his bike and a hard rain pounded on the home's tiles. "Mommy, is Pappy getting wet?" she asked Pauline.

"Don't worry, I'm sure he will find shelter somewhere."

"But Mommy, what about Oom Piet? Is he outside getting wet?" Eline continued to ask her mother about Piet: where he worked, who cooked his meals, and what he did all day. Pauline told her daughter about the packages they sent. As Eline contemplated Piet's life at Vught, she remembered an egg that she had been recently given. She had been begging for an egg for weeks and her persistence had paid off, and she had yet to eat it. She then asked her mother to send it to her uncle Piet.

The job of caring for everyone kept Anne busy. The children continued at school. At night, the children listened in on conversations between the van Leeuwens and Anne as they talked about Piet. The winter days drifted one into the next. None of the children remember celebrating Sinterklaas.

"You have to understand that this all happened in a different time," Hanneke had said to me. "Parents didn't talk to children like they do today. They didn't sit down with you and explain things."

Around the same time Piet left Vught's hospital, the Dutch underground newspapers had printed the news of the ten women murdered at Vught. When the story became public, news of it eventually reached the upper ranks of the SS command; they were not pleased. The Nazis had no use for an excessively violent concentration camp commander. It created too much attention. They wanted their camps run quietly and efficiently. In response to the deaths, they demoted Grunewald to the rank of infantryman. He was then sent to the Russian front where he died in battle.

In his letters to Anne, Piet never burdened her with the horrors of Vught. Nor did Anne burden Piet with the war outside the prison.

Despite his absence, the work Piet had begun at the Soetendael continued. His wife now continued without him, and the traffic at the farm never slowed.

The recently restored boundaries of Camp Herzogenbusch,
known commonly as "Vught."

Chapter 12

I SAT ON A BENCH in San Clemente, California, watching the gentle Pacific waves collapse on the sand. Mothers herded young children across the beach while seagulls fought over dropped French fries and ketchup packets next to the snack stand. I was early for my meeting with a Jewish woman named Carla Polak. Soon after Piet was transferred to Vught, Anne had received a desperate call from Carla's parents. They had been in hiding but Carla's father feared the Gestapo knew their location. I stared at the horizon where the blue of the water met the blue of the clear sky. San Clemente seemed a nice place to retire.

I had found Carla online, through Yad Vashem's Central Database of Shoah Victims. She had written a testimony and had included her address. I sent her a letter asking if we could meet. Carla wrote back, her stationery bordered with yellow daffodils and pink petunias. A Teddy bear with a summer bonnet and carrying a flower-filled watering can smiled in the bottom left corner.

I turned out of the beach park and rode my motorcycle above the seaside cliffs. Carla's house was one of a neighborhood of similar homes. Not similar as in similar-era, but as in mirror image: the same color, same floor plan, same mailboxes lining the curbed street. I concentrated on the address numbers. I could still smell the ocean.

Carla greeted me with a smile and invited me inside. She reminded me of my eldest aunt, Hanneke: the same rosy cheeks, round face and white hair cut above her neck. And also like my aunt, Carla didn't look or move like a person who had been a teenager during the Second World War. I added the years in my head. She had to be soon approaching eighty. She looked in her sixties. "Would you like some coffee?" she asked.

The home had a familiar feel—wood furniture, old clocks on the wall, rich colors, orderly, and markedly clean. It reminded me of my childhood home, more so perhaps than any home I had ever been inside. We sat at her small kitchen table. "I don't remember much about your grandparents," she said. Carla had a forwardness: her voice strong and eyes steady. I pulled my recorder out of my bag, pressed record and sipped my coffee.

Carla held nine pages of memoir in her hands, the type all in capitals and printed on the backside of yellowed sheets of Newsletters for the Lawnchair & Picnic Society: Carla Polak, Treasurer. We talked about my grandparents. "I don't remember exactly how I met them," Carla said, "but I wrote in here, 'at the Bennekom time I got to know Annie and Piet Schoorl ... they had five children, the oldest a few years younger than I.' So that was Hanneke," she said looking up.

In the first letter she sent me Carla said she was willing to talk about her memories of my grandparents. But it was really Carla's own life that I wanted to know about. I hadn't made a point to tell her. "So what year were you born?"

"I was born in '28."

"Your name wasn't Polak then."

"No, it was van Leeuwen."

"So you were related to Pauline and Leo?"

"Yes, Leo was a cousin of my dad." That explained Carla's blue eyes.

"If it's okay with you, why don't we start at the beginning . . . I hardly know anything about you. I don't even know your parents' names."

"My mother's name was Estella."

"And your father's name?"

"Leo."

"So another Leo van Leeuwen."

"Yes. You see the grandparents had six children. My dad was the son of the oldest. The grandfather was Leo, so all the boys were named Leo."

The nine pages rested on the table between us, single-spaced—just like my mother's. She had typed the words nearly a decade earlier. The memories were important to her. Carla looked relaxed. She started from the beginning.

ESTELLA WAS TWENTY-FIVE when she gave birth to Carla in the cosmopolitan city of Berlin, Germany. She was a slight woman, and the child had stretched her small belly tight. The family of three began their lives together in the upper story of a pleasant apartment building overlooking a large park. Berlin was a beautiful city. When Carla grew tall enough, she could peek out the apartment windows and see her father playing tennis in the courts below.

Her parents had met in Holland. Leo's father wanted his son to marry a wealthy Jewish girl. Leo insisted she be a pretty, wealthy, Jewish girl. The two were introduced at a family gathering. They wed shortly thereafter. Leo was two years older than his new bride.

Leo took his wife to the sprawling German city to start a company manufacturing sausage casings. On sunny weekends, after the couple's daughter learned to walk, the three would amble through the park next to their home, across the open grass and beneath the shadowy canopy of old deciduous trees. Squirrels ran from trunk to trunk, and songbirds flitted in the branches above. There was a pond in the middle of the park. Ducks swam in the sunlight, and frogs jumped from the pond's edge into the safety of the murky water when passersby came too close.

Carla remembered her father as a happy man. "He was a fun person . . . my mother was more serious. People told me, 'no . . . no . . . he wasn't always fun-loving. He could be very serious,' but I have never seen that serious side. He was always very optimistic." Leo's blonde hair grew thick. Carla would be the couple's only child.

Hitler was appointed the Chancellor of Germany the same year Carla's mother watched her daughter disappear inside the kindergarten classroom for the first time.

There was nothing outwardly different between Carla and her Aryan classmates. Her blonde hair and bright blue eyes suggested she was as purely German as the next child. And one could easily argue that she indeed was, but not according to the Nazis. Though not yet old enough to fashion a sentence or read a book, Carla already understood how dangerous Hitler was for her people. The National Socialists had already infiltrated the schools, and during class Carla was required to line up next to the other children. "Heil Hitler," the kids repeated, snapping their small arms upward.

Afraid to stand out, 5-year-old Carla slowly raised her arm partially in the air and mouthed the words.

Since moving to Berlin, Leo had succeeded in creating a prosperous business, but it wasn't to last. On April 1, 1933, the Nazis organized a planned boycott of all Jewish businesses and Hitler's stormtroopers took to the streets. The brown-shirted thugs blocked the entrances to Jewish stores and painted black and yellow Stars of David on their doors. On his way home from his factory Leo passed propaganda posters pasted to the city walls. The dark sneering faces of large-nosed Jewish caricatures with menacing eyes and pointed ears leered at him.

Acquaintances stopped visiting the van Leeuwens. Some of Carla's friends were told by their parents they couldn't play with her. "I was very blonde and blue-eyed, so nobody expected me to be Jewish ... I was very shy, but I would always tell people I was Jewish so that if they didn't want to play with me or talk to me then at least I would know beforehand. I looked very German," Carla said.

As Hitler's Nazis grew increasingly powerful and ruthless not even the family's close German friends came to their apartment anymore. "Everybody was so afraid ... you never knew who was going to tell on you. It could be your own wife or your own husband." The terror of the Gestapo lurked in the background of every public setting. Hitler's enemies silently disappeared into concentration camps or worse. It became mandatory for German children to join the "Hitler Youth." Sometimes school children told teachers when their own parents did something the government outlawed. Loudspeakers played Hitler's speeches on street corners. By 1936, life in Germany had become intolerable for the van Leeuwens.

Jews packed the consulates in Berlin desperate to obtain exit visas. Fortunately, Estella and Leo were citizens of the Netherlands. They could enter Holland without legal permission. The family packed their possessions, boarded a train and left their apartment by the park forever.

Carla stayed with her grandparents in Hoogeveen, Holland while Leo and Estella looked for a new home. The family eventually settled in a second-story apartment in Rotterdam in a neighborhood on the edge of town.

Leo had been forced to relinquish ownership of his factory in Berlin, but he opened a new one in Rotterdam. The family settled back into an ordinary routine. Carla made friends in school. Winter fell twice on their small peace-time apartment building. The snows of '39 were particularly heavy. The day the Nazis followed Carla to Holland remains vivid in her mind.

"On May 10, 1940, we were awakened by the sound of planes—lots of them, all over. It was a beautiful day, and the sky was black with planes." After five days of fighting the Germans bombed Rotterdam. Sirens wailed. Leo took his wife and daughter down the stairs and into the cellar. Stuka dive-bombers dropped from the sky toward the heart of Rotterdam. The bombs ripped through the city. The explosions ignited fires and the flames leapt from building to building.

With the family living on the outskirts, their apartment escaped harm. When the rise and fall of the sirens ceased, Carla and her parents left the cellar and walked towards downtown to see if Pauline and Leo van Leeuwen and their children survived. There had been little rain that spring. As they neared the city the family watched distant flames consume entire blocks.

Smoke blackened the sky. The bombs had destroyed the water system. The firehoses hung limp and the fires raged unmolested.

The family walked amongst thousands of newly minted refugees. People carried what they had managed to save from the bombs and the fire. Carla and her parents came to Pauline and Leo's home. It was intact and the family unharmed.

"Then the Germans walked in. We were in town. They told us 'hands up and go home.' I remember my mom telling me 'Don't you dare cry. Don't you dare cry.' If her eyes could have killed somebody they would have. She was so angry. So we went home. We had no water, no electricity, no gas."

Before running to the cellar, Carla's father had filled up their large bathtub. The family rationed the water. Their downstairs neighbor knocked on their apartment door and asked for some water to clean her baby.

The German army took quick control of Rotterdam. Carla's family was forced to house a young German soldier. Barely out of high school, the boy arrived when the van Leeuwens were eating breakfast. He politely introduced himself and shook everyone's hand. He then left. "Stop eating and go wash your hands," said Estella.

"Those guys were very dirty," Carla said to me. The young soldier had been marching for days.

Within a few weeks the utilities came back on and Carla's grandparents moved in with them. The grandparents had received numerous letters from Estella's brother, Sam, in America urgently requesting they flee Europe for America. "It's going to get bad," Sam had written. Estella's parents agreed, but were in no hurry. They eventually sold their home, got their passports and visa, and packed all of their belongings in the hold of a ship in the Rotterdam harbor. They were to set sail to New York on May 10, the exact same day the German bombs fell on the city. The vessel never departed. The fires consumed the boat and everything Carla's grandparents owned.

The families resettled and the occupation began. Hitler didn't want to destroy Holland, just absorb and fashion the nation in the likeness of the fatherland. Carla entered her first year of intermediate school in the fall. The changes started slowly.

"First we weren't allowed in parks, or theaters, or concert halls. Then we could only shop certain times in the day, like 3:00-5:00 p.m. Since there were no supermarkets it was hard to do everything—baker, grocer, fruit and vegetables, etc. And there was a shortage of many food items. By 3:00 p.m. they were out of things. Still it was bearable. Some merchants saved certain items for their Jewish customers. The Germans were so clever: one rule at a time. So we cannot go to the parks; well, we can live with that. Next, no theater. Alright, so we'll play games. Naïve is what it was—stupid is a better word."

In '41 Carla was no longer allowed in public schools. A school for Jews was built across town. Estella sewed a yellow star on Carla's jacket with Jew written across it. When Carla boarded the streetcar toward her new classroom and walked down the aisle with her new star, a few commuters looked at her star and glared. But another passenger stood up and in a show of sympathy gave Carla her seat. Soon she wasn't allowed to ride on public transportation and Carla walked the forty-five minutes to school.

As the school year progressed, fewer and fewer of Carla's classmates arrived in the morning. The raids had begun.

Four of the six families in Carla's apartment building were Jewish. Deep asleep, Carla didn't hear the Nazis raiding the lower apartment. The next day the mother and father and two young children who had lived below the van Leeuwens were gone. No one had heard a thing. The following day Leo and Estella removed the stars from their clothing and packed one small suitcase. After dinner, after the sun set and the streets turned dark, the three of them walked down their apartment stairs, out of the building and down the road to the corner and waited for the streetcar. Carla was scared. Too many people they knew had disappeared. The streetcar took them to the central train station where they boarded a train to the quiet country town of Bennekom where Leo's cousin and his two kids were already in hiding.

Carla's short memoir still sat on the table between us. "From Rotterdam," she wrote, "we went to Bennekom where someone had arranged a place in a boarding house for us—one room for the three of us, very depressing. We could go out for walks and the area was very nice, small town, lots of woods. After a few months we found a place in a home where we had a living-dining room. I could go to the Schoorls who were very active in the underground. He found places for the Jews, and Mr. Schoorl falsified IDs. We got our IDs a different way. Somebody in City Hall somehow got birth certificates from deceased people and used those names. My parents' name was Howeler and mine was Gerda Dubios. I could play with the Schoorl kids who were a little younger than I."

Eventually, a Bennekom police officer came to the home where they were hiding. He told Leo and Estella that the Germans knew where they were and they'd better move. The family traveled a few miles north to the town of Apeldoorn to a pension where they had vacationed before the war. "My mother would help prepare meals and do some cleaning. There was a single gentleman upstairs and two elderly ladies." The van Leeuwens told the other guests their home had been bombed. "People believed our story. More difficult was the fact that I did not go to school. I don't remember what tale we came up with for that. The lady who took care of everybody got very sick and my mom took charge, happy to have something to do to. I helped and even my dad peeled potatoes. In our spare time we took long walks. There was a beautiful nature reserve close by. I found a friend my age, but it was so difficult to keep our story straight that it was hard to have friends."

After several months at the pension, German soldiers confiscated the building. They wanted it as a barracks for women soldiers. The family had nowhere to go. Leo called the Soetendael.

Anne and Leo talked. Anne might have been willing to take the family short-term. The problem was that once she did so, she'd be forced to find a long-term hiding place, and Anne had run out of "addresses." She explained this to Leo. He knew Anne, and knew that the home and the lab were filled to capacity, and there was always the problem of finding food for everyone.

Leo then found a summerhouse in the woods in the adjacent town of Beekbergen, northeast of Bennekom. But the family could only stay for a week without registering with the Germans. Before the week was even over, Leo felt unsafe. The family sensed they were being watched. He again called Anne—this time more desperate. Could she at least take his daughter, Carla? Anne could hear the fear in Leo's voice, and she promised to try. She called her father, Jan. She assured Jan that the girl would only stay at his farm temporarily. And the Jewish teenager was fair-skinned, with blonde hair and blue eyes. She would fit right in with the family. No one would ask questions.

Jan might have been a stubborn bully; however—similar to his daughter in many ways—he also had a kind streak and a large heart. Jan agreed.

Just as when the family had slipped out of Rotterdam, they did their best to not attract attention as they boarded a westbound train toward Amsterdam. They would now make that same terrible choice that was forced upon so many Jewish parents—to surrender their child to the care of another and then attempt to survive the worry, the hours anguishing over the safety of the one thing most dear to them in this world. The train out of Amsterdam took them north and into the rural countryside. They passed soggy pastures and farmers' fields, then arrived in Alkmaar and found my great-grandfather's farm. Leo and Estella met Jan and Greet Borst. The four conversed and likely in a manner that skirted the emotional gravity of the moment. Jan's remaining four daughters mingled in the background. The hard choices had already been made by each couple. Jan and Greet would sacrifice the safety of their entire household to harbor Carla.

Leo and Estella left the farm after only a few hours. They needed to return to the summerhouse before the day's end so no one would notice their absence. The sun fell behind them on the last leg of their train ride back toward Beekbergen. The future of their little girl who had learned to walk near that placid pond in Berlin was now out of their hands. The couple stepped off the train into the twilight and made their way back to the summerhouse. I expect they walked in silence. It's possible they held each other's hands. It's also possible that they felt a terrible ambivalence when the house came into view—a cold stab of fear coupled with a warmth of gratitude

Leo's intuition had been correct. The Nazis had been watching, and they were waiting for them at the residence. They immediately asked about the location of the Jews' teenage daughter.

Carla's demeanor never changed as she told me her story. My coffee cup was now cold. The recorder continued to turn the wheel of the cassette, not only capturing her words, but also documenting each silence. "I thought they went to Westerbork," she said, the transit camp that collected the Jews of Holland before dispersing them east. "They wrote me. That is to say my mother wrote. She said Dad is working in the fields. He is very busy and looks very good. He has a tan. We sent packages there. They were there about three weeks, and then they were sent to Sobibor which is a death camp." Carla's voice never faltered.

We spent another hour together. Carla brewed more coffee and the clocks in her living room chimed the hours. Carla eventually brought out a large, finely published book, the type people leave out on their coffee tables with thick pages and glossy photos. One of her cousins in Holland had painstakingly documented the van Leeuwen family's wartime struggle. He had included a biography of each member. It wasn't until Carla was in her fifties that she found out exactly what happened to her mother and father.

The Borst farmhouse in Alkmaar

Chapter 13

A FTER THE FIRST LETTERS from Westerbork, Carla heard nothing more from her parents.
As the days turned to weeks, the pastures surrounding
her new home at the Borst dairy farm softened with
the coming of spring. On May 3, 1944, the Nazis pro-
cessed another of their prisoners. Pieter Schoorl was
told to gather his few belongings. The proper papers
were stamped and inmate 1103 was transferred from
Vught to a small prison in Utrecht where he would
stand trial for his crimes against the Reich. The following night, as Piet settled into his new prison cell,
the war would again breach the boundaries of his little
farm in Bennekom.

Anne and Pauline sat together in the living room. It
was a war-time evening not unlike most others at the
farm. Hanneke had a friend stay the night. The two girls
were sleeping in Hanneke's downstairs room. The rest
of the children were slumbering upstairs. Leo was gone.
He had left the farm shortly after dinner to attend a
Russian language class. It wasn't uncommon for Leo to
leave. After he opened and closed the Soetendael's gate
and entered the streets of Bennekom he was the Dutchman, Nico de Wit. He had an ID card that said so.

Daytime at the farm could be hectic, but the nights, if not disturbed by Allied bombers, brought a welcomed calm, and Anne could rest. Only earthly sounds disturbed the home: a breeze through the new spring leaves of the tall oak trees, or the patter of a soft rain on the red roof tiles. The silence had settled peacefully around Anne and Pauline on that particular evening when the front door of the farm suddenly burst open. "The police are at Frau Broekman's," a panicked voice shouted. Anne and Pauline looked up to see their friend, Tante' Aster—the color had drained from her face. "They are demanding Carel."

The words poured cold over Pauline and pinned her into her chair. Nearly two years had passed since the widow Frau Broekman had received Pauline's son, Carel, into her home. On the same evening Anne first saw Eline's rosy, tear-stained face, Frau Broekman, who lived just a few miles away on the other side of Bennekom, had tucked Carel into a bed in an upstairs room of her small home. Pauline had not seen her son since that night. The living room seemed to collapse on top of her. Pauline could not move. She could not speak.

At that same moment Tante' Aster threw open the Soetendael's door, another member of the resistance had located Leo. Leo first rushed through the night to the home of Mr. Hartman to solicit his help and then returned to the farm. When he arrived, Pauline had regained some of her senses. The shouting and sobbing woke up Hanneke and her friend. Hanneke walked out of her bedroom. Pauline looked terrified.

"Is he alright?" Pauline pleaded to anyone in the room. No one could answer her.

Not every Dutch citizen hated the Germans. A neighbor in Bennekom had informed on Carel. Tante'

Aster believed the boy was still at Broekman's. For reasons no one could explain, the police had left the home without Carel, but they were planning to return, this time with the Gestapo.

Anne and Leo left the farm almost immediately. They pedaled their bikes through the dark roads. Mr. Hartman was already en route to Frau Broekman's home. Anne and Leo rode frantically toward the Gestapo's Wageningen headquarters in case the Germans already had the boy. Neither Anne nor Leo knew exactly what they would do once they got there. There was no plan.

Before they turned onto the road connecting Bennekom to Wageningen, they decided to detour by Frau Broekman's. They rode underneath a quiet night sky, passing a neighborhood of small homes before arriving near the widow's. A police van was parked in her driveway. The two stopped, quickly hid their bikes in the woods and slowly approached by foot. They found Mr. Hartman hiding behind shrubbery close to the driveway. The three were unable to clearly see the home's entry. Anne decided to move closer to get a better look. As she edged forward she could see a driver behind the steering wheel. She continued still closer until she could see the man's face. A Gestapo officer stood in Frau Broekman's open doorway; another Dutch policeman stood behind him.

After Anne and Leo had left the Soetendael, Pauline struggled to pull her mind into order. Hanneke and Iet both stood in their nightgowns and watched as Pauline ascended the broad staircase. Pauline opened the door of her daughter's room and gently woke her little girl. No one knew what the evening would bring. Before Leo and Anne left the farm, it was decided that the Soetendael was—again—no longer safe.

Eline raised up her arms as her mom pulled a shirt over her head. Pauline dressed her daughter against the cold night and packed a small suitcase. She led Eline down the stairs and passed her daughter into the care of another member of Bennekom's underground who was waiting to take the girl away. Dividing the family when danger lurked was now a habit.

Pauline went back upstairs and packed her own bag and prepared to leave the farm. She walked through the old garage, next to the unused animal stalls, and onto the gravel drive. She traveled east that night toward Wageningen, toward another safe house, a farm named "Elisabeth."

Pauline had endured a far different war than the other inhabitants of the Soetendael. She suffered like her sister, Adele, suffered, and also the German couple, Kurt and Lisel Dannenbaum, who hid quietly in the attic of the lab. Since the first day her family decided to go into hiding, Pauline had become a passive witness to whatever dark twists fate would bring. She had relinquished both her children to the care of others. And she had relinquished her own care. Her Jewish blood and her Jewish features had rendered her powerless in almost every regard. From the egg on her morning plate, to the pillow under her head, Pauline depended on others. Leo had the luxury of being able to hastily dash out into the night after his son. Pauline could only work to stave off the horrible possibilities raging in her mind as the stubborn hands of the clock slowly ticked forward.

She continued across the flat, dark landscape. She passed a few homes with the muted glow of a reading light showing through a window, but most were black silhouettes against the dull night sky. As she neared her destination, the images fell upon her. Pauline could not help it. She pictured Carel in the hands of the Nazis. She pictured him alone at the transit camp Wester-bork. She pictured her 7-year-old boarding a cold cattle car bound for Poland . . . alone . . . amongst doomed strangers . . . with no one to care for him. She pictured his thick black hair, his broad smile, his large dark eyes. The images played relentlessly over and over, again and again.

The owners of the Elisabeth farm took Pauline into their care. But she found no respite. She knew there was nothing she could do for her son. Every minute was agony. It felt unbearable, until . . . finally, during the last hours of May 4, 1944, Pauline found a small peace. She made a decision that when dawn broke, if her son had been captured by the Germans, she would venture out into those first morning rays of light and start walking toward downtown Wageningen. She would travel openly on the day-lit streets until she came to the Gestapo headquarters. She'd open their door, walk inside, and turn herself in. And she'd then be with her son, and could run her fingers through his thick hair, and tenderly hold him as a mother should, until they met their end, together.

Frau Broekman blocked the doorway with her wide frame. She was an animated and robust woman and, like my grandmother, she could be fierce. Her flushed features shone in the dim light. She looked into the Gestapo officer's eyes with a steady gaze. She didn't deny that the boy was in her home. He was upstairs sleeping, as was Frau Broekman's only daughter, Titia. The officer was trying to reason with her.

While the two spoke, Anne got the attention of the driver. She knew the policeman, and she knew he was on the right side. Anne asked him to signal with a flash of his car lights if they had Carel when they left.

"The child will be well taken care of," the Gestapo officer assured Frau Broekman. "He will be taken to an orphanage." The Dutch policeman standing behind the officer and off to one side looked at Frau Broekman while the German spoke. He silently shook his head side-to-side to assure Frau Broekman what the woman almost surely knew—that the German was lying. Broekman looked back at the Gestapo. She told the officer that the boy wasn't feeling well and she absolutely refused to wake him. She needed time to pack his bags. She promised him that she would personally deliver the boy to the Gestapo headquarters in the morning.

Anne, Leo, and Mr. Hartman waited behind the shrubs and watched the van pull out of the driveway. The driver didn't blink the lights. As soon as the vehicle was out of sight, Mr. Hartman dashed inside the home and ran up the stairs. Carel was still half-asleep when Hartman appeared back outside carrying the boy. He had rolled Carel in a carpet and threw him over his shoulder. Hartman never stopped running, and Anne and Leo watched him disappear into the forest. The village butcher lives only on the fringes of the memories of Piet and Anne's children. He seems to arrive at the direst moments—always faithful, bold, and resourceful. His own story now fades, just as my grandparents' story had before my mother brought it back to life. Hartman had a wife and children just as did Piet and Anne. He risked everything to save the Jews and when the Schoorls needed help Bennekom's butcher was the man they trusted most.

Hartman knew where Pauline was hiding. He continued through the night until he arrived at the Elisabeth farm and carried Carel inside the home. The boy was sleeping when he set him down into his mother's lap. Pauline wrapped her arms around him. Carel's droopy eyes looked into Pauline's. Despite the passing of two seasons, and the gauze of sleep still thick in his head, Carel recognized his mother. This time, the slender margins of chance had favored the van Leeuwens, and, for Pauline, the night resumed its dark quiet. This was not the case for Frau Broekman and her daughter.

NO ONE KNOWS for sure why the Gestapo believed Frau Broekman. She was a convincing woman, and she loved Carel. Maybe the German had tired of his job and didn't relish the idea of tearing the boy from the woman's arms, which he would have had to do. Maybe he doubted he could rely on the two Dutch officers for support. But in all likelihood he was willing to wait until morning because he doubted Frau Broekman's allegiance to the Jewish child—he knew the price she would have to pay to save the boy, and he doubted she'd pay it.

After the police left, Frau Broekman went to Titia's upstairs room and woke her. Together, she and her daughter packed up their most necessary and precious possessions, probably not the most expensive, but those they could never replace: a photograph of Frau Broekman's late husband, a locket passed from generation to generation. In fact, the German had underestimated Frau Broekman. She never suffered a moment of hesitation.

The mother and daughter had until dawn. When they finished packing they would have to walk out of their home and into the same forest that had so recently enveloped Carel and the butcher Mr. Hartman.

Leaving behind a fully furnished home and the bulk of their material possessions, the two carried their bags out into the earliest hours of dawn. The village roosters had yet to announce another day of occupation. As they drove off, they left the only home Titia had ever known. Mother and daughter were now refugees and newly identified enemies of Hitler's merciless Third Reich.

The van Leeuwens

Chapter 14

THE NIGHT OF Carel's rescue still loomed in Anne's mind as she dressed for the cool May morning. She left the farm by bike as usual, met by the quiet, picturesque neighborhoods of Bennekom as she, again, pedaled to the train station. Since her husband's arrest, Anne faithfully followed him—first to Euterpe Street in Amsterdam, then south over the Rhine to Vught, and she would now board a train and head due west. She had hired a lawyer to defend her husband. Her children had listened quietly in the background as Leo, Pauline, and Anne discussed legal strategy at the dining room table.

The patches of white spring clover dotting the farmers' fields soon gave way to the concrete and steel of Utrecht. Anne had not seen her husband since the morning of his arrest. It had been eight months. She felt the train slow as it neared the busy city station, and she stepped into the morning bustle.

Anne located the old prison; an expansive lawn surrounded the stone building, and the early sun worked to raise up the morning's dew. Anne could see the narrow bridge which spanned the stagnant waters of the building's ancient moat. In comparison to the industrial

sprawl of Vught, with its perfect rows of electrified fencing and rifles point down from the guard towers, this
new location felt benign. Anne walked across the bridge
and faced a tall wood door.

My grandmother died in Holland on March 8,
1995. I never attended the funeral. My last memory of
Anne occurred eleven years earlier on my nineteenth
birthday. She sat in a chair in the same living room
where I had watched her spin wool when I was young.
I remember a winter sun shining through the window
behind her, illuminating the edges of her sweater. Anne
handed me a present. She had softened a bit in her later
years. Her hair was no longer thick and coarse, but silky
white and thinning. She seemed less surly. I unwrapped
the narrow box. Inside was a royal blue Parker pen. It
would be the last gift I received from my grandmother.

Anne visited our family several more times, once at
my parents' new home by the Hood Canal. But I don't
remember her. We could have sat together on the deck
of that home, and, in the gentle company of my parents' pine forest, talked about the war. But I had little
interest in my grandmother back then, and I had yet to
understand the war she endured. Which is to say, I had
yet to understand Anne.

My grandmother had the same sad eyes as my mother—weighted, soulful eyes—the same as all of Anne's
daughters. When relaxed, the edges of her mouth
looked as though they were pulled down in a perpetual
frown, adding a dramatic contrast to her smile, which
seemed to lift her entire face. The light in her eyes
sparkled. Anne was proud of her grandchildren, and
the ones who lived in Holland had fond memories of
their grandmother's company. Had we sat together and
talked about the war, she would have smiled a lot as

she told me all of the funny war stories Anne liked to recount. And I think she would have indulged a few of my questions. "Did you see Piet on the day you first went to the prison in Utrecht?" I could have asked. "Was he behind bars? Could you touch him?" It seems she had to have talked to him.

After that first visit, Anne returned regularly to the prison. On days she wasn't scheduled to enter the building, she'd take a few of the children to visit the grounds. Anne would lead them to a specific location on the prison's large lawn. "Wait here," she instructed. "Your father will come to that window." Anne pointed to one of the upper stories. The children remember the sense of hope the impending trial had brought to their lives. The news had lifted everyone's spirits. They remember the blades of grass and the sunlight and the murky water in the moat. Iet had sat down on that lawn and fastened her eyes on the window. She couldn't see her father, only shadows. Hanneke remembers a hand waving.

I assume that on Anne's first visit to Utrecht, she walked through those heavy wood doors and down some dim stone corridor and eventually met her husband. But like so many bits and pieces of this story that I've tried to patch together over the years, I cannot be sure. Anne could have answered so many of my questions, and I think she would have.

The days of May turned slowly as the family waited for a trial date. The calendar flipped to June. Anne had visited the prison several times.

On the fifth day of the month a bright moon rose in the night sky above the farm. While the families slept, it played across the silent pastures of Bennekom. It also illuminated the rolling waves of the North Sea upon which the largest armada in modern history powered toward France. Five thousand vessels left the safety of English harbors that night. When dawn greeted the farm, Allied soldiers swarmed the beaches of Normandy. The Soetendael rose to the call of the rooster, and the children's warm feet slipped out of their beds and onto the cold wood floor as heavy German machine-gun fire cut into the invading Allied forces. Young men dropped lifeless. Their limp bodies drifted in the sandy surf.

The Schoorls had a radio hidden beneath their living room floor. By the time the news of the invasion had trickled over the airwaves and into the family's home, the Allied forces had battered their way through the German defenses and into the French countryside. The liberation of Europe had begun. But Anne knew the soldiers could not come soon enough. Piet's lawyer had called. A date for the trial had been set, and on one of those afternoons on the lawn next to the prison, just days after the Allied assault, Anne held up a white sheet of paper with June 15 written in bold letters for Piet to read. Nine days after D-day, his trial would begin. It's a day burned into the memories of all of Piet's children.

NONE OF MY AUNTS or uncle, nor my mother, remember the words Anne used when she explained why she wanted all of the kids to attend the trial. But they all clearly recollect the reason. Or, at the very least, as adults they now understand why it was so important. No matter the outcome, Anne wanted her husband to see all of his children at least one last time.

Hans, Iet, Ruud, Marianne, and little Helene left the farm on foot with Anne, all of them dressed in their nicest clothes. The six ambled slowly toward Bennekom's main avenue and eventually boarded a train and rolled toward Utrecht. This time the children also crossed over the moat and through the great doorway. Once inside, they ascended a wide stone staircase that opened to a large second-story waiting room.

A crowd had already gathered. Hanneke hadn't expected so many people. The mood was solemn, and everyone spoke in hushed voices. A row of benches lined the sides of the room. A single doorway with a transom separated the waiting room from the courtroom.

The relatives of the prisoners on trial continued to pack into the waiting area. There were very few children. Without warning, a side door into the waiting room opened, and a line of prisoners passed through the room in a trotting march, their feet stamping in unison. They all wore the same drab uniforms and their hair had been shaved short. Iet watched them disappear through the courtroom door. She hadn't been sure at first, but then thought she recognized the narrowed face of her father.

After the prisoners were seated, three judges, surrounded by their various assistants, ascended that same stone stairway. The already quiet crowd silenced as the group walked across the waiting room. Chief Justice Dr. Meyer, Judicial Judge Modersohn, and visiting Judge Dr. Berg passed in front of the Schoorl children. They wore long dark robes.

As soon as the door closed behind the judges the crowd pressed up against it as everyone tried to peer inside the small transom window. After a few moments of jostling a line formed, and the children found their place in it. Hanneke, Iet, and Ruud waited patiently. All were tall enough to stretch their legs and peek through the glass. When their turn at the window finally arrived, each of them had trouble recognizing Piet. Their eyes scanned the row of prisoners from one end to the other before returning to the man who, after a long look, they realized was their dad. Though always trim, his face had drawn tight, and he looked weary. His lack of hair and the lines of his skull added to the confusion.

"I needed to be lifted up to see through that window," Mom said to me as we sat together in her sewing room, my tape recorder between us. "It was a room full of families who didn't know what would happen to their loved ones. There was a fantastic amount of pressure. That room was loaded—loaded with emotions. Not just for our family, but for everyone."

"Do you remember someone pushing you up?"

"Mom lifted me up. There were a lot of people. You had to wait. It makes me cry." Mom's eyes turned glassy. She swallowed. Then the tears started falling silently down her face. I can count the times I've seen my mom cry on one hand. She wiped her cheek and forced an embarrassed smile as though she was being melodramatic. "That's all it was. It was emotions. I remember the feelings, the tension, the gut . . . the pain, the anxiety. You hadn't seen Dad for nine months and you were lifted up and you could see him, and it was hard to recognize him. He was in a jail suit." The tears continued down her soft and wrinkled cheeks. She caught them with the back of her hand before they fell from her chin. "I think I picked up the emotions from Mom. She realized a lot more what was going on. I think my brothers and sisters knew more. But I knew enough. I remember a lot of the other people. I don't remember the details, but I remember how crowded it was in there, how everybody wanted to look through that little window. Isn't it interesting how you start crying about that now when you start talking about it? There was just so many emotions during that time, and you couldn't express them. There was nobody who would hold you. It wasn't done. People didn't cry. We didn't complain. We did nothing. He looked thin. His face was a lot thinner. He was wearing prison clothes."

"Did he see you?"

Mom looked up and away and her brow furrowed as she searched harder for that waiting room and that moment by the window and the prisoners lined together. "I think he did . . . yes . . . they were all looking toward that window." The tears slowed.

After Marianne, Anne held up Piet's youngest daughter, Helene. Piet's eyes remained fastened on that small doorway. He had missed his daughter's third birthday. When Helene finally recognized her father, she put her small hands against the glass. Her weight against that window pushed it open and the sounds of the courtroom wafted into the waiting room. "Hi Papi," Helene yelled. The voice echoed into the chamber. Terrified, Anne quickly pulled her daughter away.

THE NETHERLANDS INSTITUTE for War Documentation doesn't allow visitors, and it's not particularly easy to locate. The front door of the ornate stone building faces a canal. It's just one of several lavish structures, likely the previous home of some wealthy Amsterdam businessman, built several centuries earlier. I walked past the entrance several times.

In contrast to its old world exterior, the institute's insides resemble a high-tech bank. I explained my purpose to the gentleman behind the counter. He relayed my story to his superiors, and eventually two guards unlocked the heavy glass doors leading into their sanctum. "Secure all of your belongings in one of the lockers," I

was told. "One of our historians will meet with you."
The security and formality felt intimidating. I was directed to a row of metal desks where I was met by a
young man.

I again explained my story to the historian. He wrote
Piet's name on a tablet and disappeared behind more
locked doors. Fifteen minutes later he reappeared. He
had in his hands the court transcripts from the day of
my grandfather's trial—not a copy, but the actual transcripts that were pulled from a typewriter on that very
day and had then been filed away in some dark cabinet belonging to Hitler's Third Reich. Those files were
eventually the property of the victorious Allies and had
likely been transported to and fro until finding their final resting place here at the institute. It seemed highly
probable that I, and the historian at my side, were the
first to read the words. The typist had created a few er-
rors and later corrected them with a pen.

Mr. Straube from the Public Prosecutor's Office introduced the facts. "The accused, Dr. Schoorl, a Dutch
National citizen, is suspected of providing identity
cards to a Jewish woman," he began. "Based on his
confession, the following is known: Schoorl attended
public elementary school, high school, and higher agri-
cultural college, followed by the eight years he worked
as an assistant at the college. He then started his own
laboratory, studying the nutrition value of food products. From the fall of 1942 until spring of 1943, he
worked in a laboratory in Amsterdam where he became acquainted with the Jewish woman, Hildegard
Sara Wittner. They worked together. She occasionally
told him she was afraid of being deported, and asked
if he could help her and her fiancée go underground.
Dr. Schoorl stole two identity cards from one of his

employees by the name Pieter Wouter van Soest. He gave these to the Wittner woman. Schoorl therewith committed a theft (penal code article #242), and further—through another independent act—the transfer of identity papers to another for which they were not issued, with the purpose of going underground (penal code article #74). Therefore he is guilty of article #281—the abuse of identity papers."

The judges listened. They conferred briefly, then came to a unanimous decision. "Taking into consideration that the accused does not deny the charges, and that he was not politically motivated, but acted solely out of compassion, and also taking into consideration that he has no prior record, and has five underage children, ages thirteen to three, the senate has for the theft—in spite of the fact that the accused was not afraid to steal from one of his employees, exposing that employee to grave danger—sentenced Dr. Schoorl to five months in prison, and for the abuse of the identity papers, another five months. For both . . . a combined sentence of eight months is considered suitable and sufficient. Taking into consideration the detention of the accused, the court refrains from further punishment."

"This is very unusual," the historian said to me. "I'm surprised they even gave him a trial." The fact that the prisoner they would soon release had, at that very moment, two homes filled to capacity with Jews further adds to the unlikelihood of the day's outcome.

After the judge read his statement, Piet stood up and walked through the courtroom and toward the door where his family patiently awaited the court's decision. Still accompanied by guards, he stepped through the threshold and toward his wife and children. "I'm free," he said as he knelt down. My mom watched her father as he hugged her siblings then felt his arms wrap around her small frame.

Mom was six-and-a-half years old that summer. She didn't cry when she saw her father go into that courtroom and she didn't cry when he came out. After holding all of his children and embracing Anne, Piet left the waiting room for final processing.

The children descended the stone stairs with stoic faces. Anne had told the children not to celebrate if Piet was freed. She didn't want their joy to further upset any of the less fortunate families who shared that cramped room. But that wasn't the only reason for their calm. Over the last year they had witnessed one of the world's most terrible wars unfold quietly within their gentle home. It did not drop its blood on the living room carpet, nor fill the air with the smell of its lingering dead. When it came to their farmhouse door, it did so politely. It never disturbed lunch, or kept the children from their evening tuck-ins. When the Wagenaars escaped to the farm, Anne served them tea. When the Nazis murdered Ben and Joost, the deaths were only words spoken softly. My mother's war had been reserved and well-mannered and the children acted in kind.

When the children saw their father a few hours later, he was wearing his own clothes. The sun glimmered on the water in the prison's moat as Dr. Pieter Schoorl walked across the prison's bridge a free man. The family left the grounds, together once again. The seven of them stopped at the home of Piet's widowed mother in Utrecht and ate lunch before boarding the train to Bennekom and back to the Soetendael. For two short summer months they would be a family reunited.

Chapter 15

PIET RETURNED HOME to a party. Friends and family gathered on the back lawn next to the swing set and fruit trees. Bennekom's baker had scrounged together the ingredients for a mocha-torte and delivered it as a gift. The children watched their father closely as he chatted in the afternoon air. They couldn't help notice how Piet had changed. There was no fat on his arms, and his muscle rippled underneath ropy veins. Everybody wanted to be with him and talk with him. He looked very tired, but also cheerful. During the weeks in Utrecht, his hair had grown a bit, but it was still shorter than the children were used to and a cold reminder of Vught.

Iet watched her father eating cake. Standing on the edges of the party, she wrestled with feelings of ambivalence. She was happy to have her father home. But she didn't feel the warm affection she was used to from him and had longed for since her father's arrest. Despite his standing there in front of her, that longing didn't leave. She was also struck by the color of his hair. In nine months Piet's full head of brown hair had turned completely gray.

Soon after the party ended, Piet and Anne, and Leo and Pauline discussed everyone's safety. It was possible that the Germans would be watching Piet, and by the end of the night it was decided that all of the Jews should leave the farm. For the second time in as many months, Pauline packed Eline's suitcase and sent her away to stay with a member of the underground in the town of Ede. After Eline was gone, Pauline said goodbye to her husband and son, and then made the same trip to the Elisabeth farm to which she had traveled on the night of Carel's rescue. Leo and Carel were the last to leave. Leo washed a chemical into his son's hair to turn Carel's black hair blonde. The two would perform the parts of a vacationing Dutch father and son, and they traveled through the rural countryside booking rooms in pensions. When other vacationers asked about his mother, Carel said she had died under a German bomb.

The lazy days of July and August passed peacefully. There were no midnight knocks on the Schoorls' front door or German raids rippling through their small community. News of the Allied advance continued on the airwaves. The British and Americans had taken the French beachheads. They had fashioned a makeshift port, then poured their men and war machines into Europe. The Allied air force had nearly decimated the Luftwaffe, and their fighters now savaged German ground forces with near impunity. Within only a few weeks of landing, the Allied tanks were pounding the Nazis east, and by the end of summer the Germans had nearly retreated to within their own borders. But the American and English forces had yet to push north into Holland. As the Germans had learned four summers earlier—the Netherlands, with its numerous rivers and near endless canals, was particularly hard to invade. Yet the Allies' progress did have an ancillary effect on life in the little village of Bennekom—distracted by their failure to hold France and the might of the army bludgeoning them eastward, the Nazis' grip on Bennekom had loosened. It soon became clear that the Germans had larger concerns than the comings and goings of Dr. Pieter Schoorl, and midsummer, the four van Leeuwens returned to the farm.

Though there seemed a brief respite from the war that summer, for my grandfather, the newfound peace was not easily navigated. He spent more and more time alone. The lost weight had hollowed his eyes and the lines on his face drew deeper. His short hair had grown an inch but remained a whitish-gray and would for the remainder of his life. But he had lost more than those pads of fat and his auburn hair. The rosy ideals that had guided his youth and the faith in humanity that had acted as his personal beacon had been cut loose of their moorings within him, and Piet struggled forward. The family respected his need for solitude, and Piet would often absorb the long summer hours alone in his study. He refused to discuss Vught with anyone. It looked as though Piet had aged ten years in the last two.

From across the English Channel the BBC hosted a Dutch program named Radio Orange, and Piet and Leo would sit together in the living room in the evenings to listen to the latest news. Leo was convinced Holland would be liberated before his upcoming birthday. But no one could be sure. Though the Germans' attention had waned, the day-to-day life for the Schoorls had become increasingly complicated. The Nazis, who had once harbored hopes of winning the support of the citizens of Holland, were fed up with the Dutch and their stubborn resistance, and had since decided that if they couldn't placate Holland then they would plunder and punish it. Every day trainloads of Dutch resources poured out of Holland and into Germany, and it became quickly evident that if the war wasn't over soon, the family would need to prepare for a hard and hungry winter—the Schoorl family, the Schoorl land, and all of their guests were soon mobilized to this singular end.

The edges of Anne's garden had widened over the last two years. On moonless nights Kurt Dannenbaum and his wife would leave the lab's cramped attic and walk to the Soetendael to escape the confining monotony of their life in hiding. They'd sleep at the farm and then spend the next day tending the rows of produce—picking beans, discarding weeds and soaking in the fresh air and sunlight in close company with Anne's bees who also contributed to the war effort. Before the war, Anne had taken a bee-keeping class. She had learned to build hives from reeds that grew on the riverbanks. Piet had stores of an inedible industrial sugar at his laboratory, and Anne's bees transformed the blue crystals into usable honey. The farm's rich soil fed the Dannenbaums' spirits as they worked in tandem, and the two would again wait for night to fall before sneaking back into the lab.

Every day the war progressed, Anne's black-market connections became more valuable. In the 1940s, Europe still endured the vestiges of the strict class system, but Anne's life as a farm girl helped her build relationships with the region's farmers. She spoke their language, and they saw her as one of their own. That summer, she bought as much food as she could get her hands on. Sometimes her family in Alkmaar sent potatoes and onions to add to the Soetendael's stockpiles. Bread was particularly hard to find. On the rarest of days, a loaf appeared on the morning breakfast table, but usually the kids ate porridge.

Piet and a friend, Kor Bekker, designed and built an electric press that squeezed the oil from beechnuts, which could be used as a cooking oil. The trees were abundant and the press worked well, and after finagling a way to get extra electricity rations to run their invention, the two men worked steadily until they had produced enough oil to last a year.

Iet also remembers foraging for food. The woods had always been her friend, and in midsummer, she wandered the narrow trails with a basket in hand, picking blackberries. Toward fall, after the first rains fell, she hunted the woods for mushrooms. She knew in exactly which parts of the shadowed underbrush the fungi grew. Walking in the woods alone, underneath the forest's old trees, reminded her of those afternoons before the war with her father. Her body could feel those memories. A breeze through the meadow, or the sight of a butterfly with its wings pulsing as it weighted a blade of long grass, helped unwind the knots in her gut and provided a refuge. The fact that the Germans strictly forbade anyone from entering the woods didn't concern her. The forest was one of the few places she felt safe. Even as Iet made her way back into the relative security of the Soetendael, her stomach would tighten. She'd always scan the property for signs of trouble before pushing through the hole in the hedge.

By the summer's end the family was ready for what they thought would be the worst-case scenario. Anne had worked tirelessly canning row after row of fruit and vegetables. Even if their nation wasn't liberated before winter, with the farm, their food stores, and friends in the community, they could survive. But on September 5, a day remembered by the Dutch as "Mad Tuesday" it appeared that all of their work had been unnecessary.

* * *

THE EXODUS BEGAN as early as September 2. The highways were choked full with all forms of vehicles. From lumbering horse-drawn wagons and men pushing carts, to sleek staff cars, military half-tracks, and heavy trucks, the traffic continued east day and night. German soldiers were seen shedding their uniforms and begging for civilian clothes. Nazi politicians looted their offices, packed up their girlfriends and frantically searched for transportation. By Tuesday, rail stations spilled over with desperate German civilians and their Dutch sympathizers standing next to piles of luggage, anxiously awaiting anything heading east into Germany.

On September 1 the *Reichskommissar* in Holland, Dr. Seyss-Inquart, had issued an evacuation order to all German civilians. Seyss-Inquart had been nervously monitoring the Allies' swift thrusts into Belgium and decided it was time to implore his countrymen east toward Germany. Anton Mussert, the infamous Dutch Nazi party leader, delivered the same message to his underlings. Two days later, Brussels fell to the British, then Antwerp. Allied tanks were only miles from the Dutch border and seemingly poised for an easy rout of the less-than-battle-ready German forces Hitler had left to defend the Netherlands. The Dutch Queen Wilhelmina announced on a radio broadcast from England that the liberation of her country was underway. General Dwight D. Eisenhower followed the Queen's address with his own, stating: "The hour of liberation the Netherlands have awaited for so long is now very near." Holland's prime minister in exile told radio listeners that the Allies had indeed breached the Dutch borders. A fever-pitched pandemonium ensued.

Just as the Soetendael shielded its occupants from harm's view, it also muted the swelling hysteria seizing the nation. But the news was impossible to ignore. Dutch flags rose to the tops of their flagpoles. Pockets of Dutch commandos who'd patiently awaited this day for years, descended on their enemies, arresting any Nazi they could find and holding them until the Allied troops would arrive. Crowds of Dutch civilians celebrated in the streets, and rumors ruled the day. Allied troops were reported to occupy various Dutch cities, and what had begun as a calmly planned exit east by the Nazis on the first of the month turned to frenzied bedlam. Both sides, it appeared, had abandoned all rational faculties.

There was, of course, not a thing wrong with a mass celebration on the part of the Dutch, or a mass exodus on the part of the German invaders, if there had been good reason for either. But as the dust settled on Mad Tuesday it became painfully apparent that nothing in Holland had actually changed. Despite the influx of news to the contrary, not a single Allied tank—indeed not a single Allied soldier—had stepped beyond the Belgian border. The reason was as simple as it was sad. Though the Netherlands was ripe for an easy invasion, the Allied tanks had run out of gas. Their push into Belgium had exceeded their supply lines and they hadn't sufficient fuel to mount a further advance. By the time the sun had dropped beyond the trees on the Soetendael's western horizon, Hitler's generals, in their predictably efficient manner, took control of the situation. Veteran German paratroopers were rushed into Holland to buttress defensive positions. The German troops that had abandoned their posts were collected up and restored to duty, and the Dutch Prime Minister again spoke on the airwaves apologizing for his misguided and premature speech. The euphoric celebrations ended as abruptly as they had begun.

On Wednesday, the Schoorl children fell asleep to another day of occupation. But "Mad Tuesday" wasn't compelled by complete aberration. The war was turning in a way that the children could see and feel. The Nazis were crumbling. It appeared only a matter of time until the little village of Bennekom would be free.

Piet's new identification, issued after his release

Chapter 16

A S THE EUPHORIA of Mad Tuesday drifted into memory, my mom prepared for the start of school. Anne combed her hair and tied the bows around her pigtails. "Everyone was talking about the end of the war," Mom told me. "But I didn't understand what it meant for the war to end." Mom had two orange ribbons—the official color of the Dutch royalty—waiting on her dresser for the day the Allies rolled into Bennekom. "That's really all it meant to me—the end of the war—that I could wear the orange ribbons."

The school year had barely begun when Mom walked home from her classes on the Friday afternoon of September 15. The farm was just beginning to undress in preparation for the cold winter months. The oak trees had started to turn, and most of the farm's crops had been harvested, but the sun still held strong in the clear blue sky. It wasn't an unusual day. It could have drifted off into obscurity, except that it marked the last day that the little girl would make the trip from school to home for a very long time. The next day's events would change the war, and my mother, forever.

* * *

"IT WAS OVERWHELMING," said Hanneke, as she recalled that very weekend. Two days had passed since I had first arrived at my eldest aunt's home, a two-story town house built in an upscale retirement community where she lives alone. Several old clocks announced the hours at more or less the same intervals. Hanneke's boyfriend, a soft-spoken, retired doctor of psychology who lived in an adjacent building, sat with us. Hanneke held a cup of tea. She spoke of that weekend with an awe that had remained in her despite the passing of so many years.

In her seventies, Hanneke looks the part of the Schoorl family matriarch. She resembles her mother, but only partly. Her high cheekbones, rosy complexion, and carefully groomed hair distinguish her from Anne. In many ways, I think my eldest aunt is the woman Anne had dreamed of becoming when Anne was a young lady milking cows on her father's dairy farm. After completing high school, Hanneke received a college education, and then married a successful dentist. I visited their home when I was a child—the largest residence in the town of Medemblik, a lavish stone house built on the edge of a canal leading to the stormy waters of the IJsselmeer. Hanneke's husband, Eddie, was president of the yacht club; their family of six could walk across their back yard and board their boat.

As a child it was Hanneke who shared her mother's love for music, and she had her mother's voice. The two spent hours seated side-by-side on the narrow piano bench in the living room of the Soetendael playing and singing the old tunes Anne loved. When Iet and Ruud were lost in the woods, Hanneke busied herself inside the home. She liked to help her mom organize the china and crystal on their dining room table when the family entertained guests. Hanneke would pick flowers and arrange them between the place settings. As an adult in Medemblik, she hosted her own dinner parties and moved with a social grace her mother could never quite manage.

I still remember the columns of stone leading to the entrance of Hanneke's large home and the salty air of the IJsselmeer blowing a thick dark lock of her husband's hair as he stood smiling behind the wooden wheel of his boat. Sadly, after Hanneke and Eddie finished raising their four children, Eddie died in a car accident and Hanneke has lived alone ever since.

Hanneke had guided me along much the same roads as I had traveled with her sisters. The memories came easily. We walked beside the freshly pruned trees and underneath the hayloft. She described the ornate stairs and the ladder leading to a cramped attic. She remembered the long breakfast table, and her mother's simmering soups. "My father loved to take us with him on walks," she said. But Hanneke never much cared for them. She preferred remaining at home and embroidering with her mom. She recalled that it was Iet and Piet who shared a love for nature.

She took me through those first days of invasion—that first time she saw a German soldier, the large home in Arnhem, and the bombing of Rotterdam. She described the evening Eline arrived and the time half a year later when Pauline, dressed as Black Pieter, briefly reunited with her daughter. Just as with Iet, these were memories she hadn't visited since they first wrote themselves on her mind.

When she talked about those winter evenings during the occupation when the families gathered by the piano and sang, a wistfulness warmed her already kind voice. "I loved that," she said softly emphasizing each word. Her eyes seemed to be watching the scene playing out in front of her, and she remembered the Jewish couple, Kurt and Liesel Dannenbaum, with that same tenderness.

"Your face lights up when you talk about them," I said.

"Yes, I loved them." It was Anne who had made Hanneke visit the dentist and his wife in the attic of the lab. The Dannenbaums often talked about their teenage son in England, and how when the war was over Hanneke could meet him. They thought the two could make a cute couple.

Hanneke filled my coffee cup repeatedly and served cookies between breakfast and lunch. Her boyfriend remained a fixture in the living room. He joined us for breakfasts and dinners out. He had also survived the war as a Jewish child in Holland.

I asked if she remembered that weekend.

THE PLEASANT WEATHER my mom enjoyed as she made her way home from school held for two more days. On Sunday, Anne spread a cloth over the table on the back patio of the Soetendael and served brunch outside in the warm light. It was a beautiful sunny morning. From the patio, beyond the hayloft, the farmer's cows could be seen grazing in his fields. Everyone sat together for the meal. It was one of those pleasant pastoral settings that could fit nicely in an oil painting.

The sound of the planes didn't build in the usual manner. This wasn't the barely discernable drone bombers first made as they navigated the thin air thousands of feet above the green Dutch landscape, that ethereal buzz that slowly built to a roar. This was an earthly growl. The firing of pistons and the slap of the propeller chop were close enough to feel against your chest. The aircraft appeared almost instantaneously, so low the children could read the white lettering and see the wings trim and bobble against the bumpy air. Hundreds of British and American transport planes lumbered only a few hundred feet above the family, shadowing the village pastures as they passed. Spellbound, none of the family moved or said a word. Thick ropes sagged between several of the planes and the fat gliders they towed behind. The bright sun blinked repeatedly as the crafts passed overhead. Some of the gliders cast off their ropes, and the thick cords slowly dropped like dangling tails from the rear of the C-47s that had pulled them over the channel. The sky was alive with a symphony of aircraft.

Inside the immense wooden gliders the men of the 1st British Airborne Division braced for hard landings in the farmers' fields only a few miles east of Bennekom near the town of Oosterbeek. The Schoorls and van Leeuwens watched in stunned amazement.

The clusters of aircraft seemed without end. They spread across the entire southern horizon. With their gaze still fixed upwards, the children soon recovered from the awe and jumped up from chairs, shouting "we are free, we are free," in unison. As one swarm of planes passed beyond the trees on the eastward end of the farm, another emerged from the west—they filled the sky in layers. Gliders descended toward their landing zones as their tugs ascended back into the blue atmosphere to return to England and repeat the journey. And then the lines of paratroopers started streaming out of their planes in long horizontal lines, rows of black dots with ribbons dangling above them that then exploded into blossoms as their white, orange, and khaki parachutes caught the wind. Plane after plane dispersed their human cargo into that sunny afternoon light until thousands of chutes drifted in that gentle air like dandelion seeds.

The spectacle unfolding in front of the family continued unabated for hours. Code-named "Market Garden," it was the largest airborne invasion in history. Over 4,700 aircraft navigated the crowded skies. Waves of explosions could be heard coming from the direction of Arnhem. Distant clouds of smoke rose above those trees where the children lost sight of that first wave of liberators. Burst of German anti-aircraft fire from a battery near Bennekom cut across the sky.

After Leo realized there was no apparent end to the invading formations, he hurried inside and called a family living closer to Oosterbeek to get a report. He remained on the phone, calling out the news—more planes had been sighted south of Arnhem and Allied shells were leveling parts of the city. The children all remained outdoors. Entire families had climbed to their rooftops to watch the splendor unfold. Adele, who for two years had only braved the outdoors under the cover of a dark night, descended the attic stairs, stepped out of the front door of the lab, and walked openly on the sunny avenue and toward the Schoorl farm. Crowds of Dutch took to the streets. This time it wasn't rumor and innuendo. This time the Allies were here, and they'd arrived in breathtaking fashion.

"IT WAS OVERWHELMING," said Hanneke. "And then the rumors began. Where are they? Are they coming our way?" A large sliding-glass door in the living room opened to Hanneke's manicured gardens and the natural light ripened the colors of her imported rugs. "They were so big," she remembered. "And they flew so low. It was so impressive. We shouted, 'we are free,' and 'there they come.' That was a big event. I remember seeing it, and the feeling."

THE INVASION WAS the brainchild of Britain's Field Marshall Montgomery. He had relentlessly hounded his superior, the Supreme Allied Commander, General Dwight D. Eisenhower, for the resources to launch an attack on Holland. Eisenhower was reluctant to authorize such a bold push, but eventually gave in to Montgomery's dogged requests. And the plan had some merit. With a massive air assault on Arnhem, coordinated with a push north with the tanks and ground forces massing in Belgium, the Allies could secure several key bridges leading across the Rhine. Once over the river, they would have outflanked the German defenses and could swoop down into northern Germany and capture the Nazis' key industrial centers in the Rhineland. Montgomery was confident the Allies would occupy Berlin by Christmas. The initial landings went better than expected.

The 1st Airborne Division, dropped north of Arnhem, was tasked with securing the main bridge spanning the Rhine. They needed to capture it intact and hold it for at least four days until XXX Corps' tanks blasted their way north from Belgium. Despite a failing radio system and the fact that only half of their forces actually arrived on that first afternoon, the 1st Airborne managed to take the bridge. The landings to the south were equally successful. The Germans had been caught completely off guard.

With the phone system still intact, Leo was able to stay abreast of developments. He remained for the most of that first day sitting at the bottom of the staircase holding the black receiver to his ear. The sounds of war continued unabated. That night, the crack of rifles and the deep rumble of heavy artillery continued to travel the several miles to the farm. The children listened from their beds until each finally slipped into sleep with the images of their liberators filling the sky, and they snuggled against the warm hope of a life returned to them.

The following morning the children again awoke to the bright blue horizon, but it quickly succumbed to a thick cover of clouds. The air traffic had now completely stopped, yet the house still buzzed with excitement, and everyone speculated as to the condition of those brave paratroopers who had come to save them. Leo's phone calls provided few specifics. The fight had continued east and away from the farm and into the city of Arnhem. The family had no way of knowing that the tenacious British soldiers, attempting to keep the bridge open for XXX Corps, had come face-to-face with the results of what can be accurately described as a fluke of historic proportions.

On September 4, nearly two weeks before that spectacular Allied air invasion had arrived above the farm—and only hours before Hitler ordered that he be replaced—Field Marshal Model had made a flurry of decisions in reaction to the Allied pummeling his forces had received since the invasion of Normandy and the subsequent push into Belgium. Model leaned over a map of Western Europe. He ordered troops to reinforce the ports of Dunkirk, Boulogne and Calais and he also strategized a counter-attack against the Allied armored divisions. He scrambled to make radio contact with his generals. His command center was chaotic. Doing his best to manage that chaos, it would be one of the Field Marshall's last decisions—the seemingly benign choice as to where he should rest and refit his severely battered 9th and 10th Panzer divisions—that would most influence this recent Allied onslaught. After a few moments pondering over his map, he made his choice. He ordered the Panzers to slowly disengage the enemy and move north to a location he chose primarily because it was peaceful and out of harm's way—the Dutch city of Arnhem.

Before the 1st British Airborne had boarded their gliders and strapped on their parachutes, intelligence reports noting the presence of several tanks near the Arnhem countryside had reached Britain's top brass. But no one recognized their significance, or at worst, those in charge were so taken with the audacity of their pending invasion they were unwilling to squarely face the possible threat. The Panzer divisions were spread thinly throughout the area, with most hidden in the woods. But it only took one day after those first planes interrupted Sunday brunch at the Soetendael for the tanks to regroup and crawl toward the lightly armed British paratroopers.

By the close of the second day of the invasion the family had little new news. The bellow of heavy artillery could be heard at all hours. It seemed that all of Bennekom was in the grips of speculation. By Tuesday XXX Corps had reached the Dutch town of Nijimegen, only ten miles from the Rhine. As they passed through one Dutch town after another, they were met by streets overflowing with elated Dutch citizens, cheering and waving flags. But the tanks were severely behind schedule.

Leo remained in touch with friends near Oosterbeek. There were reports of German tanks blasting through downtown Arnhem and heavy casualties on both sides. Neither Anne nor Piet, nor any adult at the farm ever spoke to the children about the specifics of the war. But over the years, all of the children had learned an unspoken language. They could fill the details by the look in their parents' eyes. The children's elation only lasted two days before it started to leak out of them. The cloudy skies hampered further airdrops, and the men of the 1st Airborne were using up their supplies fast.

The sounds of battle waned as the days progressed, and the children more or less settled back into their routines, unsure of the exact outcome of the invasion. The rumors that had made their way from Arnhem to Bennekom were not good, and it was toward the end of that week that Iet decided to walk to the lab and climb up the chestnut trees that grew between the house and the road. She carried her basket with her as she walked. The fall sun had burned away the blanket of clouds that had hung over the family all week and again shone clear. Iet arrived at the lab and began climbing the tree. Foraging for food helped her feel useful. She cradled the basket in the crook of her arm as she steadied her feet on one of the thick lower limbs and reached to a narrow upper branch, pulling herself further into the foliage. There was an element of solitude when surrounded by all those leaves, a peace similar to that of the forbidden woods. Iet worked her way to the outer branches where she could reach the last of the tree's nuts. The almost constant din of the battle for Arnhem had nearly stopped. Only the occasional thumps of a distant artillery blast interrupted the otherwise quiet afternoon.

While filling her basket with nuts, Iet heard the sound of an unfamiliar vehicle approaching from the south. Its stiff suspension rattled against the stone road. Iet wasn't able to see it until it passed directly beneath her—it was an open vehicle, olive, army-green, small and compact. She did not know it at the time, but it was the first Allied jeep to pass over the roads of Bennekom. She also watched a mini-bike pass. Both had flown over her home in the bellies of the fat gliders on that wondrous Sunday. The mini-bike folded in half for easy transport. Iet recognized the uniforms of the drivers.

The British soldiers needed to hold the bridge in Arnhem for four days. Nicknamed the Red Devils, they were some of the best warriors Britain had produced. Armed with only the light weaponry they could carry, they took on the Nazi Panzers. The German tanks pushed forward repeatedly to retake their bridge but couldn't dislodge the tenacious Red Devils. The men of the 1st Airborne succeeded with their mission. They captured the bridge over the Rhine on that first day, and they held it for the following three while waiting for the tanks of XXX Corps to reinforce them. But XXX Corps never arrived.

The soldier behind the wheel of the Allied jeep passing underneath my aunt was German. So was the one squatting on the diminutive mini-bike. More Germans passed on foot with weapons drawn. Beside them marched those Red Devils. They passed underneath Iet with heads bowed. Some had bloodied bandages wrapped around useless limbs. Some carried their wounded comrades. They had fought to their last bullet, then the survivors surrendered. They were dirty, dejected, and exhausted. Iet's knuckles whitened as she tightened her grip on the old tree and her eyes filled with tears. Though highly unlikely, Iet felt afraid the Germans would shoot her on sight; she held her breath as she watched hundreds of battered British prisoners of war passed beneath her.

Nearly sixty years later, when she recalled the moment, Iet would have to stop mid-sentence as those same tears resurfaced. "It was a terrible moment. The men that had come to free us were prisoners." Her aged elbows pulled in toward her body as she wept.

A small number of the soldiers of the 1st Airborne had escaped across the Rhine at night in rubber dinghys. As they walked the few miles south toward XXX Corps their eyes scoured the roads in vain for their friends. In one short week their division was annihilated. The Germans had stopped the approaching Allied tanks only a few miles short of Arnhem at the Dutch town of Driel.

Of the more than 10,000 men of the 1st Airborne division who had dropped into Holland, 1,485 lost their lives. Another 6,414 were taken prisoner, of whom one third were badly wounded.

Leo at the Soetendael with a black-market goat, with
Ruud in the background

Chapter 17

THAT INVASION MARKED a new type of war for my mother. This one was not content to lurk in the shadows. The Germans re-fortified the northern shore of the Rhine and for the coming weeks the heavy guns of the Germans' 25th Army blasted away at the Americans' 82nd and 101st Divisions entrenched across the river. The Allies responded in kind. A fury of heavy artillery dropped on both sides. Dutch families with homes close to the fighting retreated into the dank safety of their cellars. Many perished under the fire. My mother now lived just a short bicycle ride from the newest front of the Second World War.

On the last days of September, the Nazis ordered all villages close to the Rhine evacuated. The citizens of Renkum and Wageningen packed only what they could push or carry. Forced to choose between belongings that had both material and sentimental value, and those they needed to survive, the families prepared for the exodus. Anything with wheels—bikes, strollers, farmer's carts—was piled to capacity. On October 1 the roads north swelled with thousands of refugees—all on foot and moving slowly. Bennekom was the first town to receive them.

The gate to the Soetendael was closed as usual on that morning. The doctor's sign warning against diphtheria still hung prominently. A mat of freshly fallen leaves covered the edges of the gravel drive, and—despite the war—Iet woke up with a tinge of excitement tickling her belly. She turned fourteen years old on that day. It was her fifth birthday since the Nazis had invaded Holland.

No matter the circumstance, Anne always made sure birthdays were special. And with her usual stubbornness, she refused to let the war dissuade her. My mother remembers all the kids gathering on Piet and Anne's bed, and the birthday boy or girl snuggled tight and warm between their parents. On that particular morning, Iet opened a large, flat, rectangular package. Inside was a copy of Hans Christian Andersen's *Fairy Tales and Stories*. The book sat heavy on her lap, and Iet turned the thick pages carefully. It was going to be a birthday she would never forget.

Friends of the Schoorls who had walked the several miles from Renkum knew that, despite the doctor's signature, the sign by the entrance of the farm's driveway was fraudulent. Their children were tired, and they needed a place to sleep before resuming northward. They carefully swung the gate open, pushed their belongings inside and closed it behind them.

The phone lines were down, and Piet and Anne had no idea how many would arrive. The first refugees were offered space inside the house. Later, beds were prepared in the old animal stalls in the attached garage where the Dutch soldiers had slumbered on that snowy winter evening nearly five years earlier. Before midday the Schoorls and van Leeuwens would be preparing beds in the squat barn across the driveway. By nightfall the little farm would house over fifty people, and Anne and Piet did their best to keep things in order. They put the children to work tearing old newspapers into toilet paper, and coordinated use of the kitchen and laundry room.

Even my grandfather's closest friends were unaware he had several Jews living in his home. But he didn't have time to worry or even explain their presence. The evacuation had created a larger problem for Piet and the van Leeuwens. There were the seventeen Jewish children Piet had hidden in the attic of Ms. Bos' cottage on the old Keyenberg estate in Renkum. When the bombs started falling, Ms. Bos took the children to a nearby cellar in the isolated woods. Word had gotten back to Piet that the children were now alone. Simon and Adele de Leeuwe's two children, Ruth and Ruben, were two of the seventeen. A little after one o'clock, Iet and Hans overheard Leo, Simon, Piet and Anne discussing the children. Leo suggested they smuggle them through the woods and to the farm.

"DID YOU MEET Ms. Bos?" I asked Hanneke.

"Yes, I did. Iet thinks I didn't. But I think I did. I didn't like her. She had one child of her own—a girl."

Leo rode his bike to the estate and had found the children in a remote cellar, but soon after they started through the woods toward the Soetendael, some of the children collapsed.

"Ms. Bos was paid a lot of money," Hanneke said. The children lived in her attic for two-and-a-half years. They were all poorly cared for.

It became quickly obvious many of the children could not make the trip through the woods, so Leo decided they should head for the open roads and hope to blend in with the rest of the refugees. But still, several of the smaller children could not walk. They were malnourished. Some were sick. They were already in poor health when living in Ms. Bos' attic, and the last two weeks in the damp cellar had depleted whatever reserves their little bodies had to begin with. Anne told Hanneke and Iet to get on their bikes and ride toward the estate and ferry the worst of the children back to the farm.

The sisters pedaled side-by-side. They rode for nearly twenty minutes, winding their bikes through the constant stream of oncoming families. It was another crisp, clear fall day. Hans and Iet both felt a glow of pride. It felt good to help—to be needed.

"What were the names of Simon's and Adele's children?" I asked Hanneke.

"Ruthy and Ruben."

"Are they still alive?"

"Yes, they are."

"Are they in Holland?"

"Yes."

"Do you think they remember?"

"Ruth does. I met her. She remembers."

THE FOLLOWING DAY, Hanneke dropped me off at the train station in Wageningen. I walked beside the morning commuters. A man in a dark business suit glided past me on an odd-looking bike with small wheels. The train slowed to a stop beside us. He stepped off the bike just a few yards in front of me, bent down to release a clasp, then folded the bike into the size of a large briefcase and walked through the open train door.

Ruth de Leeuwe now lives in Groningen, a college town close to the northern border of Holland. She had seemed eager to meet me. I looked outside the window at the flat pastures. Within an hour the train had emptied of most of the professional-looking men and woman, and was now filling with young adults. Ruth's voice had a smooth sweetness on the phone—a velvety voice reaching into a higher octave than most. The sound of hard heels upon the stone floor of Groningen's 19th century train station echoed off the cathedral-like ceilings, and the stained glass windows grabbed at the morning sun. Ruth pulled up in her car only moments after I left the station. She also looked much younger than her sixty-six years.

We parked on the cramped roadside next to her apartment-like home near the station. Rows of shelves lined her hallway, packed tight with books and stacks of paperwork. Ruth writes for several Jewish publications. The home had a cozy, eclectic feel with fine-art prints and paintings on the white walls. She cleared space on her living room table, made some tea, then sat across from me. She looked more somber than her sprightly voice suggested. Her short brown hair curled upward and was only just tinged with gray. She wore a black sweater and a silver necklace with a small Star of David.

Ruth removed an old photo album from one of her shelves and placed it between us. "My father, amongst many other things, was a photographer," she said as she opened the pages. The images were fixed on heavy black paper with a thin transparent leaf separating the pages. There was an image of Ms. Bos holding Ruth's little brother Ruben. Ruben looks to be around three. His blonde hair bushes up around his soft forehead and his two ears stick out. He has a half-smile and is holding a small wooden train. Both are wearing overcoats—Ms. Bos' black, Ruben's white—Ms. Bos' thick brown hair is up behind her head. She also has a half-smile, and her eyes squint thin. There's a casual intimacy in the way her arms fold around the child.

Ruth turned the pages from the other side of the table, explaining the inverted photographs. "May 5th, 1940" was written in white chalk beneath seven images of a tulip field. Five days after Simon had snapped those shots the Nazis invaded. Nine days later he would hold his daughter as the two watched Rotterdam burn.

"So you were born in Palestine."

"I was born in 1936, on the eighteenth of November."

"And then you left Palestine."

"On holiday for half a year. My father planned to take a course in motor mechanics in Driebergen. They wanted to visit their family. They had no clue what would happen to them. Nobody from Holland told them not to come, or stay where you are, there's going to be a disaster. Either nobody knew, or they didn't want to tell them—this I don't know. Anyway, they came. We lived in Driebergen for half a year, then we moved to Rotterdam. All my mother and father's family lived in Rotterdam."

I could hear and see the city traffic outside Ruth's large living room window. She explained how the family lived off savings and the income from the cinema her mother and Pauline inherited from Ruth's grandparents.

"My father had a good job in Palestine. He was a bus driver, which was really a good job at that time. He was a member of the Palestinian Philharmonic Orchestra. He played the violin and percussion in the orchestra. His whole family were musicians. He was a very good violin player."

On one of the pages in her photo album, Ruth's father is holding his daughter much the same way Ms.

Bos held Ruben. His large arm wraps around Ruth and she is leaning into his shoulder. Simon has a full, confident-looking face, with an easy smile and strong jaw. His hair recedes a bit. Over his solid frame he is wearing a sweater with a thick collar like one would take to sea, and he sports a stylish rectangular wristwatch. There is nothing Jewish-looking about his features, and he appears more like a man cut from the same cloth as Ernest Hemingway. Above that photo is another of Ruth. She is lying on her bed, nestled in a thick quilt, her dark hair matted against the pillow. She is grinning, with her thumb partly in her mouth.

"We moved to Rotterdam. Then my brother was born in 1940—February. Two months later there was the bombardment. And I remember being so terrified that—in my memory—I was screaming for days and days. My father tried to show me outside. He tried to make a game out of it. 'Doesn't it look nice, all those lights in the air.' But it didn't make any kind of impression on me. I was just terrified. They let me sleep in the bathroom and make my bed in the bath. There were no windows. This I remember very well. But it didn't help. I was completely hysterical."

Ruth was so hysterical her parents asked the family's doctor to come see her. The doctor suggested the family leave Rotterdam as soon as possible. They followed his advice and stayed with friends and family, eventually renting a home in Bennekom. For several months Ruth's parents would find her hiding underneath the furniture.

"We stayed in Bennekom till the summer of 1942. And then went into hiding. We were brought away—my brother and me."

"And what was life like prior to that?" I asked.

"It was nice. My father was away a lot. I remember

he went fishing in the middle of the night. And I think he was playing in an orchestra somewhere. We had a happy life. I wasn't aware of a war. I was five years old then. I became five in November 1941. I was very busy with my brother. My mother was busy with two kids. And my brother had a lot of ear infections. So the doctor came a lot. We had a nice garden and a place where we could play. It was nice—what I can remember. My brother had to be in this box."

"A playpen."

"Yes. I was very fussy I think, a very dominating child. I really liked to tell all the other children what to do, and what not to do."

"Who were the other children?"

"Eline and Carel, and there were other children which you do not know—Carla, Albert, and there was Bonnie who also came from Palestine. There were quite a lot of families that came together, had dinner together, and were probably talking about the war a lot. So this Bennekom period was really nice. Of course there must have been a lot of tension between my parents and other grown-ups, but this I didn't pick up."

On May 18, 1942, Ruth's grandmother came to Bennekom. She and Ruth were born on the same day and her grandmother came to celebrate their shared half-birthday. She arrived in a rented horse and carriage. "She brought me a beautiful present," Ruth said. "I remember it very well. I saw her coming and she stepped off this carriage like a queen and she gave me this little plant—a deep red geranium. And I was so happy. I was so happy that she came. That was the last time I saw her. She died in the camps."

Less than a month later the family went into hiding. "We were not prepared. And I realize now that you cannot prepare a 5-year-old child for such a thing. But my mother and father decided not to prepare me at all and just told me that I was going to go out on a kind of holiday to stay with a nice aunt. So I was of course asking, 'Who is she? Why don't I know her?' This I don't remember exactly, but I was this kind of child—always wanting to know what was going to happen. I remember my mother crying all the time and hugging us for no reason obvious to me."

"And you said you remember being driven there."

"Yes." The family turned into the Keyenberg estate. "We came up this huge lane with high trees, and on the right side this big house. My mother said, 'No, you're not going to live there. There is another house, another cute little house.' I don't know, maybe she had been there before to discuss the money. Because that was the most important thing to Ms. Bos—the money."

"How do you know that?" I asked. I remembered just a few days earlier that Hanneke had told me the same thing—that Ms. Bos charged a lot of money for each child.

Answering my question, Ruth embarked on a story about a national conference held in Amsterdam in 1993 to bring to light the stories of Jews hidden as children during the Nazi occupation.

"It was the first time after the war that there was any attention to the hidden children."

"And during this conference they made mention of Ms. Bos?"

"No. Before this conference there was this television program called 'Behind the News.' And eight weeks before the conference they had a story about people who were attending and their past." Ruth was ambivalent about signing up for the conference. "I know what happened. It's integrated in my life. I don't suffer from it anymore," she told me. And she didn't see the point of attending. But friends implored her to go. So she registered, and shortly after was contacted by the reporters from "Behind the News." Ruth told me about how they asked if her experience was a good one, or bad. Ruth said it was very bad. The show did a preliminary phone interview. Apparently in the process of corroborating Ruth's story they found Ms. Bos. They asked Ruth if she was willing to meet with her. Ruth flatly refused. But Ruth did agree to visit the Keyenberg estate and meet with a reporter and television crew.

The program sent a driver to Groningen and he drove Ruth toward Renkum. As the car neared the estate, Ruth felt unsettled.

"It was the first time, ever, after the war that I went there. And I must have made me very nervous because I got this skin rash." Ruth recognized the wooded estate. "So we drove on the exact same lane with the huge trees." She remembered the grounds and directed the driver to the mansion. "So we went into the house and waited for the reporter. And there were photos on the wall from this caretaker's house." It had since been demolished.

The reporter arrived. He interviewed Ruth as they drove to the site where the reporter believed Ms. Bos hid the kids in the cellar. Ruth told her story. They stopped in a clearing in the woods and found an underground shelter and descended into it. "We went down a small stairs and there were potatoes lying around." Ruth looked around, then told the reporter this wasn't the right place. "He said, 'Well, you know. It's so long ago. Your memory is mixed up.' I said, 'No, I am convinced that it is not this place.' But he didn't want to accept this. So that was that. And then I was brought home. But then a few days later, or a few weeks later I was phoned by the television station."

A woman had heard Ruth's voice on the TV. She was in her kitchen feeding her pets. The voice coming from her living room made the hairs on her arms stand up. She recognized Ruth's voice from 53 years earlier when they both hid in the attic of that small caretaker's cottage. The producers of the program gave Ruth the woman's phone number. The two met. And the woman, Ester, confirmed many of Ruth's memories.

"Ester said terrible things happened there. And the only reason Ms. Bos did it was not because she wanted to save us, but because she wanted to be rich. She asked for a lot of money from the parents, and she even threatened parents to throw their children on the street if they didn't pay in time. That's what she told me, this Ester. I never knew because my parents didn't tell me. I was too young."

"Also, before the conference, they called me—these television people. They said they met a man who had seen my interview. He told them he knew Ms. Bos, and he had been in her home. He also told them that the place they took me was not the right place. It was much further in the woods. I was very happy because, again, it confirmed my memory."

Five-year-old Ruth, her little brother, and Simon and Adele continued in the car toward Ms. Bos' home. The woods were quiet. Ruth's parents took her by the hand and stepped inside the cottage. The first thing to strike Ruth was the smell. The thick odor of an unplumbed toilet seeped into the small kitchen. Ruth noticed Ms. Bos' 10-year-old daughter in the corner of the room. The girl looked slightly mentally handicapped. Ms. Bos welcomed the family. She offered a place to sit and a cup of tea.

To Ruth, Ms. Bos looked to be around the same age as her mom and dad. Ruth doesn't think there was ever a Mr. Bos. Ruth sat on one of her parents' laps—she forgets which. Ruben was next to her. The adults shared tea. "I don't remember what I was doing till my momma said, 'listen, I think it is a good idea if you take a nap because Ruben also needs to take a nap. It's his time.' I definitely didn't want to. I was a big girl—five years old. So, they tried to get me to sleep. Which really made a big scene. I didn't want to go. Maybe I sensed the danger. I don't know. They succeeded in getting me to sleep on her bed. I don't know how, maybe they put something in my drink."

When Ruth awoke she was alone. She looked around the unfamiliar room. "I needed to pee. So I get out of bed and called for my mother. But nothing happened. I immediately panicked. And I really had to pee. And I was screaming for my mother. And after a while Ms. Bos came in. And she was very rude to me. She took me from the bed by my arm and said, 'if you ever behave like this again you will be punished.' And she kind of kicked me to the kitchen and said, 'your mother left with your father and they are not coming back anymore.'" Ruth remembers almost vomiting from the smell inside the small restroom. "When I came out she said, 'go upstairs now to the other children.' And I thought, other children? I didn't know. 'And your brother stays down.'"

Ruth followed Ms. Bos from the kitchen into the living room. Ms. Bos walked to the far end of the living room, reached up to a cord hanging from the ceiling and pulled down a folding stairway. "She took me up, and there were all these other children. And she just pushed me up the stairs and said something to the children like—here is another one. And that was it. And then I don't remember very well what happened next. We slept on the floor." There were fifteen other children in that attic. "We were the last. After us there were no more children."

Ruth lived in that attic for over two years. She remembers remarkably little. Two older girls in their early teens watched over the younger children. The attic spanned the length of the small cottage. The children could lie down on their bellies and look out either of the attic's two small windows. They took turns. "I was one of the youngest—maybe the youngest. My brother was downstairs." Ruth remembers watching the seasons pass through those small panes of glass. Snow clung to the bare branches in the winter transforming them a skeleton white. In the spring the trees budded. The only daylight the children knew came during their moments next to those two windows. The buds blossomed twice, bathed in the summer sun twice, and fell twice before the children would leave that attic. Ruth remembers on two separate instances a plane crashing into the adjacent woods.

Ruth has vague memories of conversations with the older girls. "I must have asked a lot of questions. And they just said something like we were there because we were Jews and it was war. Both messages didn't mean anything to me. I mean we were Jewish, but we weren't religious. We didn't do anything."

The children urinated in pots. If they had to go poop, they went downstairs. The attic was dirty. Ms. Bos signaled the older girls if there was danger. There was a space between the two floors where the children could hide. Every week they rehearsed. Ms. Bos came up, counted to three while clapping her hands and the kids scurried into their hole. Ruth remembers on two different occasions the children scrambling into the floor and German soldiers entering the home. "It wasn't just us who had to go down, but the mattresses and everything. It was really a question of maybe one minute. That's why we did this rehearsal. The older children had to keep their hands over the mouths of the youngest. We were all lying on each other and we couldn't make any noise. Then we heard these soldiers walking over our heads. I heard them talking in a language I didn't understand."

To pass the time, the older girls told stories. The children also shared a ball of yarn and two knitting needles. Each child took a turn knitting a small square. When they exhausted the bit of yarn, they'd unravel their work, re-ball the yarn and pass the needles to the next child. Ruth was too young to knit.

Ruth remembers Ruben getting very sick. The two children slept together. One morning Ruben was too ill to get up. His body was covered with red welts. Ms. Bos sent for the doctor. "I was with him all the time and I kept him in my arms and I kept telling him that mommy loved us and I loved him and that he would be better. I took care of him. He survived. I don't know how. There was no penicillin. I don't know what the doctor gave him."

When Ruth told the producers from "Behind the News" she had a very bad experience as a hidden child, it wasn't because of the two-plus years in the attic, or the dirty sheets, or whatever lack of care, or profiteering Ms. Bos either was, or wasn't, guilty of. When Ruth shared the details of her story with me, she seemed to offer them up as more of a side-note than anything, supporting facts for a main plot, the one that still seethes inside her. And as I sat across the table from Ruth, it became evident that there was really only one war remaining inside her—Ruth's remembered war with Ms. Bos.

"Right from the beginning she told me that my mother would never come back. She wanted to steal my brother. Because he was so beautiful and so non-Jewish, so blonde, and so blue-eyed. You can see in the photo—she always kept him close. That's why he was downstairs and not up with us. Several times she told me my mother was dead. And Ms. Bos thought of a nice little game to play with my brother and me. She asked my brother, 'who do you love more, your black mommy or your blonde mommy?' And then, of course, he was supposed to say the blonde mommy because that was her. Now if he said that—which he did in the beginning—she looked at me like a devil. With a face like—you see, I win.

"When my brother was upstairs with me—we slept together all the time—I told him stories over and over about our own mommy. I was convinced that she was still alive. I said that she is still alive and that she loves us very much and she is coming to pick us up from here.

"Once he said that he loved his black mommy more. She slapped me. And she kicked me and she closed me in this toilet. Because she knew it was me who influenced him. It was a war between Ms. Bos and me."

Ruth remembers her father visiting twice. "Before he came, she dressed me properly with a dress and ribbons, and she told me that if I said one word to my father over what happened in the house, or that there were any other children, I would be closed inside the toilet. When he came I was terrified. I was on his lap like iron. I didn't like him to come because it was so difficult for me not to tell him anything. And not to tell him how terribly I missed my mother. I missed him less.

"Then one night there was a fire in the big house," Ruth said, referring to the Keyenberg mansion. And after the fire Ms. Bos told me, 'your mother was there and she burned. So you don't have to tell your brother that she's alive and that she loves you. She's not there anymore.' I didn't believe her. I knew she was lying. I don't know how, but I knew she was lying.

"I think it was after the fire then, not long after the fire, that we slept together my brother and me. I woke up and my brother wasn't there. So I got out of my bed. It was the middle of the night. I looked for him around this attic, but he wasn't there. I really don't remember how, but I got down the stairs, went out and went looking for my brother outside. I was in such a panic and I was driven to look for him.

"I found him. He told me he was looking for our mother. I don't remember how we came back, or if we were found, or she found us. I only remember me waking up, missing my brother, and feeling this absolute urge to look for him—to go out and find him. He told me that he was looking for black mommy."

The sun had passed beyond Ruth's living room window. Her large eyes looked plaintive. But there was what seemed to be a stubborn anger in her—a piece of that child who despite the decades passing could not let go of the fight. She had recently told the same story to the Steven Spielberg Jewish Film Archive. Ruth had misplaced Ester's phone number. I would never corroborate her story.

Ruth doesn't remember the planes from Market Garden, or the exchanges of artillery across the Rhine.

Shortly after the Nazis' tanks rolled over the British soldiers of the 1st Airborne, Ms. Bos led the children out of the house and through the woods and to that lonely cellar. Ruth remembers Ms. Bos saying someone had betrayed the children and the cottage was no longer safe.

"It was just a hole," Ruth said, "nothing but earth and sand. We had to go on our knees to get in. There were some blankets. It was summer. It must have been the end of August, the beginning of September. But it was very cold at night. We were very close to each other—keeping each other warm. I don't know how long. I really don't know."

There was little food. The older children left the cellar during the day and picked wild berries. The kids were already in bad health and the cold and the moisture took a further toll.

Ruth remembers returning to the cottage and Ms. Bos preparing the children for the evacuation. "We were dressed properly, and had our coats on. And everybody had a little bag with whatever we had—almost nothing. We were all standing there next to each other waiting for people to come and bring us out. I had my brother next to me. We were standing in a row. And all of a sudden she took my brother from me, and she took me, and she pushed us into a cupboard—this deep cupboard. She pushed us in. She put socks into our mouths and bound our hands to our legs. We couldn't make any sound. She closed the door and then I heard my father coming in and Oom Leo, or maybe your grandfather—this I don't remember very well. The children were terrified—they didn't say a word. My father asked her, 'where are my children?' And she said they are gone. And then I could hear them arguing and then I think there was a kind of fight. In the meantime I was so terrified. I can't explain it to you. And then one of the children said, 'they are in the cupboard.' And she became furious. Then my father wanted the key. And she said, 'I threw it away.' In the end my father got the key and he opened the cupboard. And we came out. It was really . . . it was terrible. And then we were on the back of a bike and went to your grandfather's."

HANNEKE AND IET wove their bicycles through the oncoming exodus. With shoulders hung low under the burden of heavy suitcases, the newly minted refugees moved slowly. The two girls passed children who were carrying their thick overcoats, and their mothers and fathers stared down that road with a weighted anxiousness. Most of the phone systems were down, and with the heavy bombing and the Nazis' evacuation orders the families had no choice but to gather their belongings and begin northward. Few had any idea where they would sleep in the coming nights.

The sisters kept looking ahead as they pedaled through the lumbering crowd. The purposefulness of their trek felt a touch heroic. Most of the departing families that they had passed had managed to find something with wheels, and their littlest children were balanced on top of stacks of luggage that their parents either pushed or pulled forward. The girls continued to scan the horizon. Anne hadn't given Iet or Hanneke exact instructions as to how to find the children, but when they saw the small herd making their way toward them, they understood that a description wasn't necessary.

Two-and-a-half years in the dirty attic had turned the children's skin a pale white. Long curls of dark hair fell from their little heads in every direction. Black dirt traced arching lines under their long fingernails. Their clothes were filthy. The cloudless Dutch sky helped illuminate the years of neglect. Scabies had burrowed beneath the skin of most of the children to lay their eggs. The itching and scratching raised red welts on their arms and necks. All of the children looked worn and frightened. "We'll take the little ones first," said Hanneke.

The sisters retraced their way back toward the farm, each with the small hands of one of the children gripping their waists. They passed the same families they had faced on their ride toward Renkum. They made their way back to Bennekom, unlatched the farm's gate and dropped the children off with Anne and Pauline, and then returned for another trip.

That afternoon still lives vividly inside both of my aunts. It was the first time either had directly assisted in the work of rescuing the Jews. Both assured me their efforts were less than essential, but it still felt important to both of them—and they felt proud. They met the group a second time, and again took the smaller of the children on their bikes. By the time the girls had dropped off the third and fourth child, the other thirteen were just down the road from the farm.

That October afternoon was the busiest the Soetendael had witnessed in years. Between the Schoorls and the van Leeuwens and all of the refugees and now the children, over fifty souls found sanctuary in the isolation of the small farm. Despite the daylght, Adele had snuck across the meadow between the lab and the Soetendael and through the hole in the hedge. She had not seen her children since the day they had all driven down the lane next to the Keyenberg mansion. Her son had doubled in age. When she found her daughter amongst the children, Ruth turned away when Adele tried to hug her. "My mother was crying. I think she hoped for more. But I was completely—I don't know—ruined or something. I just wanted to stay with my father."

Anne was shocked at the sight of the children. They looked deathly pale. She guided them into the sunny backyard behind the flower garden next to the beehives. Pauline went inside to get something for the children to eat and drink. One of the men resting at the farm for the night with his family remarked that the children looked too Jewish. "You need to cut their hair," he said. It was obvious something needed to be done quickly. Anne sent for the family's hairdresser in Ede, Mr. Zomerhuis.

Hanneke helped prepare beds for the children in the old barn. The next-door farmer brought fresh hay. Hanneke spread bed sheets and blankets over the soft dry lawn for the children to sit on. Anne had asked Marianne to find some toys for the children. Marianne stood inside her room and anguished for a few moments over which toys to part with. She chose a few of her less favorite things and also brought out some comic strips for the kids to read. Iet sat among the children. None of them talked much. They appeared intimidated by the air and the light and the nervous attention surrounding them.

Mr. Zomerhuis arrived while the afternoon sun still hung high. Another member of the underground from Ede had brought new clothes for the children. A chair was placed next to the tall row of flowers which provided a modicum of shelter if a passerby happened onto the Schoorls' property. One after another, the children took turns in the chair. Their dark locks dropped on the grass next to the busy feet of Mr. Zomerhuis, lice still clinging to the black strands. Each child was bathed and their fingernails clipped. It looked as though they were moving through an assembly line. Along with the new clothing came travel bags filled with toiletries. The kids moved from caretaker to caretaker. When they were finished they again sat quietly on the back lawn. Their eyes looked vacant. Some read the comic books my mother had brought them.

By late afternoon, the shadows lengthened and the air chilled. Adele and Simon had received Ruth and Ruben off the end of that assembly line, the children's hair clipped and bodies scrubbed. The smell of the cottage was mostly gone, left in the pile of soiled clothes piled on the edge of the cold lawn. But there were other stains not so easily exorcised. Ruth had trouble looking in the eyes of her own mother, and Adele could not explain away her daughter's angry bewilderment. The reunion both had longed for was tainted: the reasons too slippery for a child to understand or a mother to find an easy peace with. Mother and daughter had fought a war every day they were separated. And just like a young soldier who returns home fresh from the killing fields of war, the peace of home did not exactly feel like peace. Adele kept her daughter and son close by her side as the reunited family walked through the meadow and to the lab. Behind them, the farm continued to buzz with activity.

The house, the garage, and the few outbuildings were filled with people. There were so many distractions and so much to do, it was easy to slip into the comfort of the tasks at hand and think that the same war the Schoorls had been fighting for years was somehow diminished. But the threats were as real as they had ever been, and the burden of Jewish lives directly dependent on my grandparents had more than doubled in a matter of one day. After the remaining children were properly cleaned and fed, Hanneke took them into the stand-alone barn on the other side of the Schoorls' driveway. The building bore a gentle resemblance to the attic the children had so recently fled. The sidewalls were just above waist high with a couple of windows allowing in some light. Bales of hay were placed strategically inside the barn to shield the children from view. Toward the back were small arched openings meant for the pigs to meander in and out of their stalls. Hanneke explained that if the Germans came toward the barn the children should escape through the small holes and run to the neighbor's farm. She had brought a table and chairs and stayed for several hours with the children. The older ones told her stories about Ms. Bos.

The Schoorls put out the word that no one was allowed to leave the farm without authorization. After the children were tucked away, someone saw a German soldier on a bicycle ride up to the gate. He read the doctor's warning, then turned and left.

Before dusk settled into dark, two more refugees would arrive at the farm. Piet's mother, Johanna, whose rheumatoid arthritis had confined her to a wheelchair for most of her adult life, slowly made her way to the farm alongside her longtime caretaker. Since Piet's dad's death from cancer in 1942, the two women had lived alone. Both were elderly. When food became increasingly scarce, Piet had moved his mother from Utrecht to a house in Bennekom. That afternoon, the Germans demanded the house to billet troops. A small suitcase rested on Johanna's lap as her caretaker pushed her wheelchair down the bumpy roads and toward the farm.

Hanneke was outside when her grandmother appeared on the bend of the driveway. The front wheels of the chair caught against the dirt and gravel. Despite all Hanneke had seen that day, there was something exceptionally cruel about this particular moment. Hanneke used to visit Johanna often in Utrecht, and the two were close. They played board games together and knit. As Johanna aged, she suffered more. But she never complained. There was always a frailty and vulnerability to her, and the image of her grandmother cast into the streets made Hanneke cry. Anne took her mother-in-law into the busy home and found a place for her to rest.

The home was in constant flux that evening, and Anne moved centrally in all of the busyness. She mothered over that farm and the needs of everyone within it with a care bordering on compulsion. Since the beginning of 1944, the Soetendael had been, in many ways, Anne's, and from her pastoral headquarters she had met the war head-on. Whether lucky or shrewd, or a mixture of both, she had always found it her lesser, a fact that only served to more fully awaken and strengthen that iron will that had always hummed inside her. Anne worked to keep all of her guests comfortable that night. She made another bed for Johanna and continued to have her eldest daughter check up on the children in the barn.

After the evening settled, Anne worked alone in the kitchen. She boiled some potatoes and chopped endive and made Iet's favorite birthday dinner. For dessert, mother and daughter sat together at the dining room table and ate chocolate pudding.

The following morning, the flurry of activity continued. The fifteen Jewish children awoke to the foreign setting, their young minds needing to shake off the last bits of slumber before fully recognizing the barn walls and the hay and the reason for their shorter hair. Some of the Dutch refugees had left at first light; others were preparing for the open road. Towns to the north had temporarily opened school buildings and set up beds. The motley exodus of civilians continued through Bennekom as hundreds of families hop-scotched their way from village to village making their way to the homes of distant friends or relatives.

As the day wore on, there was a bit more elbow room at the Soetendael. The space and time afforded Piet and Anne allowed both to consider the problem of the fifteen children. Plans had to be made quickly. There was no way for the Schoorls to care for them safely. The German armies were consolidating in Bennekom and the adjacent towns, preparing to repel another Allied push northward. The short reprieve created by the fighting in Belgium had ended, and the streets began to again fill with soldiers. In fact, at that very moment, one particular group of Germans had marched down the main avenue, then turned west onto the side road that led to the Soetendael, and soon neared the shade of the large hedge. The soldiers slowed as they reached a Y in the road and could see the closed gate, with the words "de Soetendael" carved into it, on their left. And it was as though the men had been given specific directions to the farm, for they continued directly to the gate, and, ignoring the doctor's sign, unlatched it and swung it open.

Chapter 18

THE SCHOORLS' PIG hung upside-down above the kitchen sink; its hind legs, bound to a wood frame, angled up to the room's ceiling. The stream of warm blood had filled the home with a thick unfamiliar odor. The blood collected in the sink, and soon the stream diminished to drops, each sounding out in lengthening intervals, much like the hands of all of the Schoorls' many clocks had only hours earlier—each tick and tock growing further apart until the entire farm seemed to move in an agonizing slow motion.

The sound of the gravel driveway often announced the farm's visitors. The grind and occasional pop created by a car's wheel occurred more and more rarely. A child's foot was discernibly different than that of an adult; a bare foot could be easily differentiated from one within a shoe. The sound of several grown men in heavy boots had set off instant alarms, the first moments of which began without words or thoughts but as an electric jolt of fear that tremored through the many bodies. Before any of the minds at the farm could piece together a single shred of information, their hearts pulsed hard and fast; the gait of each soldier seemed to slow as the adrenal glands of the Soetendael's residents quickened their every thought and movement. Hushed warnings reverberated throughout the home and farm, the near silence and the piercing alarm augmenting each. In seconds the warnings had reached throughout the farm, informing every soul within its boundaries of the emerging danger. The children in the barn pressed their bodies against the bales of hay. Anne, Pauline, and Paya, one of the older Jewish children who had been so recently rescued from the woods, were together in the kitchen when the soldiers finally arrived at the door. There wasn't time for the two Jews to make it up the stairs and behind the relative safety of the false wall. Anne hurriedly pushed them inside one of the large kitchen cupboards. A few ticks of the clock later and the Germans' boots could be heard on the wood floors.

The home's many refugees watched the Germans, silently following the soldiers' every move, and, as they did, felt the heat of a familiar anger well up in them. But newly complicit in Piet's and Anne's underground world, their minds were less familiar with deceit, and they likely strained to not look toward the barn filled with children, or toward the cupboard or even at the little blonde-headed girl they now knew belonged to Pauline. They watched the Germans and tried to act as natural as possible.

Pauline pressed her body against Paya's. She could hear the soldiers' voices. One had demanded to speak with the owners of the farm, and Piet and Anne now stood in front of him. The Soetendael seemed suspended in one gasping inhalation of fear as the man started to speak. "You have forty-eight hours to vacate your home," the officer told Piet. "Leave the furniture, leave the clothing, and leave the food." The Nazis were taking over the farm to use as their headquarters. They looked at Piet and Anne sternly as they underlined that everyone was allowed to pack one bag and one bag only.

WHEN THE LAST of the pig's blood drained from the animal's opened neck, the butcher poured scalding water over the skin and began scrubbing off the thick hairs. The Schoorls were simultaneously recovering from one trauma while enduring another. Had the Germans been looking for Jews they'd have found plenty. But they didn't search the home. They simply informed Piet that they were taking the farm and then left, and the home drew a deep breath of relief while its owners also wrestled to make sense of all of the implications of the Germans' orders. There was little to celebrate—nor was there time to mourn.

The family began immediately packing anything they thought unobvious—anything they thought they could get away with removing from the property. Butchering a black market pig had already been illegal for some time. Piet and Anne were now hedging their bets that none of the soldiers had seen the beast. Once the pig was rid of its hair, the butcher cleaved it open and removed its entrails.

The Schoorls, the van Leeuwens, and the Jewish maid and her boyfriend would all join the other families already living in the lab. The children began making trips back-and-forth between the two homes. Anne could often be found standing silently as she agonized over what she could get away with keeping and what she'd have to leave. She stood under the thick beams of the Soetendael's small cellar in the garage looking at the rows of glass canning jars she had slaved over all summer long. She had picked, peeled, and preserved most of the orchard's fruit. The thought of leaving all that food in the hands of the Germans made her ill. It was one of many moments during that war that would remain alive in Anne until her last days. After Anne turned her back on the rows of jars, she would never be able to bring herself to can another item again for as long as she lived. The loss of the farm felt more like the loss of a friend.

Two of the five Schoorl children were born in the upstairs of that farmhouse. For all of the children, it was the only childhood home they had ever known. But those distant childhood memories—the farm as their plaything, their dad's terrarium and salamanders, and the lazy summer days playing in the shade of the hayloft within the innocent isolation of their farm— seemed perhaps too distant. As the children grew up the war had grown up with them, and it seemed so had the very farm itself. The home they would miss would be the one where the morning breakfast table grew unpredictably larger, and where there was always someone somewhere in the home offering their warm company. When my mother told me that the war was all she ever knew as a child she was in earnest. And the only early childhood she could recall was the one that had unfolded in that home and in the shadow of that war. It was as tender as it was horrific, and Mom would miss it terribly. The Sweet Dell had always seemed an impenetrable refuge, as if its seven acres had contracted a blessing with the better parts of our world. In a way, by nature of its unique geography, it was the land that commandeered Piet and Anne into its service and pushed them forward into the front lines of this quiet and deadly war. The silent pastures and the unruly hedge had faithfully sheltered dozens of lives. It provided food and warmth, and, for so many, its calm and quiet acted like a balm, a rural respite from the Nazis' bloodletting. Losing the farm was in a way like losing family—but there was no time to reel.

Piet had made plans for the Jewish children which were now hurried forward. Through whatever mysterious channels he had always done his work, Piet made contact with another arm of the resistance somewhere in the north of the province. A Red Cross truck would arrive that evening at the now-abandoned school about a mile down the road. Piet's only remaining duty to the children was to get them safely inside that truck. He and Anne decided that one of the fifteen, the teenage girl, Paya, was too sick to make the journey. Despite their care, the girl could still hardly summon enough energy to walk, and the family had decided to take her with them to the lab.

Piet was uneasy with the children remaining in his barn. There were too many of them and no place within the structure to effectively hide. Bennekom was thick with German soldiers. Piet talked to the farmer who owned the land between the Soetendael and the school where the Red Cross truck was to arrive. The farmer agreed to stack the bales of hay in his pasture in such a way that would create a large cavity inside. The children could hide in the hay while waiting for the truck.

As the night fell, the hasty evacuation of the farm continued. Leo and Piet worked side by side in the vegetable garden, digging two large holes. Their shovels cut first into the soft cultivated soil and then deeper into the wet sand. The holes were shaped like fat graves. Both families collected their valuables and keepsakes and placed them carefully within two fifty-gallon barrels. Iet's one-day-old birthday present—the book by Hans Christian Anderson—was sealed inside along with the rest of the belongings. The barrels were lowered and the holes filled. The moon rose as the men spread the excess dirt evenly across the farm's latent garden.

Under that same moon, Hanneke led the remaining fourteen children out one of the small openings in the rear of the barn and into the pasture and toward the neighbor's field. The children, as quietly compliant as they had been since they had come to the Soetendael, followed single file. They each carried their new bundle of toiletries. In the last two days, Anne had fed them as much as their hungry bodies would allow. And when she looked at each of those children her mind probably wandered in much the same direction it had over two years earlier when Anne first saw little Eline sleeping next to Marianne—imagining the mothers of each Jewish boy and girl, and what the women had gone through to part with their children, and then, possibly, what it was they were going through at that very moment. Piet may have known the faces of a few of those parents, maybe even a piece of their story. But he would have tried not to and would have shared nothing. And it is a cold statistical likelihood that several of those young sons and daughters were now, as they followed my aunt across that dark field, orphans.

Hans found the freshly stacked hay and directed the children through a small hole. The farmer had placed knee-high bales inside for the children to sit on. They waited to be signaled that the truck had arrived. Hanneke remained with them, but it wasn't an easy night for her. She worried that if the German soldiers discovered their hole, she would be swept up with the rest of the children and then shipped by the Nazis to Westerbork.

After the truck arrived, Hanneke led the fourteen across another moonlit pasture and down a side-road. The vehicle had the familiar thick Red Cross painted on a white square. Piet was waiting next to it. The children were helped into the rear. The truck's engine rumbled, and it turned out of the school parking lot and rolled northward to the city of Garderen, leaving father and daughter behind in the silence.

That evening would be the last anyone saw of the children. The war was now moving at a different pace, and it didn't pause for moments of reflection. There was little conversation between Hanneke and her father as they walked together back to the Soetendael. Both were tired, and once home they went to bed. When the new day dawned the family awoke to the pressure of each hour's passing as the Nazis' deadline loomed. Everyone hurried about the home.

A bit after breakfast another farmer arrived at the Soetendael. He sat atop his heavy cart pulled by two muscular draft horses. The farmer turned the cart in a large U so it pointed back out the drive and then halted. Piet's mother was wheeled out of the home. Two of the men lifted Johanna out of her chair and up onto the chest-high cart upon which a soft living room sofa that had been strapped in place. Once Johanna was comfortably settled, a few of the Schoorls' belongings were also added to the cart, and someone draped a thick wool blanket over Johanna. Once the load was secured, the farmer signaled his horses with a flick of the reins and the load started forward. The wheel chair had been tied to rear of the cart, and it wobbled back and forth as its little front wheels struggled to find their center. Piet and Anne had found a home further north where Johanna would be safer. Both Iet and Hanneke cried as they watched the cart disappear beyond the gate. The journey would take the better part of a day. Everyone hoped it would not rain.

THE FAMILIES HAD been busy preparing to leave the Soetendael for nearly a day and a half. During the last week it was as though the war was collapsing around them and they were all being pushed from one dire moment to the next. Perhaps a part of each one of them envisioned a calm after this unrelenting storm, that the war somehow owed them a momentary respite. But it did not come.

The Schoorls worked to make good use of every minute they had to prepare for the evacuation of their farm. Hanneke had asked her mother if she could pack the sheets and linens, and was busy folding the edges of the sheets sharp and stacking them neatly in a box. Marianne and Eline were close by, and Pauline and her son, Carel, were also still at the farm as was the ailing Jewish teenager, Paya. But, compared to the day prior, the farm was now practically empty. The refugees had all departed and most of the Schoorls and their guests were busy organizing the lab. This time, no one was near enough to the driveway to hear that ominous sound of soldiers' boots marching on the gravel drive. The Germans had arrived nearly half a day early, and it wasn't until they had nearly entered the garage that they were spotted.

The same hushed alarms of panic again shot through the Soetendael. The soldiers entered the garage and walked next to the old animal stalls and toward the doorway leading inside the home. The moment marked the last a Jew would hide at my grandparents' farm.

As the Germans pushed open the garage doorway, Pauline, Paya, and Carel rushed out the front door. The three ran toward the orchard as they heard the door slam behind them. The black paper covering the living room window had long since been removed and Pauline and the two children were clearly visible from inside the home. But it was as though the Soetendael had bent the margins of chance in favor of its habitants one last time—a last benevolent act, granted by a trusted friend. None of the soldiers looked toward that window as they walked down the open hallway, and the three Jews slipped unnoticed through the safety of the hole in the hedge.

Anne looked at the Germans with disregard as she continued packing, and casually told Marianne and Eline to leave to the lab together. The two girls walked down the street holding each other's hand. Anne gathered the last items she could manage and then left her little farm.

The Soetendael's ornate oak staircase

Chapter 19

THE LAB WAS a mess of boxes and luggage when Anne walked through the front door, carrying the last items she had packed from the farm. True to her nature, she did not rest, but immediately began the task of unpacking. Refugees could still be heard outside as they traveled the main avenue in front of the lab. From the house's tall first and second story windows and between the few leaves that still hung on the chestnut trees, one could see them passing by.

Piet's lab equipment was no longer in regular use. The desks and tables and spiraling twists of glass were pushed against the wall to make room. Anne's two sisters, Ety and To, still lived on the second floor as well as Dr. Gorter, but the home now needed to house thirty people, nearly half of them Jews. Anne organized the cupboards and shelves in the kitchen, and after a few of the boxes were emptied she realized she forgot a few necessary items. She asked Iet to return to the Soetendael and retrieve them.

My aunt took the popular shortcut across the browning meadow and through that well-traveled hole in the hedge. The front door of the Soetendael was open. As was her habit, she didn't knock. She entered the house, walked through the hallway past the kitchen and living room and stepped up the broad wood staircase. As she passed the open door of her parents' bedroom she saw two German soldiers standing next to the bed. She could see her father's wardrobe was opened and his suits hung neatly in a row. The soldiers were posturing in front of the mirror and laughing at each other while they took turns trying on Piet's collection of caps.

The buzz of activity that had swarmed about the Soetendael was now at work at the lab. The home wasn't as expansive as the farmhouse, but it was large. The clean lines of the smooth stucco walls reached up for two-and-a-half stories where they met the roof's ceramic tiles. The attic spanned the full length of the lower stories, and every inch of it was put to use. The stairway was like a crowded thoroughfare that evening. Remnants of the Schoorls' pig were packed in the cool of the lab's cellar, mattresses and luggage were pulled through the hallways, and furniture was carried from one room to the next. Beds were made for the twenty adults. Piet and Anne's room looked out the back window. Eventually, as the hallway traffic slowed, someone started dinner.

The family now lived closer to the heavy report of German guns firing shells from a battery near Bennekom, and they continually sounded through the house's thick walls. By now, the blasts were common. The Germans aimed their shells just south of the Rhine into the Allied front lines. The Americans and English responded in kind, and errant shells regularly exploded throughout Bennekom.

At night, the children listened to the bombs rising and falling. For four-and-a-half years now, the noise of war had invaded their days. But it was only recently that the sound had, for them, turned potentially lethal. By mid-fall, the Germans were launching their V-2 rockets—the world's first sub-orbital rockets—from nearby railcars. Hundreds had passed over the English Channel and erupted on London, and the Germans had recently pointed them at the Allies in Antwerp. The less sophisticated V-1 rockets made a telltale buzzing sound when they streaked across the village sky, easily discernable to the Schoorl children listening to them passing overhead. But the rockets were notoriously unreliable. Sometimes, a few moments after they took to the skies, the rockets silenced and then fell. They could land anywhere. In daytime, when the kids heard them, they would run for a ditch or hide underneath a home. At night, they simply listened. When a V-1 exploded, it left a truck-sized crater.

After the children finished eating dinner that first night at the lab, they all descended the narrow stairway into the tiny cellar. It was the safest place for them. The cellar's wide shelves were cleared to make room for small mattresses, and the younger children were stacked one atop the next. My mom slept on the top shelf.

The cellar was like most—a cold concrete room, dark and musty. The air didn't move and old cobwebs clung to the harder-to-reach corners. There were ten children in the room. Baby Helene, now three—and really hardly a baby at all—slept upstairs between her parents. As Marianne tried to fall to sleep, she looked up at the hard ceiling and worried that the shelves would collapse beneath her. The older children slept on mattresses spread across the hard floor. Some of the newly packed luggage was stacked against the wall next to boxes from Piet's business. Hanneke didn't mind the cramped quarters, and the children talked as their bodies slowly warmed their sheets and blankets. For Hanneke, the room felt intimate like a slumber party, and, one by one, the children drifted into sleep.

AS ONE DAY passed to the next, life at the lab began to fall into routine. It did, however, have some very obvious drawbacks. Besides the number of people living so close together, there was the simple fact that the house rested just a few paces from one of the busiest roads in town and lacked the safety of the farm. Kurt and Liesel Dannenbaum had rarely moved from their room for the two years they lived in the attic. Adele also hardly ever traveled below that third story.

On one of those first days at the lab, Marianne and Eline pushed their doll buggy on the sidewalk in front of the home's iron gate. Their make-believe worlds were perhaps the only thing completely predictable in their lives, and despite the endless tumult the girls still played regularly. They parked the buggy while their babies napped, and the girls played beside it with a jump rope, wiggling it on the cobblestones like a slithering snake. Their imaginations were suddenly interrupted when an old woman came down the sidewalk from the direction of Ede to the north. My mom looked up. She could feel the woman's eyes on her. It was attention my mother wasn't used to, and she sensed malice in the woman's stare. Marianne reached for Eline's hand as the woman walked up to the girls. The old lady pointed a finger at Eline and said, "I know who she is." Mom scooped up their dolls and hurried through the gate and inside the home pulling Eline behind her.

Mom was six in 1944. Her hair had grown long since the beginning of the war. When Anne tied her pigtails into braids, the two locks fell nearly to her belly button. My mother had always been a quiet observer. Her parents had told her to keep a look out for strangers.

After the door closed behind her, Marianne let go of Eline's hand and hurriedly searched the lab for her father. She told Piet what the woman had said, and he quickly took Marianne to the living room window and asked her to point the woman out. As soon as Mom identified her, Piet shot out the door. Mom watched him run down the sidewalk and in front of the woman. He stood blocking her way. From behind the glass Marianne could see Piet's mouth moving. The conversation ended briefly and Piet walked back inside the home. "Everything is alright," he said to his daughter. He could see the weight of concern in Marianne's eyes. He again reassured her that everything would be okay and said he was proud of her.

WITH EACH PASSING DAY, the bombs fell with greater frequency. A siren sounded when incoming shells were expected, and the children either rushed into the cellar, or if they were outside, ran toward an open field and lay on their stomachs.

Bennekom's infrastructure slowly deteriorated. The schools remained closed. The phones were down. Power was down. The mailman no longer delivered.

Hardly a week had passed since moving, when Iet heard someone knocking on the lab's front door. She opened it and standing in front of her was a man dressed in black. He introduced himself as the village undertaker. He was making his way down their side of the street, stopping at each home to read a list of names he carried with him of the recently deceased citizens of Bennekom. He read the list with the deliberate and learned reverence of a man well versed in his trade. The forgettable names passed through Iet until she heard one she recognized. It was a friend of Piet's from his college days who was also the father of one of Iet's classmates. He was a Jew married to a Dutch woman. Though the undertaker continued reading from his list, his was the last name she heard. The man had survived the genocide in hiding. And he had probably felt the same exultation as Adele just a few weeks ago when the hundreds of Allied planes darkened the skies above Bennekom. He probably hugged his wife and child. And even with the Allies defeat in Arnhem, everyone believed it was only a matter of time before the American and English armies overwhelmed the Nazis. The war, it appeared, was nearly over. The man was working in his garden when the Allied shell dropped. The shrapnel had pierced his flesh and cut through his insides. The undertaker finished his list and made his way to the neighboring home.

Compared to the weeks prior, those first few at the lab passed without event, and the family worked to adjust to the new setting. Outsiders seemed to pay the home little attention. The days grew shorter, and the chestnut tree was soon nearly bare. And only a short bike ride south, the Allied liberators worked to defeat the German occupiers.

THE AMERICANS' 101ST DIVISION was dug in on a five-kilometer strip of land, locked between the North Rhine and the Waal rivers called the Betuwe, a rich farmland thick with orchards. The 101st had expected to be pulled out of the fighting after Market Garden failed. But the English, charged with holding the south banks of the Rhine, needed more manpower.

The Americans called that strip of land "the island," and their 105mm howitzers pointed toward Bennekom.

Every day and every night the bombings grew more fierce. On one particular evening, after nearly two weeks in the lab, Piet and Anne decided to carry Helene into the safety of the cellar. They made up another small bed, and tucked her under the covers alongside her brother and sisters. They walked up the cellar stairs, through the kitchen and to the main staircase and then back up to their second-story bedroom. My grandparents lay down together on the large mattress on the floor by the window. Piet had made candles in his lab and the light flickered against the walls. One of my grandparents blew out the candle, and they both fell to sleep.

The muzzle flash of a howitzer illuminated the pockmarked fields of the Betuwe and lofted a single shell up above the dark waters of the Rhine. It twisted silently as it drew a long arc in the night sky. It passed over the recently evacuated villages and the lonely woods before beginning its descent near the farmland to the south of the village of Bennekom. When it finally broke the city limits, it was just a hissing piece of slender metal forged around gunpowder that had been first birthed into this world back across the Atlantic Ocean in the United States of America. It had slid off some assembly line with its newly machined form and was then packed into the bowels of a freighter and rocked in the ocean swells before it arrived at the Betuwe and was sent forth by the tug of a gunner's arm. The skill of the gunner had combined with the elements—the thickness of the air and the whimsy of a night breeze—and when the shell finally returned to the dark earth its furthermost tip pressed against the windowsill of Piet and Anne's bedroom and ignited the explosives lodged in its belly. It first burst the glass into a spray of splinters and then tore into that second-story wall sending a shock wave rippling through the lab. The entire home seemed to lift it up off its foundations. The concussion slapped against faces and eyes flashed open in unison. The debris crashed down on Piet and Anne and pinned their limp bodies beneath the wreckage. The children stared wide-eyed into the dusty blackness; the smell of burnt sulfur filled the home. Dr. Gorter rolled off his bed and onto the floor just seconds before a window crashed onto his bed. Iet tried to draw a full breath of air and choked on the dust and burnt powder.

And as suddenly as the shell had exploded upon them, a long silence followed. The children first heard nothing, then a shuffle of feet, then voices yelling in the night. Ruth looked over at her brother. He didn't move, but it took only a few seconds to realize the boy had somehow remained sleeping. Someone opened the door to the cellar and yelled down for the kids to stay put.

Piet and Anne were lost beneath the debris. Shrapnel had pulverized every part of the bedroom above three feet. Someone brought light into the room. The air had yet to clear and the remnants of the third story and pieces of the roof lay heaped in the haze in front of them. The cool night, moving freely through the room, slowly cleared the air. After the mangled beams and mortar were carefully removed, Piet and Anne's bodies were pulled from the tangled mess. Both were conscious. A piece of the hot shrapnel had lodged inside Piet's head, and shards of glass glistened in his face. Blood dripped down the back of Anne's neck. Both were able to stand.

The children could still taste the blast. The chemicals burned in their mouths and throats and their limbs were covered with a fine layer of dry dirt. One of the adults came into the cellar with a candle. Anne and Piet were helped into their overcoats and guided out the lab's front door and down the cobblestone sidewalk and to the hospital. The rest of the adults joined the children in the cellar for the remainder of the night. They could hear the rumble of more shells dropping around Bennekom.

After the literal dust had settled, Hanneke helped organize a place for everyone to sit. Lines of wax dripped down the sides of the candle and puddled at its base. The cellar was now packed tight, the bodies pressed together shoulder-to-shoulder. After the initial shock of the explosion waned, some started recounting the moments after the blast. The conversation helped drain the trauma from their bodies and soon a gentle levity joined the candlelight. My mom, however, remained silent and frightened on her shelf, and the next moment she remembered was when her mother and father walked down the steps of that crowded cellar just before daybreak. Anne's head was wrapped in gauze like a turban. A bandage covered Piet's left ear. They told the children they were fine. The doctors had pulled the steel splinter from Piet's head, and removed the shards of glass from the skulls of both parents, then stitched closed their broken skin.

Though no one could tell at the time, that shell had unleashed its lethal fury just about belt high. The spray of shrapnel had penetrated every surface of the room at or above the height of the windowsill that it first struck. The fact that my grandparents slept on the floor had probably saved their lives. As the story is remembered by the family, the shrapnel that had damaged one side of Piet's head and the opposite side of Anne's had mainly penetrated the space between them, that same space where, for all of the days at the lab prior to that one, their youngest child had slept snuggled tight between the two.

Before my grandparents had returned to the lab, and while that candle had dripped its wax in the company of all who huddle in the safety of their cellar, Piet and Anne had faced the fact that they could no longer remain in the village. They had to get their family out of Bennekom as soon as possible. They stepped out of the hospital and into the stillness of the dark morning and discussed the painful implications of their decision.

Two-and-a-half years had passed since my grandfather and Leo van Leeuwen played tennis on that grassy court in Ede. The little girl Piet had promised to care for was sitting on a shelf close to my mother and safe. Piet had placed himself between the Nazis and every Jew in that cellar. He had navigated on the outer edges of chance and, more than once, was left to rely on a grace beyond his own. Despite everything he had endured, the good in my grandfather remained. The Nazi command occupied his farm. The Allies inadvertently blew a hole in his second home. His wife was bloodied beside him, and within twenty-four hours, he and his family would join the legions of others swarming north, and the Schoorl family would own no more than they could carry.

Before they reached the lab, Piet and Anne prepared to explain their decision. They could no longer care for the Jews hiding in this home. My grandparents' situation was painfully obvious—they simply had nothing else they could give.

Book Three

Chapter 20

A FULL DAY had passed since the bombing, and the morning's first light worked its way down the tips of the trees toward the house. The bomb's wreckage remained shadowed. Much of the second-story corner had simply vanished—the bits and pieces of the bedroom wall so small you could pour them from your hand. No attempt was made to cover the wound. There was no time. By morning's end, the lab would be empty.

Simon and Adele were the first ones ready to leave. Simon lifted his son up into his arms, and the two walked over to Simon's heavily laden bicycle. The three-wheeler had a large box on the front filled with a careful selection of the family's possessions. Ruben wore a heavy coat. His father set him atop the luggage. The family of four was now lined up in front of the lab and ready to brave the open road. Simon had fastened two thick wood blocks onto the pedals of Ruth's bike so her feet could reach.

Ruth's knuckles showed white as she gripped the handlebars. The family called out their last goodbyes and then pushed forward. Ruben's blonde curls bounced as his father navigated those first bumps on the sidewalk in front of the lab. Ruth tried her best to follow them. Her bike wobbled as she pushed against the wood blocks. Had the girl not been robbed of her childhood, this bike would have been an old companion. But she had been robbed, and the contraption was almost completely novel. The seat seemed too high and she struggled to keep her balance. It also did not help that the bike her father had found for her had wooden tires.

Once her daughter started forward, Adele followed close behind her, and as she did so, the safety of that laboratory—that sanctuary—with its careful, attentive hosts and their manifold efforts to help her and her family survive, slowly disappeared behind her. But there was no other choice. It had made more sense to depart casually in the bright morning light than to try to sneak out of Bennekom at night—to try to lose themselves in that stream of refugees. They had made every possible preparation.

Before leaving the lab, Simon and Adele made Ruth repeat her new last name over and over again. Despite all Ruth had endured, she was still chatty and precocious, and her parents worried that she might say the wrong thing around the wrong people.

"De Lange, De Lange, De Lange," they said so many times that the name rang like a bell in Ruth's head.

The four of them slowly made their way down the sidewalk and north toward Ede. When her daughter teetered, Adele reached forward and Ruth could feel her mother's hand on the small of her back.

It had been several years since Adele had felt such a wind on her face, and though the morning sky was clear, the air still bit at her cheeks. The family had no specific plans. Like all the other refugees, they would head north beyond the reach of the Allied guns. Simon led the way. His wife and daughter's dark hair turned in the breeze.

MY MOTHER STILL clearly remembers those last days in Bennekom and the events that had led up to their evacuation. She still remembers the wounds on her father's face, illuminated in the unsteady light of the candle, and she remembers the sad tone of his voice as he stood on those stairs—"Get dressed. We're leaving." The steady rumble of distant artillery in that early dawn hour helped punctuate the urgency. Marianne slipped off her shelf and put on her clothes. By the time she walked up the cellar stairs and into the kitchen, the home was already busy. And though this day seemed in many ways to mimic the events two weeks earlier when the families had scrambled to leave the Soetendael, it did not feel the same. This time, there was no home to go to. This time, their wartime family would be fractured, and all of their futures were uncertain. There was less conversation than normal, and the mood felt heavy and dark as each family strategized its departure.

Piet and Anne had secured space on a Red Cross truck for themselves, Pauline, Paya, Helene, Eline and my mother, which would take them to the town of Zeist. Leo and Carel and the three eldest Schoorl children would travel the twenty miles by bicycle and meet them there. And from Zeist they would all continue to Vreeland to the home of Piet's father's former mistress—once a student of the college professor—the home Nicolaas Schoorl had built for the younger woman before he had passed. But they weren't expected, nor did they know how they would be received. There was no way to contact the residence. The remaining members of the laboratory made similarly insecure plans.

After the last bags were packed, Piet and Leo pulled one of the laboratory's heavy shelves into the kitchen. They pushed it against the door leading down into the cellar and readied to secure it to the wall. Everything the families were leaving in Bennekom had been carried below. This time, deciding what to take and what to leave didn't weigh so heavily on Anne. The choices were simple—she would take what the family could carry and leave what they could not. The cellar was now filled with valuables—furniture handed down through generations, Piet's expensive laboratory instruments, imported carpets, and Ruud's violin. Before the shelf was secured, Piet added two small suitcases belonging to two elderly women from Wageningen who were also leaving Bennekom. They had asked if Piet would be willing to hide the cases along with everything else in his cellar, and Piet agreed. After he secured the shelf in place, he filled it with cartons of chemicals, books, and glassware, and it was as though the door had disappeared.

Iet packed her toothbrush along with a few clothes and a wool blanket. The side-bags on her bike bulged full and the back rack was loaded with as much as she could reasonably manage. There were five more bicycles awaiting departure. They were all top heavy and looked clumsy.

As usual, the children weren't told the exact plans. They gleaned what they could from the adults' conversations. They had watched as their same family doctor arrived just before their departure and inspected Piet and Anne's wounds. He then covered Pauline's face with fresh bandages. Pauline also worked to lighten Paya's dark complexion with baby powder and cosmetics.

After fixing the shelf in front of the cellar door, there was one last task that remained before the lab was abandoned to the war. A recessed window beneath the ground level let a trickle of light into the cellar. It was the last clue suggesting the room existed at all. Piet filled the hole with dirt, then raked the ground flat. The three eldest Schoorl children then mounted their bikes; Carel climbed on the back of his father's. Leo steadied the heavy load before pushing off the sidewalk and slowly pedaling forward. Hanneke, Iet and Ruud followed behind. The Jewish maid and her fiancé rode with them. My mother left the lab on foot, walking close to Eline and Piet and Anne, and she watched as the six bikes glided toward Ede.

"Don't say anything to anyone," Anne had repeated to Marianne and Eline over and over again before leaving the lab. All of the families were tense and scared. The parents explained that the Germans were after Pauline and that no matter what happened or who asked the questions the two girls were to remain silent.

Piet, Anne, and Pauline all carried large suitcases. Marianne wore a button-down overcoat and a skirt and wool tights. The truck was waiting for them at the hospital about a quarter mile from the laboratory. Anne repeated her instructions one last time to both children before they neared the crowded parking lot. A German soldier was standing by the rear of the Red Cross truck checking identifications. My mom looked up at him. She kept her mouth closed tight. The man looked at Pauline while studying her forged papers and asked where she had been injured. Pauline accidentally pointed to the wrong side of her head. The soldier seemed not to notice. Someone helped the children into the truck's bed. Paya was still very ill.

Two wooden benches lined the sides of the bed; luggage and boxes were stacked in the middle and up against the cab. About two dozen people were packed inside. The truck's canopy shadowed the passengers. The engine soon sparked to life and Pauline and Anne shared a nervous smile, each watching the German soldier from the corner of her eye. When the truck turned onto the main street, the family's view of the village slowly diminished.

It had been over six years since Piet had carried my mom down that broad staircase at the Soetendael, her newborn body wrapped tight in a blanket in his arms. My grandfather had a spark in his eyes that late evening, and I think he not only enjoyed the moment for what it was, but I imagine he also luxuriated in the entire scene while considering himself from a distance, contemplating his life—his fortune as a father and husband, as a scientist and businessman. From the rear of that crowded truck, I doubt Piet's mind wandered much at all. He was now too much a veteran of war. It was possible that the next bend in that road toward Ede could conceal his last moments. Thinking too much about any of it could drive a man mad. At best, he could now relax and enjoy perhaps an hour or two of rest as the stiff suspension beneath him rattled against the bumps in the road toward Zeist.

The truck eventually rumbled past Leo and Carel, and the three children riding single file behind him on a bike path beside the road. The maid and her fiancé had already turned down a different avenue. The parents stuck their heads out the back of the truck and yelled "hello" and whistled. The children looked up and waved.

The home that the family had dubbed the lab would remain empty. The small attic window facing the street would never again reflect the shadowed features of Adele de Leeuwe, or Kurt and Liesel Dannenbaum.

For months on end, the three had endured within its confines. Maybe that first morning spent under the fall sun had been a touch exhilarating. But leaving the safety of the home and the trusted care of Piet and Anne and all the others in Bennekom who had helped them survive had to have been—at the very least—a melancholy event. At worst, I imagine it was terrifying.

Logistically, it made sense to divide the household. Everyone evacuating together would have been too conspicuous. And the price of failure—complete. The war had taught that the odds favored smaller groups. I have no idea how the conversation among my grandparents and the Dannenbaums and the de Leeuwes transpired. But it couldn't have been easy for any of them. I doubt anyone questioned Piet's heart, or Anne's. Both had proven they were willing to do most anything to help. But circumstances forced the hard decisions, and Piet was sensible enough to know it. When he left with his wife to meet the Red Cross truck, he had relinquished all responsibility for either family. He had little choice.

It's possible my grandparents had a hand in whatever arrangements the Dannenbaums made, but not probable. There was almost no way to communicate on such short notice. Even Piet's own plans were shaky. I know that Simon and Adele and their two children fled that morning into complete uncertainty. I have to believe that the dentist and his wife did the same. The two left Bennekom that same day, also forced to brave the light of day. They may have traveled only a few short miles. They may have crossed most of Holland. No one remembers.

The specific paths of the many souls who had played various roles in the lab and the farm now diverged. Anne's younger sisters left Bennekom together and

worked their way back to their father's farm in Alkmaar—no one is exactly sure when. And then there
was Tante Chiel—the crazy aunty whose presence
seemed to drift out of the Schoorl children's memories
sometime after Market Garden. The always-faithful
Dr. Gorter also left into obscurity that morning.

Up until those last few days, Piet and Anne's lives as
members of the underground had continued, and the
children saw so many people come and go that they
can no longer place them in time. Along with the specter of Bart Bes and his radio, there were also Allied pi-
lots—men whose planes were shot down by those German guns that seemed to blast away only a few blocks
from the Soetendael. Ruud once saw his father at the
lab with two of these Allied airmen. Piet was bent over
a large map, his index finger tracing the route the two
men needed to take to escape the Nazis. The other
children remember airmen at their breakfast table at
the farm. A letter, signed by Eisenhower, thanking my
grandfather for his "gallant service in assisting the escape of Allied soldiers from the enemy" hangs on my
wall above my desk; the seal from the headquarters of
the European Theater of Operations is pressed into the
parchment. The children of Piet and Anne would never
know all of the details of their parents' efforts; however, the fact that their parents' role in the underground
came to its end on the day of their evacuation was glar-
ingly clear. But their parents would not shed all of their
responsibilities. Piet and Anne would continue to tie
their fate, and that of their five children, to the van
Leeuwen family. Why? The answer isn't complicated.
The families had grown very close, and were in many
ways like one. The hardships of war had forged an intimacy beyond anything comparable during peacetime.

None of the four were willing to let go of one another, and no matter the peril, they'd decided to remain together until the end.

The American howitzers in the Betuwe continued to launch shells over the Rhine and errant bombs continued to fall on the small village. In two weeks the local German command made the decision—probably from the comfort of the Soetendael—to force a complete evacuation of the region.

That day on the Red Cross truck would mark the end of my mother's childhood. The further it rolled north, the further my mother was from whatever innocence life had ever afforded her. If her war had ended on that day, she very well may have been able to hide from it for the rest of her life. But it didn't, and the following months would cut deep, creating wounds that would never properly heal.

Chapter 21

LEO AND THE CHILDREN had reached the town of Ede then turned west toward Zeist. After leaving the city limits, the scene turned rural. The tilled soil of farmers' fields flanked the road on both sides, and the sky remained blue and clear. There was still a bike path beside the main road, and the five continued single file. The refugees, who had left their homes in Wageningen and Renkum two weeks earlier, were already far gone, and the quiet landscape punctuated the squeaks and groans of the bike's frames laboring under weight. The children pedaled patiently. It would have been safer had there been crowds.

Leo slowed and the three children braked behind him. He turned into the driveway of an anonymous farmhouse, knocked on the farmer's door and asked for some water. The break was short. The children didn't talk as much as usual. The uncertainty of the road ahead and no clear sense of the days to come had struck a solemn note in all of them. With her toothbrush and blanket near her side, Iet sensed her new fragility. Theirs had always been the farm offering a drink of water or a moment's refuge. The open landscape ahead disappeared into the lonely flat horizon.

Iet felt sad. And to her, the lot of them looked sad. Leo thanked the farmer, and the children leaned into their pedals and continued on.

The setting remained the same and would for some time. The five continued, mostly silent, one following the other in an orderly line. For Hanneke and Iet, in many ways that outer journey coincided with a more arduous inner one. Their former life had been anything but quiet, and their days had always been anchored in place by their trustworthy farm. Each girl could feel the uncertainty ahead, and it felt as though their lives had lost its orbit. In short, they were scared. And the raspy sound of the diesel truck that soon came up behind them didn't help.

As the truck neared, the driver downshifted and the vehicle slowed. The girls turned their heads to the left. It was a large German transport. The driver looked over at the bicyclists then stopped the vehicle. Leo braked, and the children lined up behind him. There were two soldiers. One leaned out the truck's window and began to ask questions.

THE RED CROSS TRUCK must have arrived in Zeist around the same time the Germans stopped Leo and the children. It pulled into a church parking lot and the many passengers stretched their legs. Someone helped the Jewish child, Paya, down to the pavement.

Anne and Piet and Pauline carried their suitcases inside a large auditorium-like room. The facility had been transformed into an evacuation center, with straw and rough wool blankets provided for temporary beds. The family partitioned off a small section of the room with their belongings. After they settled, they were offered a bowl of hot soup. It was also at this point that

Paya figuratively disappears from the story, lost in the memories of my family. She was likely transferred into the care of a member of the underground more suited to ensure her safety, and I cannot provide her a more elegant departure.

After the brief meal, Marianne and Eline were allowed to wander outside the church. They were soon playing together on the sidewalk in front of the building when Marianne noticed two older girls approaching from across the street. She watched the two suspiciously. There was something odd about them and the fact set off alarms inside Marianne. The two strangers continued toward them, looking awkward, and then stopped within an arm's reach. One of the girls hesitated, then handed Marianne a coloring book and some crayons. The teenagers then turned abruptly and scampered back across the road and into a house facing the church.

THE DIESEL IDLED while the soldier talked with Leo. The truck's throaty growl rolled across the fallow fields. Both men raised their voices. The children watched closely. Leo could feel his son behind him. The trick was—for just that moment—to forget you were a Jew, and to forget your wife, your son, your daughter, the dead, and the war. Leo explained they were refugees. He moved closer to the German as he talked. It was an instinct Leo had cultivated over the last two years. Fear has an odor; confidence disarms. But as it turned out, these two soldiers weren't threatening—they were just a couple of guys stopping to help, and they offered the families a ride.

Leo hesitated. The road ahead disappeared straight into the blank flatness. The cloudless sky loomed. Leo worried about Allied fighters that now freely roamed the Dutch skies. The planes hunted German targets. The large truck on that lonely road with its khaki canvas stretched tight invited attention. But he accepted the ride. And the soldiers helped pull the laden bicycles up onto the truck's bed. The children could not manage Leo's detached reserve. Fear worked through Hanneke and Iet's young bodies as they watched the Germans cautiously.

The truck eventually passed through the farmland and into the outskirts of Zeist. The soldiers never took a second look at Leo's son, and there were no Allied planes. The Germans had cut the children's trip in half, and when they helped them lower their bikes back onto the road it was still early in the day.

The families had planned to rendezvous at the home of one of Piet's close friends, Kees Tasman, a comrade in the underground. The home would be safe for the van Leeuwens, and Leo led the children through the corridors of the city peddling deliberately toward Tasman's neighborhood. The bikes turned the last bend before Tasman's home and Leo could then see a unit of German soldiers blocking the road ahead. Another unit was executing a search of all the homes on Tasman's street.

Leo continued toward the road block, and the children followed obediently. He stopped right next to two soldiers and, again, struck up a conversation with the men as though the scene behind them was as ordinary as a routine traffic stop. Both Leo and the German were smiling as they talked.

By the summer of '44 everyone had noticed a marked shift in the attitudes of the Germans. Somehow Leo seemed to draw out their better halves, but by and large the troops in Holland had turned mean. Compared to the way they treated most countries, the Germans had exercised restraint when dealing with the citizens of Holland. But the constant Dutch resistance and their embrace of the Allies during Market Garden had drained whatever goodwill the Nazis seemed to entertain. The orders had come from the top down— make the citizens of the Netherlands suffer.

At one point one of the soldiers draped his arm over Carel. Iet felt like her heart stopped. Leo again appeared oblivious. The children's eyes darted between the two Germans talking with Leo and the several searching the row of homes. Leo seemed in no hurry. He explained they had just evacuated from Bennekom and were looking for a place to sleep for the night. One of the soldiers recommended a nearby school for the blind. After a slow goodbye, Leo and the kids pedaled off in the direction the soldier suggested.

No one had talked about the fate of Kees Tasman. It's possible the Germans hadn't arrived at his doorstep simply by chance, and equally possible that the raid was block-wide and routine. Had Leo and the children arrived a few minutes earlier, they would probably have been on the wrong side of the Germans' barricade. Survival, the war had proven, was often simply a matter of cold luck.

The five of them soon found out that there were no blind children at the Institute for the Blind. The school, like the church, had been hurriedly transformed into another refugee way station after the first influx of homeless swarmed into the city. But the long rows of beds were now nearly all empty. To the girls, who had spent the last weeks sleeping in the lab's dark and dusty cellar, the row of beds looked regal. The building's large windows drew in the daylight and the room seemed extraordinarily bright. It was orderly and clean, and the high ceilings seemed to enhance the sun's rays. The children were offered a simple meal before slipping between the clean sheets and drifting to sleep.

The next morning, the girls and Ruud took little time to make their beds, gather their few belongings, and head back out into the streets of Zeist with Leo and Carel. Though only away from their parents little more than one day and by hardly more than a few miles, both the time and the distance felt severe to the children, and they were glad to be underway and searching for Piet and Anne.

Piet must have learned that his friend's home had been raided, and he and Anne had the good sense to remain at the Red Cross shelter and let Leo figure out how to find them. It didn't take too terribly long. That afternoon, Leo and the children eventually rode their bikes onto the church lawn and the kids saw their parents relaxing outside in the sun. It felt good to be together and for the children to enjoy the one way that Anne had always nurtured them.

Though Holland was already beginning to feel the coming hunger that would become epidemic that winter, Anne's knack for making the best of any circumstance, especially those involving food, remained an enduring trait. That afternoon, despite the fact that all of the area's restaurants were closed due to the lack of available food, Anne contacted one of the restaurant owners and talked him into letting her use his facility. Anne had carried a piece of their last pig with her to Zeist. She scrounged up a few additional ingredients and set about cooking dinner. Soon the restaurant again filled with the savory aromas of a well-crafted meal. The food and the close company of their parents helped sooth Hanneke and Iet, and for a few moments, the families lost themselves in the warmth of the meal and the balm of their familiarly loud conversations.

The family would spend one more night sleeping on the hay in the Red Cross facility and then resume their trek in the coming morning.

Chapter 22

THE TRIP FROM ZEIST to Vreeland, and the home that Piet's father had bought for his mistress, had been short. The twelve still had most of the day in front of them as they stood in front of the residence's iron gate. Slightly elevated on its several-acre estate, they could see the white house standing proud against a backdrop of large deciduous trees. A long circular driveway surrounded the moist expanse of a manicured lawn. They opened the gate and walked toward the home. Brown leaves littered the grounds, and they pushed the four bikes up the gravel lane past a row of snowberry bushes and set their suitcases underneath the portico.

It was an elegant residence; carefully-milled corbels adorned the top of the structure's first story and filigree decorated the stucco above each window. They knocked. No one answered. And after a few passing moments, Piet and Anne let themselves inside. The burdensome wool coats fell quickly.

The children knew this home well. They had visited their grandfather and his lover on holidays. They addressed her as Tante' Ans, and the fact that the children also adored Piet's crippled mother, Johanna, had never caused them pause. This romance had always been presented to the children as the most normal of circumstance.

Tante Ans owned a significant tract of land surrounding her residence. Waterways connected her property to the canals and lakes that typified the area. Vreeland was rich in homes like hers. Popular among both the wealthy and the country's truly elite, the region's mansions and near-castles shadowed the shorelines. The children used to untie the small rowboat from the grassy edges of the narrow stream that bent across the front of the property and drift with the current to a pond. Lily pads flowered in the summer and the children's oars would mark the placid waters with a feathering ripple of waves. The children often rowed to a small island in the middle of the pond where there was a dainty teahouse, and the kids could tie up the boat and eat lunch under its shade.

After situating their luggage, someone started a fire, and Anne made quick use of the spacious kitchen. It took but a few minutes for the clamor of children to quickly drift up the wide first-story stairway and soon they could all be heard scampering across the second floor. The older Schoorl children knew exactly where they were headed, and the small herd hurried up another, narrower, set of stairs. The pond and the boat and that dainty teahouse had partly occupied their former summers in Vreeland, but all three could do little to compete with what resided at the top of that stairway. It was a room unlike any other the kids had ever known.

Like the lab, the finished attic of this house also spanned the entire footprint of the structure beneath it. Dormer windows opened south toward the autumn light, and from wall to wall the attic was filled with toys. A swing set dangled from a roof beam. There were dolls of every size and shape, poised precisely, and their glass eyes seemed to animate the room. There were baby buggies and a miniature kitchen and board games and puzzles and enough of everything that the eight children needn't pay any mind to sharing. It was a vast collection of toys and likely generations old.

In the last month, too much had happened and too quickly. The memories of their farmhouse, of their own beds, the absence of Simon and Adele and the Dannenbaums, the weighted look in their father's eyes, the dust and cordite, and the certainty of uncertainty—none of it had settled, and this oasis seemed timely. The almost magical room distracted the children from the tumult, and each child found a momentary refuge in the excess of toys and the balm of imagination. The children played as the day's sun dropped, and the last rays climbed slowly up the home's dignified lines, last touching the ornate ironwork atop the two chimneys, then darkening to dusk.

The family had found a true respite. Beds were made. There was ample room. And most significantly, Piet and Anne's ties to the underground were now completely severed. The couple would no longer be wakened to the rapping of their front door. There would be no more Jewish children to worry over, or cannons and tanks. For the first time in a long time my grandparents had the opportunity to truly rest. They had travelled beyond the reach of the Allied guns and into a region with no military significance, and no one knew how to find them.

The Germans had cut the power grids, and the dark of that night was undisturbed by man's electricity. The children each drifted off knowing with some measure of certainty what the morning would bring, images of the attic joining their dreams. Their faces relaxed into the innocence of most every sleeping child's face, lost to some other place, and so vulnerable. But the war would be over soon. Or so it seemed.

"WHAT DO YOU THINK about when you see it?" Iet asked Hanneke. She had driven off the pavement and onto the gravel shoulder. Beyond a marshy ditch and across the lawn stood the house. "Oh . . . the toys," Hanneke cooed. It was spring and the white snowberry bushes had blossomed. Both my aunts smiled.

The waters of the narrow stream still moved behind the residence. A delicate iron sundial in the shape of an orb had been placed in the middle of the lawn. A naked flagpole stood sentry over the yard. Nothing much had changed. There were no cars in the driveway. The gate was closed. It could have been 1944. My great-grandfather, Nicolaas Schoorl, had named the home the Slotzigt, meaning, "with a castle view." Just a few days after the families had arrived at the home, Tante' Ans returned. She wasn't pleased.

I looked at the house's cold stone. I had thought about this place often. "The house was big enough," Iet had said only days earlier while sitting with me in her living room. "Everything was there." And it surely was. And as I looked at the home, I thought of my mother. The five attic windows stared back at me. I imagined my mom in that room. When she played with the dolls, the ends of her thick braids would brush against most anything belly-button high. This home could have been Mom's sanctuary, and I still don't understand exactly why they left.

"I don't think at that time I liked her very much," Iet said. "I must have felt we weren't really welcomed.

We thought this was the right place for us to go. It easily could have been. I liked her better when my grandfather was still alive."

The spring sun hid behind a soft layer of clouds as the three of us quietly pondered what could have been. The base of the sundial lilted to one side. I walked along the side of the road; the gravel crunched beneath my feet. In my grandfather's very brief written account of the war, he states that they had to leave the home because of a lack of food. But it didn't add up. "I'm just trying to picture it," I said to Iet. "If there was an old lady that was in the house that my father built, and I needed to care for my children, and it's a huge home, and we're in the middle of a war, and we have no place to go, it would take a lot of influence to get me to leave. And it seems it would take a lot of influence to get your mother to leave. I don't know. You tell me." I already had my suspicions.

"You're never safe if someone doesn't want you there. And having the Jews there . . ." I had nearly put the words in her mouth. But that's the only reason that made sense to me.

Despite Ans' disapproval, the Schoorls did not leave immediately, and I don't think Anne had any plans to leave whatsoever. She had enrolled her children in school, and they were already attending classes. Anne was not burdened with much social grace. The war had galvanized her confidence, and I doubt she paid much mind to Ans' sentiments. I picture Anne simply ignoring her. When the refugees streamed into the Soetendael just over a month earlier, Anne never considered her own safety or convenience. Anne marshaled her resources and did her best to provide for all of the families that needed her care. The years of war had trained her mind to exclude the superfluous luxuries of convenience and space, and I think she probably expected the same from others. For my grandmother, I think Tante' Ans was little more than a nuisance. I also cannot picture Anne worried about finding food. She had nearly perfected the art of scrounging for food long before any of her fellow Dutch had felt the first tinge of hunger. Anne could have travelled north to her parents' farm if things got really bad and ferried food back to the estate. But this was not to be. And maybe it was for the best. Anne was nearly fearless. But she also lacked what some might consider common sense. She had a habit of putting herself and her family in danger. Maybe she had a justified confidence in her power to simply will the scales of chance in her favor, but it certainly appeared that more than once, she had relied too heavily on the slim margins of luck to survive. Her husband had more scientific sensibilities.

"They weren't going to give up Pauline and Leo," Iet continued. "I think we could have stayed on if we didn't have the Jewish family." From across the lawn, I could see inside the tall front windows. A light had been left on next to a side table. Iet remembered making candles in the home with her father in the kitchen, attaching lengths of copper pipe to squares of wood, then centering a thread of cotton inside and pouring melted wax into the tube. The children followed the flicker of a candle when walking through the home at night. The war was turning. Every day, Hitler's war machine suffered immense casualties. Allied planes had reduced entire German cities to wisps of ash. The war was very close to over.

* * *

A FEW WEEKS after first arriving at the Slotzigt, Piet worked alone in the garage as he built an axle and attached it to the underside of a large wooden cart. He had found two old bicycle wheels and secured both to the new axle. When finished, the weight of the cart balanced nicely over the wheels. He then filled the cart with heavy suitcases. The bikes were again awaiting departure in front of the home just as they had nearly a month earlier at the lab, and the families set off down the driveway next to the rows of pampered flowerbeds tucked in snug for the season. My mother and Eline sat side-by-side on back of the cart, and Piet pedaled hard to pull the weight. Marianne's legs dangled over the edge. None of the children knew where they were going. They rarely did. Their parents said they were leaving, and they left. The swing in the attic of the large house remained limp and lifeless and none of Piet and Anne's children ever stepped into that home again.

The families travelled slowly northward. There was no rubber on the cart's new wheels and the bare steel clattered over the pavement. Soon, a sleeting rain came down at an angle. Someone pulled a wool blanket over Mom and Eline. The air had a bite. It came out of the north from over the cold sea and brought with it a hint of what would come. Before the turn of the year, those winds would freeze the Netherlands rock solid. The canals would become impassable, and foods that normally floated into population centers would stop. Everyone in Holland remembers that winter.

The Slotzigt in Vreeland

Chapter 23

DOUBLED UP on bikes, the families followed the path of the river Vecht as it wound its way northwest toward the open waters of the IJsselmeer. With each pedal stroke the children pushed further from their home. The banks of the lakes of Vreeland gave way to a tapestry of farmland, each small pasture divided by ditches that drained the wet soil. The cold continued to blow from the north.

Toward the day's end, they found a road following the northern edges of the river. The pavement matched the water's every turn, and both made a slow, looping twist eastward toward the city of Weesp. The wheels of Mom's cart clattered against the hard road. To the left, the river's levee blocked the children's view of its frigid waters.

Facing backwards, Marianne watched the landscape disappear behind her. As her cart turned, a railroad track appeared on her left just beyond a small field. The tracks were elevated on a wide bed of earth and stone, matching the levee in girth and height. The track cut a straight line east.

Trains leaving downtown Amsterdam passed through the village of Weesp and into the green pastureland, then by this small bend in the river, and onward through Holland and into Germany. Several now carried the spoils of war, plundered goods heading to Germany, which the Nazis' propaganda machine declared "gifts" from the supportive citizens of the Netherlands. The passing trains also transported able-bodied Dutch men. Any adult males who could not prove they were necessary to the Nazis' war effort in Holland were conscripted into slave labor and sent to the factories in the Rhineland. Many would never see Holland again. And these were the same rails that had suffered the weight of cars transporting Jews out of Amsterdam and east to the transit-camp Westerbork—not the notorious cattle cars stuffed full and headed toward Poland, but with the families still together, wearing their best coats and seated comfortably with leather suitcases between their legs and children still nestled on their parents' warm laps. The polished rails still glimmered despite the heavy clouds.

The road continued its bend. The cart felt each bump. The railroad and the river eventually parted ways, and a few minutes later everyone stopped in front of a small farm.

Marianne was helped off the cart. A bag with her belongings and another with those of her older sister Hanneke were sorted from the rest. An aging farmer—a short, thin man with gray hair—met them in front of his home. Anne moved efficiently. Marianne watched closely. No one had told her this would happen. A few minutes passed. A few words were spoken, then Marianne and Hanneke said goodbye to their parents and watched them leave toward the next farm down the road.

Mr. Kreuger led them inside his small farmhouse. Arrangements had somehow been made in advance, and the old man was expecting two girls—one six, the other fourteen. The man's hands showed the decades of labor and his frame carried little more than muscle suiting the needs of his occupation. He both moved and spoke in a controlled, thoughtful manner. His wife had died during childbirth, and he had raised his two daughters alone. His girls were young women now, both still living with their father and working the farm. The Kreugers were kind but not warm, and when Marianne stepped inside, the home's wood floor felt like winter.

The girls were shown their room. It was both Spartan and tidy. A window opened to the south, toward the road and river. A large ceramic bedpan rested next to a wall that had two closet-like doors mounted waist high. The doors opened revealing a bed built cave-like into the wall of the home. There was a step on the floor beneath it and Marianne had to stretch to make the distance between the step and the mattress.

Piet and Anne had divided the families into four adjacent farms just east of downtown Weesp at a locale named Weesperkarspel. Iet and Eline stayed with the Andriessen family, and Ruud and Carel with their neighbors. The four adults, along with 3-year-old Helene, unloaded their own bags at the last farm belonging to the Posts, a family Anne had lived with briefly as a teenager. They had divided the children strategically, placing one older child with one younger.

The overcast sky remained a shade of constant gray that day. The row of farms, each resembling the next, seemed quietly poised to receive the winter promised by those biting winds. They were small, modest homes, built in the traditional manner with the kitchen, living room, and bedrooms attached to the cow barn—man and beast existing under the same roof. Their owners lived the disciplined and unyielding life of simple farmers. A generation earlier, the Soetendael had resembled these dwellings. Hanneke helped Marianne prepare for bed. The Kreugers read from their bible. The children blew out the candle and climbed into the bed in the wall. The home had neither central heat nor plumbing. The two girls cuddled together and shared warmth.

THE FOLLOWING DAY, as they had for years, the Kreugers woke early. They milked the cows in the dark of morning. When Hanneke and Marianne climbed down from their bed, the farmer and his daughters had already completed their morning chores. The three sat together at the large kitchen table, again reading from their bible. Kreuger's daughters wore modest clothes, and each wore her long hair pulled tight and twisted into a bun. They looked like their lives looked: ordered, disciplined, predictable. Hanneke and Marianne joined the family. After prayers, Mom was served porridge. It was her least favorite meal. Few words were spoken, and both children felt awkward and tentative.

The Kreugers were generous people, but they had little familiarity with children. To Hanneke and Marianne, the farmer and his daughters' lives seemed profoundly different than anything they knew. Piet and Anne's children had always lived beyond the limitations of a working-class life. The children—despite the war—had still been pampered and were accustomed to following both whim and fancy. The Kreugers followed obligation and the demands of their farm, and it was for no other reason than the above that Hanneke and Marianne could find no place to settle within the Kreugers' routine. Neither party could make much sense of the other, and the conversation was forced.

When the meal finally came to its inevitable conclusion, Hanneke offered to help with the dishes. The house had only one source of running water, a hand-pump over the kitchen sink, and while she worked the pump's lever, Marianne left the table to explore. She quickly discovered that the home was void of toys, and most of the rooms were bone-cold. The family lit only one fireplace in the early afternoon.

Eventually, Marianne wandered into the attached barn. She walked down the middle of the concrete floor, with two rows of cow rear-ends on either side. Each animal had a name painted above its narrow stall. The room was warm and the air heavy with scent. Mr. Kreuger took great care with his beasts and each stall had fresh straw. The cows faced either east or west where small windows let in the light. The farmer had tied the cows' tails to a waist-high wire running the length of barn to keep each clear of the poop and pee that collected in a gentle depression in the concrete floor. Marianne quickly discovered that the animals were not only especially clean, but also friendly.

As the days passed Marianne learned the name of each cow. When one would lie down in the hay, she cuddled against it. Those first days were the hardest. She missed her family and so did Hanneke. Neither was used to being alone. The cows breathed slowly. They felt warm like home: like Piet's lap before his arrest and like Pauline's hands when she combed Marianne's hair. The warmth felt like the baths Adele drew once a week at the Soetendael, even warm like the flicker of the candlelight on everyone's faces when they were huddled together in the cellar after the bomb had exploded and the dust had settled. The Kreuger home was cold, and that cold started to take hold in both girls, a hard angular cold that did not move. The cow and straw became Marianne's only comfort as the days turned to weeks and those frigid north winds took hold of the land.

On the few sunny days, before the winter had completely hardened the ground and spread its hoary frost on the bare tree branches, my mother ventured outside. She liked to walk beside the old fruit trees and jump the narrower ditches. On one particular day, Mr. Kreuger was also outside. The two crossed paths just before a train appeared on the tracks along the northern boundaries of his farm. Mr. Kreuger lifted his hand and waved to the passing locomotive. "Wave," the old man said gently to Marianne. "There might be Dutch prisoners on that train." The solemn farmer and the lonely little girl stood side-by-side waving together as the ground shook beneath them, and from that afternoon forward, whenever Marianne heard a train, she ran outside and waved vigorously. It felt good to the child to be able to fulfill this duty, but the thought of prisoners heading east was also unsettling. The routine lasted for many weeks, and there's little doubt that some prisoner had indeed seen that little girl in Weesperkarspel standing alone with auburn braids falling over her winter coat, waving one small hand to a stranger she did not know and could not see.

THE TEMPERATURES in Holland that winter continued to plummet, and the winds grew ever colder. Chunks of ice floated down the Vecht until eventually all of the canals and several key waterways in Holland froze solid. Marianne regularly climbed down from under her covers in the morning to find her urine frozen rock-hard in the bedpan. She would dress and carry the cold contents downstairs and into the warmth of the barn. Before lunch, the liquid would thaw and Marianne could bundle up and walk out to the outhouse and pour the pee into the dark hole.

At the dinner table, Mr. Kreuger eventually asked Hanneke if she attended church. Hanneke lied and said yes. She looked at the farmer while assuring herself that it was only a partial lie. She had gone to a friend's church in Bennekom on several occasions and attended Sunday school with her. Marianne remained quiet. Piet and Anne were nonbelievers. Or at the very least, they did not believe in a conventional Christian God. But Hanneke knew better than to dare share such a detail with the devout farmer. Her lie, however, had limited results. Hanneke's friend's church was displeasingly liberal to Mr. Kreuger, and the farmer was not able to hide his disdain.

That awkward divide between Hanneke and her hosts continued to frustrate and isolate her. She did her best to fit in and help around the home. But no matter her best efforts, she did not fit. And that fact would never change. In so many ways the Kreugers were the Schoorls' opposite. The farm seemed the very place that Anne had worked so hard to escape when she was a child. The Soetendael was a loud, cluttered, and joyously spontaneous place that coddled and encouraged its children and was permissive to a fault. The Kreugers exemplified order and restraint. Both Marianne and Hanneke internalized the tension and both retreated inward.

Anne came to visit regularly to make sure her children were treated properly and were healthy. She often combed their hair searching for lice. But that was all either child remembered of their parents. Sometimes the children could visit each other's farm, but not often and only for a short duration. No one remembers Piet visiting. Marianne and Hanneke felt abandoned. Again, no one remembers Christmas.

The New Year arrived and it was one of the coldest on record in the Netherlands. The temperatures dropped to lethal levels. After all their stored fuels were exhausted, families in the cities began burning their own furniture for warmth, and food became increasingly scarce. Though the Germans had finally officially lifted their punitive food embargo in November of '44, the severe winter weather and impassable canals made it difficult to transport anything into Western Holland. City dwellers were forced to wake early to search for food and anything they could burn. In time, the roads leaving the dense population centers of Amsterdam were lined in every direction with people pushing or pulling whatever they could find that had wheels toward the countryside in hopes they could beg or barter to save their starving families. Strangers soon appeared regularly on that road next to the river in Weesperkarspel, stopping at each farm. They often stood at Mr. Kreuger's doorway, their breath visible in the cold. Desperate for calories, these strange city dwellers offered whatever valuables they had for food. But the old farmer wasn't the sort to take advantage of anyone. He gave away what he could afford. But there were too many hungry and not enough food and like many farmers, he was forced to become an arbiter of life and death. The old usually died first, then the young. Thousands perished.

The occupying German army also suffered food shortages, and they also arrived regularly at the farm— but they didn't knock.

Marianne watched one morning as uniformed soldiers searched the home while Mr. Kreuger looked on stoically. One of the soldiers had a rifle slung over his shoulder. Marianne stood by the hallway next to the front door. The methodical old man had hidden his food well and the soldiers found nothing. As they walked toward the door, one of them reached down and picked up my mother. "Well I guess we'll just have to take her instead," the soldier said, smiling. There wasn't any malice in him. He was just a man who missed his own family, maybe his own daughter. The German soldiers were always fond of Marianne, as though she represented something beyond the war, something pure and untouched by the violence and death. But Marianne did not know this, and she felt the terror leap into her throat as the muscled arms carried her up. The soldier held her for a moment, then set her down and walked through the front door and down the short path to the chilly road. Marianne recovered from the experience and again lost herself in the mostly cold home. She had no way to understand that this frigid, isolated, and lonely place was, in many ways, her saving grace.

Marianne knew the cows that kept her alive by name. She drank their thick milk and ate the potatoes and onions Mr. Kreuger had stored for winter. During a few winter nights, after the other farms had all gone to sleep and the quiet and dark enveloped the landscape, Marianne kept lookout by the gate in front of the Kreugers' home, watching for soldiers while the family slaughtered a pig. She listened carefully. The little girl was good at listening, and when she heard the muted gunshot, she winced.

The illegal butchering went on nearly till dawn. The farmer and his daughters worked by candlelight. By the time Marianne returned inside, the home felt unusually warm. The pig was strapped to a frame; its hair had already been removed and blood collected in the sink. It was much the same as the butchering that occurred at the Soetendael except that the farmer was more adept. The blood would be mixed with a powdery meal and packed inside the intestines to make blood sausage. Again, nothing was wasted. The family cured the meat in salt and hung the hams in the chimney. Mr. Kreuger divided his pig amongst the six farms that made up their small community by the river. The other farmers would eventually do the same. A divided pig was the same as a divided family—harder for the Germans to find.

My mother was perhaps fortunate to have ended up at the Kreugers while so many in Holland starved. But it was a little like the good fortune that comes from receiving a shot of penicillin. It didn't feel like good fortune to her. Those first lonely weeks slowly passed, then a month, then longer, and Marianne continued to retreat within. She created a parallel world, one fashioned from the cows and straw in Kreuger's barn—a new, warmer, safer life insulated from the outside world. The cows were her pupils at school, or she turned them into new members of her family. She provided lavish meals and scolded misbehavers, and as this new world came alive, the real world dimmed, and each step the child took inward would eventually become one that would need to be undone. Unbeknownst to Marianne, her older sister, Iet, had done nearly the exact same thing.

THOUGH IET AND ELINE lived within shouting distance next door, it was hardly different than if had they lived across town. The four girls spent little time together. The Andriessens were also ardent Christians. The couple had four grown children, two men and two women, and like the Kreugers, the adult children remained to work the farm. Unlike Marianne, who found the warmth of the animal stalls on her own, Iet and Eline were told explicitly to play in the barn. Iet didn't feel welcome at the Andriessens, and she was convinced that she had ended up at the worse farm.

Like Hanneke and Marianne, Iet and Eline also slept together. At night, in the warmth of their bed, Iet read nursery rhymes to Eline. Iet had turned thirteen just before moving to the lab. Eline was now five and had spent nearly half her life in the care of the Schoorls. The two girls memorized the nursery rhymes and then acted them out together. They punctuated the verse with the grunt or caw of whatever animal animated the story. They worked on their skits for hours together, and then performed their creations in front of their four parents. Iet still remembers those brief trips to visit her mother and father. But she also remembers feeling desperately alone—isolated and self-conscious.

During her time banished in the barn, Iet had collected some scraps of wood. She had a pocketknife, and when she started to create her own alternate world, she did so in a more literal manner than Marianne. She carefully carved a table and then some chairs. She found a shoebox and set the furniture inside. A scrap of linen became a tablecloth. She slowly brought each piece of wood to life. Her work was careful, and she guarded that box with loving care.

Iet's relationship with her host farmers also mimicked that of her sisters next door. Iet didn't feel welcome because these farmers didn't understand her. They didn't understand any of the Schoorls. The farmer's good will could not cross that divide. The family's fresh-baked bread and raw milk felt luxurious to Iet.

And that winter it indeed was a luxury. But it did not mend the hole growing inside my aunt—the same empty hole beginning inside all of Piet and Anne's children.

IN THE DEAD of winter, after a couple months at the farm, Marianne and Hanneke were told they had to move out of Mr. Kreuger's home. Neither knew why. Both assumed they had done something wrong. Piet and Anne found a family in Weesp to take Hanneke— the home of a veterinarian. Mom moved down the road to the last of the six farms belonging to the van Os family. Ruud also moved into the van Os's home.

The change suited Marianne, for this new family did not share the strict lifestyle of the Kreugers. The clocks in the van Os home seemed to wield less power. Mr. van Os had also lost his wife during childbirth and had raised his now-adult daughter alone. Two young Dutchmen hiding from the Germans lived in a separate cottage behind the home, and the six of them shared meals together. Ruud and Marianne explored the farm in the daytime and slept together in the attic at night. Marianne still ran outside whenever she heard a train and waved.

As winter relaxed its icy grip, Marianne ventured outdoors more often. She skipped over the thawing ditches. She and Ruud could now walk across the road and take a few steps up the levee and watch the water slowly thawing. The river had endured the last of the worst winter winds. The sun began to shine more regularly on the long grass and cattails that lined the shores, and on the occasional boat or barge that navigated the river. Sometimes the days could pass with a peace that seemed to suggest there was no war. But these were only brief respites. The war still hung like a specter, and every now and again still visited the farm in true flesh and blood.

On one such night, after dinner but before bed, Ruud heard an explosion rip through the air. It felt close and was followed by the sporadic crack of small arms fire. Ruud ran into the barn and outside the back door facing the railroad tracks. The night sky partly lit the scene, and he saw a row of ten Dutch commandoes flash by on bicycles. They had blown the tracks and boarded an eastbound train. Ruud had no way of knowing why. Likely, they were liberating one of their own. The thin shiny rails were now twisted and useless, and the train traffic at the farm stopped completely after that night. Marianne's waving duty had ceased, but the new sunlight had broadened her world and she found new ways to navigate her hours alone.

Marianne now ventured outside more and more often and had found some abandoned farm equipment to play on behind the barn. She used the broken down equipment to till her own fields, sitting erect on the seat of a tractor and pulling on the rusted controls. On one particular afternoon, she stopped her work to go to the bathroom. Since living with the Kreugers, her poop had turned runny and she had to relieve herself with growing frequency. The problem had not gone away, and despite a solid diet, she had also become unusually hungry. She jumped off the tractor and ran to a corner behind the barn. She did not like using the smelly outhouse, so Marianne had become accustomed to mimicking the cows when nature called, and enjoying the same convenience. She pulled up her skirt and pulled down her leggings and panties and squatted in the mud. The cool air nipped at her bare legs. The pee puddled beneath her, and Mom's poop dripped. When done, she reached down to pull up her panties when she felt something tickle the back of her hand. She turned her palm upward and felt what seemed a piece of string dangling from her bottom. She grabbed it. It was warm and soft and too thick to be a string. As she pulled, it stretched, and she could feel it inside her as she continued to pull. She looked down. It was white and wider than her thumb. She continued to pull, and it continued to stretch until she had tugged it completely out of her bowels and threw it in the mud. Still alive, the thing flipped about in the cold. With no idea what had just occurred, Marianne pulled up her panties and stockings and ran, leaving the tapeworm to wriggle and die in the cold. Marianne never returned to that spot again, nor would the child ever tell anyone what had happened that afternoon. The event confirmed what she had already sensed while living with the Kreugers— there was something terribly wrong with her.

Chapter 24

ICAN SEE that the trees in front of Mr. Kreuger's home need pruning. The branches lean heavily over the yard, obscuring much of the residence, and the entire farm looks to be in disrepair. There are no cows, or much order, on that piece of land today. The old farmer would not be pleased. I looked down the side of Kreuger's home, or the home I think was Kreuger's. Hanneke and Iet cannot completely agree which is which. The roof sagged, and the green, iron light posts leaned eastward. The farmer probably died in the 1960s, maybe the '70s. Both of his daughters would now be either very old or dead. I walked across the road and up the levee and looked at the River Vecht. For a spring day the wind still blew cold. Grass grew up from the wood of an old, half-sunk dock; a thick layer of cattails guarded the shoreline.

Soon after the commandoes blew up the track, Piet arrived at the van Os's farm. He loaded Marianne and little Helene back into the cart next to their small suitcases and pulled them northwest toward Weesp. Anne's youngest sister had arrived a few days earlier and picked up Ruud. As usual, my mom did not know why she was being moved. But as would become her habit, she—again—assumed she had done something wrong.

From the levee, I could see nearly all of the six farms, and as I scanned the horizon I wondered why the families left. There could have been many different reasons. It's possible Anne never bothered to tell the farmers they would be hiding Jews. It would be like Anne to leave out that little detail. My grandmother had almost no compunction. She regularly sized up a situation and worked it toward her ends. When her intentions were noble, she resembled a hero; when they weren't, words like manipulative and pushy were used. From my vantage point it was clear that the farmers were forced to take a substantial risk when hiding Carel or his mother. There was too much traffic at those little farms. Their front doors were only a few paces from the road. It's also possible that Mr. Kreuger had only offered to take the Schoorl children for a couple weeks, and Anne managed to get two months out of him. I don't know. But one thing is for sure, the reason everyone left Weesperkarspel had nothing to do with that quiet girl with the long auburn braids.

I walked down the driveway of the van Os's. In stark contrast to the Kreugers' home, this farm was in fine shape. The new owner was slowly restoring the house to its original glory. He met me outside and we toured his property. He pointed out the bunker on the furthest end of his pasture that the Dutch military had built as part of its defensive strategy in the early 1900s. It was no more than a rise in the ground with a few pine trees growing in odd directions from its soil.

PIET AGAIN DROVE down hard on the pedals as he pulled his two youngest daughters. He crossed over the river and into the city of Weesp, past rows of small homes built tightly together. He had managed to put on a few pounds since Vught, but not much, and had to stand to ascend the smallest rise in the road. The three headed northwest, passing through the residential outskirts of Amsterdam, close to the southern reaches of the IJsselmeer; the winds blew unobstructed over its brackish waters. A light sleet fell, dotting the wet road with specks of icy white.

The three soggy refugees passed the busy ports of Amsterdam and then followed the River Zaan toward the town of Wormerveer. Each bit of ground Piet covered was accompanied by the constant clatter of the cart's naked wheels. Piet's body warmed from the exertion, but the little girls—no matter the number of blankets or coats—both shivered. The trip took a full day, and they arrived in the town at nightfall, navigating those last miles toward their destination—the home of Piet's late grandmother—in the dark. She had just recently passed away, and Piet and Anne, along with Leo, Pauline, and Carel, had moved into her home.

For the first time in months, Marianne slept under the same roof as her mother and father, yet Mom has no memory of that night. Nor does she recall the passing of her birthday on January 22. She had turned seven.

The sounds of battle were now almost completely behind the families, and they had no knowledge of the fact that the sleepy little village of Bennekom had become a full-fledged war zone. Despite his weakening defenses, Hitler had no intention of giving up any piece of his new empire. The Russian army had fought their way into Poland and liberated Auschwitz on January 26, while the Allied army had held strong during that freezing winter in the forest of the Ardennes and had stopped Hitler's surprise offensive. Germany was now surrounded and Hitler's demise seemed inevitable. But all of Holland north of the Rhine still remained occupied, and German soldiers patrolled the streets of Wormerveer while Mom slept.

Marianne woke up the next morning and was loaded back on the cart along with her little sister. The morning air quickly bit into their cheeks. They crossed a few old canals before leaving the town and headed east to the main highway connecting Amsterdam to the farmland north. It was another long day pedaling for Piet and another cold trip for all three. Marianne and Helene pushed up against each other. The road eventually cut straight, through flat farmland, and the two girls watched as one row of fences after another appeared beside them, then slowly faded into the green southern horizon. The brief winter sun glowed behind the thick rain clouds, and Piet continued patiently. This time, he reached his destination—the town of Alkmaar—before dusk, then turned left off the highway and into the driveway of the Borst family farm. Marianne's legs felt stiff as she hopped out of the cart and made her way inside. After the long trek, the home felt impossibly warm.

The Borst living room opened into the kitchen, and the large space brimmed with people—Mom's people. The smell of her grandfather's cigars mixed with the din of lively conversation, and the familiarity, mixed with the warmth, felt like a trip back into the heart of the Soetendael. Marianne's nose remained a cold red, but her arms and legs relaxed. Except for Anne, all of Jan and Greet's adult children now lived on the farm— six daughters and one son. The Jewish teenager, Carla, still hid in the home, and the family was also hiding two young Dutch men eluding the draft (there seemed to be a pair of these in nearly everyone's home). The living room was full, and loud, and lively, and the many bodies added to the heat created by the brick fireplace. Marianne felt her Oma's warm arms wrap around her. Greet was a large, gentle, and kind woman, and her soft embrace not only helped warm my mother on the outside, but also reached to a deeper place, a place that had suffered a harder cold.

On that evening, my mom relaxed into her Oma's lap in a way that she had not relaxed in a very long time, and as a piece of Marianne's loneliness started to melt away, her eyes grew heavy with sleep. After a hot meal, Marianne and Helene were tucked into one of the two featherbeds in Oma and Opa's room. The house was larger than those found on most dairy farms, and there was plenty of food. Before the two girls fell to sleep, their Opa came into the room. He gave his two youngest granddaughters a piece of candy. For Marianne, it seemed as though the two-day trip had transported her to another world, and as night fell, she felt as far from the cold farms of Weesperkarspel as one could possibly journey.

When Marianne awoke the next morning, she said goodbye to her father as he prepared to return back to Wormerveer. Piet's children—the ones who were going to help him change the world—were now spread throughout the country. My mother and Helene had been the last of the Schoorl children to leave that row of small farms by the river and to follow the course of each child demands close study of geography and timelines. Hanneke had left the Kreugers on that same day Marianne was moved to the van Os's, but instead of accompanying her little sister, she followed her father by bike to Weesp and to the home of the town's veterinarian who lived with his wife and their baby. Of course, Hanneke had no idea why she was moved, nor did she ask any questions. She simply followed her father until she was standing awkwardly by his side in a strange house and introduced to her newest hosts. After Piet left, Hanneke did her best to fit it, and this time she had to do it without the comfort of her little sister. Unfortunately, this new home was not an improvement over the last. Unlike her stay at the Kreugers', where she felt simply alone and self-conscious, life with this new family felt overtly antagonistic.

The family, perhaps, expected a more proper young lady. But Piet and Anne hadn't raised proper children. Their kids were smart, outspoken, and a touch coddled. They had been raised by a permissive father whose pre-war sentiments were liberal if not radical. The Schoorls, during the best of times, were playful and loud, and Hanneke's newest hosts were reserved and very strict. And they differed from Mr. Kreuger in that they didn't seem to have his kind heart. From the moment she was left alone in the home, Hanneke never felt able to relax.

On one night at the dinner table, when she disagreed with the father's opinion, she punctuated her point by sticking her tongue out at the man. At the Soetendael, the act would have solicited at least a bit of laughter from the onlookers and perhaps prodded the argument forward. Hanneke had done it so many times before, that it just sort of slipped out. The man was so incensed he could hardly compose himself and his resulting fury scared my young aunt.

"THAT WAS SOMETHING that was quite common in our family—teasing," Hanneke told me. She also recounted the time she ate some cheese without asking permission, and the family was so incensed they not only admonished her, but also recounted the event to visitors. "I felt so insecure. I feel the sadness about being there." She looked at me from her chair in her living room, and she looked sad. "I tried to do my best." Her boyfriend had fallen to sleep on the sofa, and her many clocks continued to mark the minutes. She paused for a moment and her brow furrowed as she tried to recount the memories and the toll they took. "I think during all of the evacuation addresses, I lost all my security and feeling of being safe, and joy in life . . . and the right to be me . . . everything went—gone." Her eyes looked like I remember my own mother's when she felt sad. The Schoorl women all have something within their stare that looks isolated, distant, and alone. "It's too much for a child," she continued with the angry tone of a mother defending one of her own children. "The Soetendael was quite stable and secure, and I was at home. My mother and father might have left often, but there was always other people. And they were guests in the house. It was my house. And now I was the child that always had to adapt—be kind. Iet was at a family in Weesp, and Ruud too. But we never saw each other. There was nothing done to let us be together. My father or mother visited once or twice." Though Hanneke knows they did, she cannot recollect the instance. With her back straight and her eyes looking hard, she spoke with both sadness and anger. "You could never be a child anymore. You had to be thankful for what they gave—the shelter."

JUST DOWN THE ROAD, Iet had moved in with a family who lived above one of the town's banks, close to the city's center and next to a narrow canal. She had left the farms around the same time as her older sister.

The family had two young children. Iet was also very lonely and food was scarce. She moved two more times within the boundaries of Weesp eventually ending up at another farm. This last home was the best. Though Iet had to sleep curled up in a baby crib and the home was hopelessly dirty, the people were nice and they had children Iet's age.

During the time Iet and Hanneke were bouncing from home to home in Weesp, Piet and Anne still lived at the farms by the river. But after Piet and Anne moved to Wormerveer, they—again—found new addresses for the two girls, and Iet and Hanneke were instructed to move once again. One move seemed to blur into the next and each added to their sense of isolation. It didn't matter if they were in a "good" home or a "bad" one, they were always unsure why they had to go and assumed it had something to do with a lack on their part. It was only when the girls were together that they relaxed, and both remember vividly the day— again moving to another home—that they rode their bikes together from Weesp to Wormerveer. The girls had met in Weesp to make the journey. With their few belongings strapped to the back of their bikes, they rode northward. On the way, they remember passing an old chocolate factory and both swore they could smell melting chocolate—a fragrance that had left their lives soon after the Germans arrived. Though it seems a near impossibility that such a luxury could still exist in a starving Holland, the girls reveled in the possibility and the life that the smell represented.

The bike ride together was a short one, and soon they arrived in the heart of the town. Piet had grown up near Wormerveer, and he had friends and family in the town. Iet stayed with the owner of a cooking oil and mayonnaise factory. He and his wife had a large home and nine children. Hanneke stayed with one of Piet's cousins—a younger woman whose husband had been shot by the Germans. The woman had two young children, a boy and a girl, neither of whom was old enough to remember ever having a father. It almost goes without saying that no one told either Hanneke or Iet why, exactly, they had been moved.

For Hanneke, this home was also uncomfortable. The woman had hoped that by allowing Hanneke to stay with her she would get some help with her children and keeping up her small home. The problem was Hanneke had no experience doing either. She had helped her mom at times by setting the table or folding linen, but only because she enjoyed it. For most of her life, Hanneke had lived with multiple maids. The maids cooked and cleaned and a nanny watched the children. Hanneke was willing to help the woman if asked, but if she saw a mess, or a crying child, there wasn't any part of her that naturally considered lending a hand. Her host grew quickly irritated, and the relationship between the two was almost immediately tense. However, as their time together lengthened from days to weeks, Hanneke learned to become more helpful, and in small ways, she began to mimic her own mother.

This new home was one of many built literally one next to the other with a small garden in the backyard. Food was still a never-ending problem, as was fuel. Simple survival demanded continued resourcefulness. It was impossible to find enough wood to fire up the main stove in the kitchen, so Hanneke and the young mother used a tiny stove, which they set on top of the large one, to cook their meals. The little stove needed only a little flame. It could boil water or simmer a stew.

But even that little flame demanded a little fuel, and that was hard to come by. For Hanneke, feeding that little flame was often a full-time job.

Hanneke routinely attached a sieve to the back rack of her bike and headed to the train station in Wormerveer in search of fuel. She'd lock her bike up by the station and carry the sieve down to the tracks. The trains weren't running anymore, and she stepped over the rails and walked beside the glistening rails. Several of the cross ties were missing where men had removed the iron pins and pulled the ties from beneath the rails and used them for firewood. This was after all of the trees in the city, along with the wooden park benches, had been scavenged to survive the winter. Hanneke had no hope of moving one of the heavy pieces of sticky timber. She instead walked until she found a section of track that looked untouched and set up the sieve. She dropped handfuls of dirt and rock onto the thin grate and shook it back and forth looking for the shiny remnants of coal that, for decades, had fallen unnoticed off the trains and onto the ground. There were often four or five others who had staked a temporary claim to a small section of the rail line. Hanneke would sift for over an hour before she managed a small handful of the black, shiny fuel, but it would burn for several hours on the little stove. The woman often made a dough that they could cook into bread with just the heat from boiling water. It was a brief luxury. Even if you had money for food, it was hard to find anything to eat in Wormerveer, and like her own mother, Hanneke soon learned to venture off on her bike in search of a few meals.

On one particular occasion, Piet had written a letter for Hanneke, asking a food manufacturer he knew up north to provide her with whatever they could.

Hanneke and the woman departed early in the morning, first dropping the two children off at the woman's mother-in-law's home, and then riding to the factory together. The journey took several days. On the first night, they stopped in Alkmaar and slept at the Borsts' farm. The next day they rode to the factory. It was another typically cloudy and dreary winter afternoon. The factory produced and canned sauerkraut. The owner gave Hanneke six precious kilos. The two also received some butter and milk from the Borsts.

As the girls slowly worked their way back south through the flat farmland, they continued to pass parties similar to their own—men, woman, and children foraging the countryside for food. The Dutch called them "hunger trips." Many either pushed or pulled wagons and carts. Everyone was dressed in heavy clothing.

One morning, Hanneke and the woman rode together through the village outskirts. It was a routine trip to a farm in the direction of the Kreugers' home. A farmer had supplied the woman with milk for her children on several occasions. After the cold ride, the girls approached the farmer together. They stood at his door as he handed them a couple of bottles, but as he did so, he told them to not come back for more. This was the last time, he said. He could no longer help them. The door closed; the two turned and walked back to their bikes in silence, and the young mother wept.

For Hanneke, the struggles continued to mount. Adding to the day-to-day search for food, she was also sick and becoming sicker. Beneath her heavy winter clothes, red dots had started to appear on her skin. She didn't know what caused them, and she hadn't told anyone. But the dots soon increased and started to itch terribly. She did not know that beneath each red welt lived a scabies mite burrowing into her skin. The parasites had travelled with her for months. They likely came from the cramped attic of Mrs. Bos, living within several of the children including Paya. Hanneke and Paya had slept under the same sheets in the cellar of the lab. The microscopic scabies had laid eggs under Hanneke's skin, and soon the itching became unbearable.

Anne eventually picked up Hanneke and took her to the doctor. Scabies outbreaks were widespread in Holland. Anne had Hanneke stay with one of Anne's cousins until she was well again. The cousin managed to heat some water and bathe Hanneke in her living room. She also helped apply a stinky salve to her skin. Hanneke remembers that it was especially nice to be cared for.

Chapter 25

FOR THE SCHOORL children—during that short interval of time while Hanneke convalesced—there was no greater disparity in lifestyles than that between the Schoorls' eldest daughter and their youngest two. My mother still recollects the details of her time at Alkmaar the way one does a childhood trip to the Grand Canyon or Disneyland. She remembers how her grandfather carefully managed his dwindling supply of cigars, and the wooden box where he kept his tobacco treasure. And when Jan Borst did smoke, she remembers how he let one of his granddaughters choose the cigar for him. Each had a narrow band with an emblem, which he'd slide off and let the girls keep.

Each day at the farm, Marianne would eat a full breakfast and then follow her aunts around the farm. They let their niece help with the chores. Marianne turned the hand-crank on the washing machine, and she helped make butter and cheese. Her aunts would often pick her up and hold her, and she also spent a lot of time in her Oma's arms.

During the evenings, it was usual for everyone to gather in the two main rooms. The Borst daughters liked to tease each other, and they also enjoyed a good argument. They'd banter back and forth about whose turn it was to do what chore, or they'd conceive of some lighthearted prank that would send a ripple of laughter throughout the room. With so much family, the conversations nearly drowned out one another, and Marianne liked to sit and watch the hustle and bustle.

Carla was also quiet like my mother. It had been over a year since she had seen her own parents—since their final train ride to the farm. She could still picture the moment she stood with the Borsts and watched her parents leave. Since then, Carla had become like part of the family. Greet had taught her to knit, and Carla often sat in the corner at night working on a project. She hadn't heard from her parents since her Mom's last letter from Westerbork, and none of Carla's subsequent letters were answered. But she hadn't lost hope. The war would end soon and she would find her parents.

To illuminate those dark winter evenings, the Borsts had hooked up a small generator to an old bicycle to provide power to one sole light bulb. The contraption sat squarely in the middle of the living room, and after dark the family took turns pedaling. One night, when it was Carla's turn, she took her knitting with her. She spun her legs and worked the long needles in unison. It was a little like rubbing your tummy and patting your head, but she managed to split her brain between the tasks and found a nice rhythm until the ball of yarn fell off her lap. It caught in the bike's chain and stopped the pedals dead. The light went out, and the room turned instantly dark. Then, after a brief pause, the room erupted in hysterics.

Every night, Helene and Marianne were tucked in bed, and every night after the tuck-in, they waited for their grandfather to slip into the room to give them each a piece of candy. For the last years, sweets were an unusual indulgence, and they were much more so by the beginning of 1945. But if a man owned a dairy farm during a famine, the unusual was possible. The fluffy mattress pillowed Mom's small frame, and she would carefully suck on the candy until it was just a sliver and then gently drift off to sleep. In the quiet mornings when she woke, her Oma was sleeping next to her, and the smell of her Opa's cigars lingered in the room. For Marianne, each passing day felt like it was fashioned from her dreams—a special elixir created to help heal those invisible wounds that had festered within her.

As the sun hinted toward spring, the farm itself seemed postured for warmer days. Tight buds emerged on the fruit trees. And it was as though a piece of my mother also waited in unison with them for when the sun would, again, rise high up in the sky, and they would all blossom together in that light. Mom felt safe and loved, and the war seemed very far away. The reprieve, however, would not last.

Anne and Piet journeyed back to the Borst farm after little more than a week. They came by bicycle as usual. They had left Wormerveer early and made the trip in less than a day. After Anne arrived, she sat down with Marianne and explained that they had found a nice home for her in a coastal village name Bergen aan Zee. Eline would be there with her. It would be fun, Anne assured her. Even for a child who had grown used to the chaos of war, the words caught Marianne completely by surprise.

Marianne stared at her mother. She could not manage any words—more than anything, she did not want to leave the farm. She wanted desperately to stay with her Oma and Opa. She wanted to wake up surrounded by her own family and in a place where she was cherished. She didn't want to be pulled from the farm and sent back out onto the road and to some anonymous family. The fact that Eline would be there did nothing to raise her spirits. She didn't want to face another stranger.

But it did not matter what Marianne wanted or didn't want; no one would ever know, because she simply sat there in stunned silence as her mother spoke and she said nothing. Her bags were packed for her. Arrangements had already been made to bring her away.

Within an hour a German truck lumbered into the driveway. Somehow, Anne had found out that the vehicle was heading to Bergen aan Zee, and she had asked the soldiers if they were willing to stop by the farm and pick up her daughter. Marianne's small suitcase was placed in the truck, and one of the soldiers picked her up and set her on his lap in the cab. The diesel idled, then the driver let go the clutch and the large truck crawled back out the driveway and rumbled down the road.

The quiet girl with the auburn braids sat as quietly and as still as she ever had. The shock of the German truck and the enemy soldiers would have jolted her no matter the setting. But now to be with them in the cab, on a soldier's lap—and that they had pulled her from the farm in Alkmaar and were now taking her to some unfamiliar location—was too much for the child. Her small frame remained rigid. For my mother, it was one move too many.

MOM STILL CARRIES some resentment. So do her older sisters. They all felt abandoned. In fact, after those first memories of the war erupted inside my mom and she had talked to the therapist, and after she had labored to remember each moment as best she could and type them into her memoir, Mom still didn't understand why she had been tossed from family to family. It was that particular piece of the war that still haunted her, and she was not able to let it go. So Mom decided to call Anne in an attempt to fill in the gaps. Anne resolved a lot of unanswered questions, but she also ignored others. Anne sent my mother a few pages that she had written about the war, but they did little to complete the story, and my grandmother continued to ignore my mother's more prickly questions. What followed was a battle of wills between two of the most willful people I know, which culminated in my Mom purchasing a plane ticket to Amsterdam. She flew across the United States and over the Atlantic, and eventually rode the elevator up to Anne's apartment to question her face-to-face.

At the time, Anne was widowed and lived alone. She answered the door slowly; her hair was pulled back into a neat bun. She moved about her home awkwardly, complaining that her knees hurt.

Anne listened to my mother while sitting in her favorite chair by the large living-room window; stacks of library books were piled within arm's reach. Mom noticed that Anne had replaced her houseplants with plastic replicas. Anne still didn't want to talk about the war.

After only a half-hour together, Anne said it was time for my mom to leave. But Mom still had unanswered questions, and she simply refused to walk out Anne's door. My grandmother could see that her daughter was absolutely serious. Anne softened a little and then made an honest attempt to explain why

Marianne was constantly moved from place to place. She told Marianne that people were afraid of the Jews. They were afraid of what would happen to their own families if the Germans found them hiding in their homes. She explained that Marianne helped provide an alibi for Eline.

The conversation seemed to provide my mom with what she was searching for. But it doesn't explain everything.

Piet's grandmother's home in Wormerveer was not particularly small, and it was never obvious to Hanneke or Iet why they couldn't all remain under that same roof—together. Pauline's son, Carel, stayed with them, and it didn't make sense to them why he could live there and they could not. In fact, despite never having talked about the war to anyone prior to my interviews, Marianne, Iet and Haneke all told me close to the same thing—that their parents were having a lot of fun living with the van Leeuwens, and that the four enjoyed not having to consider a bunch of children underfoot. And it is true that even before the war, Anne had a bad habit of pawning off her children, so this increased her children's suspicions as to her motives. However, it is impossible to discern Anne and Piet's complete true intentions during the end of the war. Perhaps the children's convictions are entirely correct, but it seems equally possible that every one of Piet and Anne's decisions were meant to keep each child alive during a time when many perished. I find it most likely that Piet and Anne's motives were a mix of the two. But despite one's suspicions or conjecture, there is one considerable, less seemly, fact that further complicates how each of the Schoorl children recollects this very dark time in their war.

* * *

EVERY NOW AND AGAIN, when her boyfriend drifted off, deep enough to snore, Hanneke would get up and gently awaken him, and he'd act as though no time had passed and rejoin us as audience to the interview.

Hanneke spoke carefully when describing Pauline van Leeuwen—her petite frame, her sense of style, her dresses, her long silky hair, and how her sharp wit and years of higher education made her a vibrant conversationalist. And also, how—unlike Anne—Pauline had given birth to only two children, and she still had a slim, alluring figure. "It caused a lot of problems with my mother," Hanneke said. "My father fell in love with Pauline."

The last of my small cup of coffee, resting on the table next to my mini-recorder, had cooled. Hanneke sat erect on her chair to my left, facing her garden. The softness had left her voice. She went on to describe how her father, despite his brilliance, was quiet and almost shy in a way, but how he always had a way with women. "They liked him because he was warm and good-looking, and interested in them." Hanneke was alluding to the time period before Piet was arrested and that Pauline was interested in her father. Though I will never know exactly when this romance first started, it did start. And by the time the four adults had evacuated the lab, the boundaries of their relationships had blurred.

"They had a very good time in Wormerveer," Hanneke said—meaning the four adults. "And they had plenty of food." Those last five words dropped with the weight of resentments harbored for decades, and Hanneke didn't try to hide her anger. I had heard that same indictment from my Mom when we sat together in her sewing room. Even Iet, who had a habit of defending her parents, remembers this period of the war with bitterness.

My mother had also suggested that Anne and Leo were also romantically linked. It's true that Leo and Anne were spending more and more time together, and that when Piet was imprisoned, the two had become like partners in the resistance. They had worked hard together to keep everyone alive. Since arriving at Wormerveer, they had also made an illegal trip back to the war zone in Bennekom by bike to recover some of their belongings from the two barrels buried in the vegetable garden of the Soetendael. There is no question that the two were close. But their relationship wasn't comparable to Piet and Pauline. Piet had fallen deeply in love with Pauline, and they began an affair that would outlast the war. I doubt it was Piet's first, and I know it wasn't his last. And, as odd as it might seem, Leo didn't appear to mind sharing his wife. It is possible that Leo shared some of my grandfather's unconventional sentiments regarding sex and romance.

Piet had always worked hard to live up to his ideals. It wasn't enough to simply believe in an ideal. If he thought a particular way of living to be the best, he worked to integrate that ideal into his life. He thought drinking a scourge, so he didn't drink. He believed his kids needed to be close to nature, so he brought them to the rural village of Bennekom. He thought the wealthy had an obligation to the poor, and he found ways to help. Many of these ideas were forged during his later college days as a member of the Social Democrats. And the crowd Piet ran with also had some very radical ideas about sex—ideas that provide a precursor to the popular hippie movement of the '60s in the United States. Simply put, Piet didn't think there was anything wrong with having sex beyond the bounds of marriage. His own father had provided living proof of the fact. Piet believed sex should be more open and free. It was once told to me that when Piet first slept with Anne at the Borst farm, he suggested to Anne (unsuccessfully) that a few more of her sisters should join them. However, this laissez-faire attitude does not explain everything. For Piet wasn't just enjoying an occasional roll in the hay with Pauline—he loved her, and he coveted her.

But none of this mess had anything to do with my mother having to leave her grandparents' farm, other than that it is easy to see the four parents conversing after they finally found a safe place to hide Eline, and then someone suggesting they send Marianne with her to keep Eline company and strengthen her alibi.

THE GERMAN TRUCK rolled out of Alkmaar and headed west, down a narrow road and toward the sea. The flat farms of Alkmaar, with its few windmills, were soon replaced by a forest.

There were no longer any worries that an Allied plane would dive down and strafe the vehicle with machine gun fire. The heavy bombers and fighter planes now largely ignored Holland as they flew south to the fronts that were slowly closing in on the heart of Germany. When the truck hit a pothole, Marianne bounced on the lap of the soldier. She didn't understand why she had to move and her little sister Helene was allowed to remain. She was little. She didn't eat much. She had slept in the same bed as her little sister. It was not explained. It never was.

Eventually, the smell of the sea mixed with diesel fumes. The truck ascended the coastal dunes and then rolled downward to the village. The soldiers found the address Anne had given them, and they dropped off their little charge and her small suitcase as promised.

The van der Pols' residence stood alone just inside the dunes and only a short walk from the shoreline. The couple was retired, though they still owned a farm just across the street and had hired help to work the land. Mr. van der Pol was pleasant as was his wife, and both were genuinely concerned for the small refugee. The two made every effort to welcome the girl into their home. They were—of course—already hiding two college-age young men.

They met Marianne at the road and brought her inside the home and upstairs to show her her new room. It was neat and orderly and also cozy, with toys for girls placed carefully on the shelves. A window opened to the front of the house.

The van der Pols were an educated, sophisticated couple and lived a life far removed from the daily toil demanded by the spare farms in Weesperkaspel. The two had carefully prepared for the little girls' arrival, but despite their attentive warmth Marianne would not look them in the eyes. She would not smile. Somewhere on that strip of road connecting the van der Pols' seaside village to the wet farms of Alkmaar, Marianne had turned more deeply inward—back to the world she fashioned from the warmth and the straw of Kreuger's barn. She fell to sleep under clean sheets feeling terribly alone, missing her Oma and her Opa. Eline was expected the following day.

THE SCHOORL CHILDREN were now scattered throughout northern Holland. No two lived together. Spring was just around the corner and looked to be the sixth during the occupation. Mr. van der Pol's bees had come to life and were upon the buds in bloom. The canals of Wormerveer had all thawed, and just north of Alkmaar, in the rural village of Bergen, Marianne's only brother, Ruud, played in the fields of his uncle's farm.

He had left the van Os's just before Marianne, escorted north by one of his aunts. The two made the same trip by bike to Alkmaar, then continued on to Bergen. Ruud had visited his uncle's farm since before the war and he knew the family well. One of their four children, a son, was the same age as Ruud—both eleven—and the two were close friends. Food was abundant and my uncle—the only Schoorl child to remember the war as generally enjoyable—was having fun.

Ruud Schoorl was the first of Piet and Anne's children that I talked to about the war in any detail. Soon after my mother's memoir had taken hold of me, Ruud flew in from the Netherlands for one of his regular visits to America. Certainly the most jovial of all of Mom's siblings, he sat down with me and explained how the war unfolded, and did so with remarkable precision. My mother's memoir had lacked an accurate timeline. Ruud's did not. He filled in detail after detail. Yet despite explaining his father's arrest, Vught, the trial, the bombing, he would not equivocate from his initial declaration—that the war was—in most regards—fun.

By the time Ruud was living with his uncle, rumors of the war coming to an end drifted throughout Holland. At night, the farmers in Bergen removed their hidden radios and listened to Radio Orange, broadcasted from across the channel. The news was continually good. Hitler's defenses had been pierced. It seemed the Allies would indeed prevail. But nothing was ever assured. One thing was for certain—there was no military effort to directly liberate the rest of the Netherlands. Occupied Holland would remain occupied until Hitler surrendered.

Across the open fields close to his uncle's farm, Ruud could see the elaborate defensive measures the German army had constructed to stop Allied planes from landing on Dutch soil. The soldiers had erected broad pine timbers on end just like telephone poles, which they spaced every twenty or thirty feet in a grid. They then fastened a thick cable from the top of one pole to the next, forming squares. These covered wide stretches of pastureland and would easily rip to shreds the tender underbelly of any plane or glider that dared attempt a landing. Ruud could also see where several of the timbers had been removed. During winter nights, the farmers had snuck into the fields and removed a couple of timbers at a time. They then reattached the cables to not attract attention. They carried to the logs on their shoulders and into the safety of their barns, and then cut and split the seasoned wood and used it as fuel for their fires. Ruud's uncle had pilfered his fair share.

As the days of the calendar marched slowly forward, the pleasant afternoons now outnumbered the not-so-pleasant, and Ruud roamed about the countryside. The Germans had commandeered the farm next door, and they stationed a garrison in the barn. During his wandering about, Ruud had crossed paths with one of the soldiers and the two had become friends. They now regularly met where the two properties joined. The soldier didn't speak Dutch, and Ruud didn't speak German, but they managed to communicate. The German's name was Heinz. He had children at home in Germany—or perhaps still had children, as the Allies were savagely bombing entire German cities into ashy oblivion. According to Ruud's aunt, Heinz was a "good German" which meant he didn't steal food or search too fervently for those in hiding. The two would mostly just pass the time leisurely.

The days in Holland were continuing brighter, and instead of layering the land with a blanket of unending gray, the clouds now billowed up—singular creations, passing brief shadows across the awakening fields. Ruud probably reminded Heinz of his own kids, and their moments together likely provided a brief sanctuary for the soldier, a surrogate for the moments he had missed with his own growing children.

The always-energetic Ruud stayed busy from sun up till sundown. He enjoyed his relatives—their company, their land, and their food. Unlike his sisters, he didn't miss his mom and dad. For Ruud the war was friendly like Heinz and as benign as barricades a cold farmer could burn in his stove. His father visited once a month, arriving down one of the narrow village roads on bike, and leaving just the same way.

Chapter 26

THE SPRING OF 1945 finally arrived in earnest. The North Sea still froze your toes if you braved the waters, but you could thaw them out in the warmth of the sand. Eline had arrived at the van der Pols' as promised, and the girls shared the upstairs room. Marianne felt excited and relieved when she saw Eline arrive; despite not wanting to be moved, she had truly missed her best friend. They could play again just like they had at the Soetendael. The grass for their doll's beds was growing in the new light and the van der Pols' yard beckoned their imaginations.

But with Eline also came feelings Marianne could not completely reconcile. Though alone and lonely for the several months the two had been apart, Marianne had also felt the lifting of a burden, a subtle feeling not easily identified by a child. She was too young to put all the pieces in place, but she knew in her gut that when Eline was close, her life changed. Marianne worried more, and she was more wary of everything. Her own father had asked her to always keep an eye out. And the same sense of responsibility that had trembled inside her every time she heard the sound of a train at the Kreugers' farm returned to her when Eline arrived. She could not help it. But as their days together turned to weeks, the two settled into a playful routine—though it was at times disrupted by obligations that neither child had to concern themselves with since Market Garden.

Mrs. van der Pol had decided to invest some time in the two children's neglected education. She had been a teacher and set up some art projects for the girls to explore. Her efforts, though extensive and thoughtful, did not yield the usual results. The two girls were poor students, easily distracted, and they not only didn't like to sit in one place—they weren't used to sitting in one place. Both had lived the majority of their lives during a war where schedules and routines were short-lived. Marianne hadn't attended a classroom with any regularity for over two years, and before that, she had only just begun her studies. Eline had only attended school briefly. The girls were used to musing about at their leisure. A touch wild and mischievous, they exercised the van der Pols' patience. The woman tried to interest them in knitting and embroidery. The kids didn't take to it. And it was easier to rebel together. And they both knew that once they wore out Mrs. van der Pol, they were free to leap back into their make-believe worlds.

On one of those days, while in their new bedroom, the girls had found a complete porcelain tea set made in miniature. The sun was out, so they scooped up the cups and headed outdoors for a party. The afternoon rays warmed the backs of their necks as they made place settings next to the quiet road. Understandably, the girls' minds usually drifted toward food. They had both been kept alive during that deadly winter, thanks to the farmers in Weesperkarspel, and neither had suffered true hunger. But they both dreamed of the feeling of an orange bursting in their mouths, or the sound of fresh pancakes sizzling on the frying pan, and butter and sugar melting together on the hot cakes.

While imagining food, the girls picked at the tar on the road. It looked like licorice. The sunlight had turned pieces of the road into a malleable goo, and when Marianne and Eline dug their nails into the tar they were able to pull up small pieces. They rolled each piece into a little ball, and then dropped the balls into the teacups. As they served their tea, the sun continued down upon them and warmed the cups. The balls of tar merged and flattened. When the sun began to drop, the tar hardened and the girls carried the now heavier tea set back inside.

Mrs. van der Pol saw the girls as they started up-stairs. Their little hands were flecked in black as were the porcelain cups. The miniature set had survived as playthings for nearly twenty years. The refugees had destroyed them in an afternoon. She could not hide her anger while lecturing Marianne and Eline. She sent the girls to their room. The tar on their little fingers stuck like glue.

Every day the sun shined, Marianne and Eline ex-plored outdoors. The van der Pols' flower gardens ex-ploded with color; their fruit trees had already blos-somed and were now leafing. The girls felt the spring prompting the village to life, and the light and warmth energized them. The two also continued to test the van der Pols' patience.

Despite being repeatedly told to stay out of the veg-etable garden, Marianne and Eline could not resist the temptation. Only a few paces from where they stood, bushes full of red currants beckoned, and they stepped across an imaginary line and into the forbidden gar-den. The currants were like little bright jewels—each a capsule waiting to burst under pressure. The girls ate till full. They did not care that the berries had not ripened. And they did not necessarily care when the berry stains gave them away to Mrs. van der Pol just like the tell-tale bits of black tar had earlier in the season. But this time there was a more severe price. After they were sent to their room, their small stomachs rebelled, and they both lay on their beds suffering terrible cramps.

Despite the two strong-willed little troublemakers, the van der Pols remained patient and kind. The girls continued rebellious, but it did not seem to dissuade Mrs. van der Pol's efforts. She eventually succeeded in getting Eline to learn embroidery. The food was always good and a few leafy vegetables had already made their way from the garden to the dinner table. After the shock of the move became a more distant memory, Marianne slowly warmed to the home. It felt alive to Marianne. The two young men hiding in the home were fun and funny. They played records on the van der Pols' phonograph and sang along with the music. They teased the two little girls and would sometimes entertain them with games. They were loud, and for stretches of time, when the van der Pols' home was at its most rambunctious, Marianne forgot to miss her Oma.

On one afternoon, the boys were in the kitchen peeling potatoes. They joked and laughed as they worked. Marianne smiled silently when they teased her. It was another clear day, but Marianne lingered in the kitchen. Mrs. van der Pol came in looking concerned and told the boys that there was a rumor that the Germans were going from home to home searching for people in hiding. She turned to Marianne and told her to go to the side room off the front hallway and keep a look out.

The boys had a prearranged hiding spot beneath the hardwood floor. They could move a small area rug, pull up some loosened boards and squeeze into the hole. Marianne left the kitchen. The boys had started to sing a song. She could still hear the two carrying on as she stood in front of the glass watching the pathway leading to the road. She hadn't been there for a complete minute when two soldiers appeared on the road. Marianne immediately yelled out in her little voice, "they are coming." The boys yelled something back in jest. They didn't believe her. The soldiers turned into the van der Pols' walkway. "They are coming," Marianne squealed louder. "They are getting closer." Her blood rose up in a panic. The tone caught the ears of one of the boys, but still unsure whether it was a joke, he ran toward the window to take a look. The other boy followed. Both of the young men looked out the window just as both soldiers arrived on the stoop. The four caught each other's eyes. The boys darted to the hallway. The soldiers opened the front door. Marianne watched. They carried rifles and had unslung the weapons from their shoulders and were pointing them forward. Marianne did not move.

The boys moved a piece of furniture off of the carpet and one had reached down to lift it up. But it was too late. The soldiers walked to the hall and pointed their guns at the boys. No one spoke. Mrs. van der Pol also watched. The soldiers motioned with their rifles. One of the boys dropped the edge of the carpet and it fell flat. The Germans led them out the front door and down the pathway next to the van der Pols' flowering beds. During that short interval of time, Marianne and Eline had run up to their bedrooms and hid.

Marianne eventually came back downstairs. Mrs. van der Pol was sitting on the sofa. She didn't move, and the home itself seemed to mourn in the silence. No one spoke. Marianne walked over to the sofa and sat next to Mrs. van der Pol. Mr. van der Pol was not home at the time.

The war had come one last time, and had arrived—like always—suddenly and without warning. And as it had so many times before, it left pieces of its darkness inside my mother. The silent home seemed to blame her. The emptiness felt like her fault. My mother would never see those two young men again, and the child was sure the boys had been caught because of her. It seemed a fact, one that felt as cold and real as the chunks of metal used to build the war machines raging across the continent, and it lodged itself within her young body where it would remain, just one sharp shard of darkness aside many—a collective wound that would not begin to heal until her body had grown, and she had crossed an ocean, and borne and raised her own children. Until she very much resembled the older woman who sat next to her on that day—one of the very last days of that war—the woman with graying hair and aging skin, and the better part of a life behind her.

Chapter 27

THE WAR WOULD be over soon. The underground distributed pamphlets updating the nation as to the Allies' progress, and the Queen of Holland, from her radio studio in England, assured her citizens that the war was indeed in its final throes. But this had also occurred once before, and those claims were eventually found to be rumors. So until the war actually did end—until that exact moment—it was still war. The Germans knew it, and the Dutch knew it, and each played their deadly roles accordingly. And the war continued on.

Iet was now living with the Duyuis family. Like the van der Pols, Mr. and Mrs. Duyuis were gracious. The family was wealthy and many of their nine children still lived in their large home. The couple's two youngest daughters were Iet's age and the three played together. Iet organized plays just like she had with Eline at Weesperkarspel, which the three girls performed for the parents.

Anne had recently stopped by and asked Iet if there was anything she wanted from Bennekom. Though the area was a war zone and strictly off-limits, Anne was planning to ride down to the farm with Leo. Iet asked her to pick up the collection of Hans Christian Anderson fairy tales that Anne had given her on her birthday. Anne arrived back a few days later with the large book on the back of her bike and it was now tucked away in Iet's new bedroom.

On one particular night while eating dinner with the Duyuis family, Iet looked out the window and intuited something that set off inner alarms. No one seated at the table around her was as adept at war as she. The window opened toward the front of the house and out into a busy street. She saw a group of soldiers passing by. But there was something about the way they passed—something in their gait and the way they moved that drew her attention. She saw soldiers regularly, but something was different about this group. And she didn't hesitate to disrupt dinner and blurt out a warning to the family. Everyone stopped eating. No one questioned Iet's sensibilities.

This family also had two young men hiding from the draft. The boys darted up and rushed to their hiding place—another hole in the floor between the basement and the first story. Iet's intuition proved spot on. After passing the home, the soldiers had doubled back and now stood before the Duyuis' locked door. The bell rang. The family's German maid met the soldiers at the door and tried to stall them. The young men squeezed into their hole, and someone puzzled the pieces of the hardwood floor back into place above them. The boys could hear the soldiers' boots—a lot of boots—above them as the Germans took control of the home.

The soldiers herded the family together and locked them in a room. They walked back and forth over the two boys as they searched the premises. Hours passed. Iet used a flowerpot to go pee. The soldiers remained until the first hours of morning, then left. They had been searching for a member of the Dutch resistance who had fled into the Duyuis's neighborhood. The soldiers had found fresh footprints in the home's garden. This time, the two boys had remained quiet and safe beneath the hardwood floor.

DESPITE THE IMMINENT end of the war, Holland was still starving. Piet's personal relationships with the owners of several food-manufacturing companies, and the fact that almost everyone from Anne's childhood owned farms, ensured the Schoorl family's survival. But not everyone was so well connected. The spring weather was nice, but it did nothing to stave off the hunger. Even with the waterways thawed, Holland was controlled by Germany and feeding the Netherlands was not a priority. As a last resort, families were digging up tulip bulbs and feeding them to their children. The deaths continued to mount.

During the last week of April, the Allies negotiated with the German command to allow humanitarian airdrops. The Allies stuffed the bellies of their bombers with food, and they came in low and littered the open fields with packages. Iet received a bar of chocolate that had made the trip across the English Channel, which she ate with sparing discipline. She took one bite, then asked her friend to hide the bar until the following day when she would take another.

Hanneke stood in line with her ration coupons to receive some of the gathered food. Each person was allotted half a loaf of freshly baked bread and half a stick of margarine. The Allied had also dropped special biscuits that expanded in the stomach. Sadly, some starving children came upon some packages containing the biscuits, and they ate so many that their stomachs ruptured. Even in its last moments, the war took its victims.

As the last days of April passed, the English forces gained the city of Arnhem. The German lines throughout the Netherland had been penetrated. The Russian army took Berlin, and on April 30, Hitler committed suicide in a bunker deep beneath the rubble of the once proud city.

ON MAY 5, 1945 the sun rose to a clear sky. By afternoon the bricks surrounding the white portico of the Hotel de Wereld—that hotel directly across from my elderly aunt's home in Wageningen—had warmed in the sunlight. Just a few miles to the north the Soetendael lay abandoned, its windows shattered by the percussion of heavy bombs.

Inside the hotel, Holland's Prince Bernhard looked on as the German Commander-in-Chief of the Netherlands surrendered to Canadian General Charles Foulkes. That afternoon, the war officially ended. And as the sun dropped into the North Sea, the news rippled through the countryside. Some thought it was still just a rumor.

That evening Hanneke looked out the window of her cousin's home while dusting. The neighbor across the street opened his front door and walked to his flagpole. She could see he was carrying something in his hands but could not make out what it was. It had been nearly five years to the day that the war had begun. Hanneke was nine years old when she woke up to the invading planes on May 10, 1940. As she watched the neighbor walk across his property, she did so as a 14-year-old emerging into young womanhood. The item in the neighbor's hands was red, white, and blue—forbidden colors. The man walked toward his flagpole and carefully unfurled the flag of the Netherlands. He attached it to its tether, and raised it up into the last of the evening light. After that first flag, others followed, and throughout the Netherlands the sun set upon a host of Dutch flags waving in the spring air. As much as any war can end, this one had finally done so.

Chapter 28

IMMEDIATELY AFTER the surrender, many of the Germans broke rank and began the long walk toward whatever was left of their own families or homes. Soldiers passed in front of the van der Pols' property in small groups. Many had abandoned their weapons. They looked tired, sad, and human. Marianne watched them with the forgiving eyes that come easy to children. Mostly, the soldiers had been kind to her. Their clothes were dirty and disheveled and their heads hung heavy. When nighttime came, some of the men simply stopped walking and curled up in the ditch between the road and the van der Pols' home. In the morning they arose and continued on, northward, toward the long dike that crosses the IJsselmeer, then east and back to their fatherland. The men still stopped when they saw Eline and Marianne and offered candy.

The van der Pols explained to the girls that the war was now over, and Marianne wished that she still had her orange ribbon.

THE CANADIAN TROOPS made their way northward through Holland. In every town or village, throngs of Dutch citizens met the convoys, cheering madly, as the trucks and tanks crawled slowly forward.

It took Hanneke those first few hazy seconds as she awoke that morning to remember that the war had truly come to its end. She looked outside. The Dutch flag across the street was still waving proudly. She dressed quickly and left to explore the new day. One of the neighbor ladies had made miniature Dutch flags for all of the children. She gave one to Hanneke.

It was another beautiful, clear, spring day. Hanneke gripped the stem of the little flag as she walked the one block to the town's main avenue. The crowds had already gathered—eight, nine, ten people deep. She slowly worked her way forward until she stood at the lip of the road. Before anyone could see the Allies, the low rumble of the convoy's diesel engines announced their arrival. The tracks of the heavy tanks squeaked and clattered against the pavers and concrete, and red, white, and blue flags of all sizes waved up and down the avenue. Just a week earlier no one dared wear anything with the color orange. Now the color of the Royal Dutch House was on proud display. Bright orange ribbons and bows adorned the citizens like new buds of spring. The exuberance rose to a persistent roar when the first vehicles passed. Hanneke waved her flag and smiled and watched. People jumped and screamed. A tank slowed in front of Hanneke as the vehicle ahead of it had stopped. A young Canadian soldier reached his strong arm down to Hanneke and pulled her up onto the thick iron flanks of the tank. She braced herself as the tank lurched forward again returning to speed. The crowds jumped and yelled and a swell of jubilation swayed over everyone, and from up on the tank the crowd sometimes appeared as one singular being, the chants and the motion cementing individuals together as one frenzied, celebratory beast. Hanneke's smile had fixed itself in place as she rode through the roaring streets. The soldier grabbed her tiny flag and waved it in the air. The anticipation of years continued to swell and rise, and the cheers did not diminish. Young men and women ran beside the trucks and tanks and handed flowers to the uniformed Canadians. The celebration had captured the body of every participant as it either waved or jumped or ran. It was the genuine moment of liberation, the truth of it clamoring down the streets of Wormerveer, and the smell and sight and sound of it there before all of them announced that truth to any dark part that had, the previous morning, found the idea unbelievable.

Piet and Anne partook in the same event as the military convoy passed by their temporary home. Piet had grabbed the side of a truck as it passed. His beige suit still hung baggy off his frame. A soldier with his head out the truck's window had offered his hand and the two held each other's arms as the weight of Piet's body pulled him outwards. Piet grinned and the soldier grinned and Piet soon let go and leaped back onto the pavement. The truck continued down the road with other Dutch citizens still clinging to its sides.

Iet walked through the crowds in a flowery dress gifted her by the Duyuis family. Her only clothes had been for winter, and the dress felt like the new day surrounding her. It was used, but it felt new to Iet, and also somehow right to wear during those first days of liberation. The white skirt with delicate flowers printed on the fabric fluttered against her knees. Iet still wore the wooden shoes her mother had the cobbler make for her back in Bennekom when normal shoes could no longer be found. The shoemaker had custom carved the inside of the thick wood to match Iet's foot perfectly, and the shoes were exceptionally comfortable. Iet liked the clomping sound they made as she passed over the cobblestones. The boisterous noise and her thin skirt whisking about in the warm breeze felt like freedom.

Further north, beyond Alkmaar, in the village of Bergen, Ruud saw an Allied jeep in the distance, driving on the elevated road. The large convoy never made it to their quiet countryside, but the farmers had all gathered on May 6 and raised large tents in their fields. The parties continued all night and into the next day. They played music and danced and drank. And after they collapsed into sleep, they resurrected the following day and repeated the festivities anew.

The scenes were repeated throughout every part of Holland that had been newly liberated. It seemed the entire nation lost itself in communal revelry. But that was not completely true. Some stayed home behind tightly closed doors. Too many of the Dutch had chosen to support the wrong side during the occupation, and the waves of the Dutch flags signaled a reckoning. Within just a few short days, the worst of the Nazi sympathizers were rounded up and sent to the very concentration camp that had imprisoned Piet. Some were less fortunate and suffered at the hands of angry mobs. Some swung from trees. But for the most part, the Dutch remained predictably civil. There were varying degrees of cooperation with the Nazis, and varying degrees of justice demanded. For the women who had slept with the German soldiers and who had enjoyed the privileges that came from doing so, the crowds exacted a revenge reminiscent of the scarlet letter once imposed by the Puritans.

Earlier on the morning of May 6, when she had first left the Duyuis home, Iet had watched a car pass with a girl and a man inside. A mob was chasing the car and screaming. Soon the mob closed in on the vehicle from all sides. The young woman inside looked terrified. Someone screamed out that she was a German lover-girl. The car stopped against a thick wall of angry Dutch men and women. Iet couldn't watch. She didn't have the stomach for vengeance.

After her ride on the tank, Hanneke walked toward the neighborhood where her parents lived. On her way, she came upon another angry crowd. They had collected in front of a house and had demanded that a young woman who was hiding inside come out. The girl had little choice. She was accompanied by her father, who stood close to her on the family's lawn. The crowd jeered. More gathered. And soon the mob numbered several hundred. Tears dropped down the young woman's face and dripped off her chin. Her father stood silently with his arms at his side. It was obvious to Hanneke that the father had been faithful to his nation. But he was still a father and could not abandon his girl. She was pushed onto a chair and someone brandished a large pair of shears. They grabbed handfuls of the woman's hair and cut it short to her scalp. As the hair fell on the grass, the crowd roared. The act contained a touch of Dutch civility as no parts of the girl were damaged in a lasting way. But the crowd's jeers and anger and rage seemed manifest. Hanneke looked at the father's bowed head. Like Iet, Hanneke did not have a stomach for revenge either. But she could not take her eyes off the scene, and it cut a pit in her stomach. None of it pleased any part of her, and if she were able, she would have scooped up the pair and found them safe harbor.

She continued walking until the house was out of sight and the sounds of the anger dissipated behind her.

By the day's end, hundreds of Dutch women had been marked as traitors. Little blood was spilled, and the hair would return. But the Dutch had long memories, and the following years would be hard ones for all of the Nazi sympathizers.

Chapter 29

O N THE DAY Iet learned she would return home to Bennekom, it took her only a few minutes to pack. She had carefully stowed her miniature carvings— the tiny table and small chairs belonging to the imaginary world that she had created during the icy winter in Weesperkarspel—in a shoebox. The car that would drive her to Bennekom belonged to the Duyuis's son-in-law, a doctor from Ede, and Iet had to squeeze between the man's suitcases and assorted boxes filled with whatever possessions he had managed to save during his own evacuation. Iet still wore her new dress, and she set the shoebox on her lap. Her large book of Hans Christian Andersen's fairy tales was close behind her. The vehicle pulled out from in front of the Duyuis's home in Wormerveer and headed east and toward the Soetendael.

Just days after the liberation, Piet and Anne petitioned for a permit to return to their farm. The Germans and the Allies had fought fiercely for control of Bennekom, and unexploded bombs littered the now-abandoned village. The region remained restricted. Despite the danger, a permit was granted.

The Duyuis's son-in-law received his permit just after the Schoorls, and he agreed to drop Iet off on his way to Ede. The two drove southeast between Amsterdam and the IJsselmeer and toward Weesp. They met the twists and turns of the river Vecht, passed close to the farms belonging to Mr. Kreuger and his neighbors, and then continued beside the shores of the lakes of Vreeland, near the almost empty white home belonging to Tante Ans. They drove through Zeist and down the same road where, nearly eight months earlier, Iet had sat next to her bike in the back of the heavy German truck. The doctor reached the village of Ede, then turned right and drove the few short minutes to Bennekom. The roads were quiet and mostly empty. Iet watched the now familiar landscape pass. This was home, and she knew every bump and turn. She knew the trees and the pastures and the trails winding through the woods as though they were a part of her. She stared out the window. Bennekom's outsides resembled her insides.

The Allies, who were dug in just south of the Rhine, had pushed north. The Germans had strict orders to defend their positions. During the winter, fighting raged in Bennekom. The doctor slowed as he passed the laboratory and then turned right toward the Soetendael. The little car drove through the remains of what was once a neighborhood. The houses, just a stone's throw away from the Soetendael, had been reduced to tangled rubble. A curtain draped over split timbers. Pieces of shattered furniture were scattered amongst heaps of bricks and broken mortar. Much of the debris was unrecognizable—the flattened remnants of homes now standing little higher than a child. Iet could see through one block and into the next, and again then next. The Germans had destroyed the neighborhood to open up their lines of fire. Broken bricks lined the pavement where they had been pushed back to make way for passing vehicles. A few surviving perennials that had been carefully planted by the destroyed homes' hapless owners poked their stems up through the wreckage and their blossoms caught Iet's eye; the colors contrasted against the brown, gray wreckage. She thought about picking a few as she drove by, but it wasn't safe to walk anywhere. The car jogged right then left and next to the hedge. The car idled up the gravel drive.

A brief rain had passed over the farm that afternoon, and the red roof tiles still glistened. Despite the destruction, that sweet smell of wet spring still greeted Iet as she opened her car door. The ground in front of her was littered with reams of damp white paper. She walked toward her home. It had no windows. The concussion of adjacent artillery blasts had shattered the glass and only jagged edges remained. Furniture, some recognizable and some not, sat in disarray both inside and outside the house. Piet and Anne had heard them arrive. Both looked tired and sad. The couple thanked the Duyuis's son-in-law before he drove off to see what remained of his own home. Iet walked inside the farmhouse. Forty dining room chairs lined the living and dining room areas, and shards of glass had piled up beneath the large front window frames.

The German command had used the house for their headquarters, and when the Canadians arrived, they commandeered the residence for the same purpose. Iet wandered up the wood staircase inspecting each room. Nothing much resembled the home she had left the previous fall. The Germans had made a mess of things. Several pieces of furniture had been added to the home, but many were missing. Iet came upon a few boxes of books and found her small collection of Grimm's fairy tales to compliment her work by Hans Christian Andersen. On the third floor the word "OF-FICE" had been hurriedly painted across the middle stile of a wood door in capital letters with white paint. The paint had dripped down the top of the "C" and the bottom of the "E" before drying. It was obviously the work of the Canadians.

Iet was the first child to arrive home, and that night she fell to sleep on a mattress in the dining room. The following day, she set about helping her mother and father put the home into order. She swept up the glass under each window and then worked loose the remaining shards that still clung to the edges of the frames. The chore left a small cut on one of her hands. As she worked, Piet and Anne organized beds and furniture.

When done with the more labor-intensive tasks of the day, Iet enjoyed searching the property for missing items. It satisfied that same part of her that enjoyed foraging for food in the woods during the war. There was neither rhyme nor reason to the scattering of their belongings. She located her silver napkin ring on the ground outside the home.

For nearly two weeks, Iet lived alone with her parents. This had never happened before, nor would it ever happen again, and Iet luxuriated in the attention of her mother and father. Her sister, Hanneke, would be the next to arrive.

IT HAD TAKEN over a month for Hanneke to receive her permit. It was stamped on June 15. Oom Louis, a cousin of Piet, had agreed to drive her home. Hanneke had perhaps endured the greatest hardships of any of the children that winter. She lived almost independently,

and for the last several months had been more a care-
giver than receiver, helping with the children and still
searching for food. She was terribly excited to return to
her mother and father and the farm.

The morning she departed Wormerveer was doubly
significant. As chance would have it, it not only marked
her homecoming, but also her emergence into womanhood. She had her first period. She didn't tell anyone
except for Oom Louis's wife Mieke who helped her
with the particulars. Hanneke was fifteen years old, and
she felt proud.

She arrived home to find her mom organizing pots
and pans in the kitchen. The Soetendael looked far better than it had two weeks earlier when her younger sister arrived, but there was still much work to be done.
Anne never slowed, and Hanneke took her place beside her mother. With each passing day, the family was
closer to restoring the home they had left.

BENNEKOM WAS STILL mostly uninhabited. To
receive a permit, you had to have a dwelling and many
were destroyed. Nearly all of the NSB'rs—those members of the political party who had sided with Hitler
and helped the Germans occupy Holland—were now
locked up in concentration camps and their homes sat
empty. The Germans, for obvious reasons, had left the
NSB'rs homes intact. But that was not to last.

The Dutch government, incensed at the ill-gotten
gains of most of the Nazi collaborators, clearly stated that any citizen of Holland could enter the empty home of any NSB member and remove from that
home whatever they needed for themselves. Hanneke
joined her mother on a short trip to one such home.
Anne had an eye for antiques and the two found a

beautiful old cupboard and brought it back with them to the Soetendael.

The baker soon returned to the village and fired up the brick ovens for the first time since the evacuation. The greengrocer followed, and Anne again had reason to go to the village and shop. It would be some time before the schools reopened, but the empty building had been put toward another use. The Germans had made such a mess of the village and scrambled everyone's belongings to such an extent that measures were needed to restore order. The villagers were instructed to bring any item they found in their home that wasn't theirs to the school. The Schoorls brought whatever orphaned furniture they could find and returned regularly to relocate their own missing valuables. When they found one of their own pieces, they attached a white card to it. After a few weeks, if no one else had made a similar claim, they were allowed to return the item to the Soetendael. They found several of their belongings. But many more were to be lost to the war forever.

RUUD HAD LEFT his uncle's farm soon after Hanneke had left Wormerveer. He was now thirteen and old enough to help rebuild the farm. Shortly after his arrival, he walked with his parents through the neighborhood of flattened homes and to the lab. The home still had a gaping hole where the bomb had fallen, and it was in the same general sad state as the Soetendael had been when Piet and Anne first returned to Bennekom. The bookshelf Piet and Leo had fastened to the wall had been pulled away and the doorway to the cellar was plainly exposed. Nearly all of the cellar's contents—all of those carefully hidden valuables— were gone.

Ruud found his violin on the ground next to its case in the backyard and amongst the rubble that had fallen on his parents. He was convinced that the two old ladies who had asked Piet to hide their suitcases had returned to retrieve them earlier in the war and in doing so had shown the Germans the hiding place. Obviously, the Germans took what they wanted.

The Red Cross set up a station in the village and handed out both clothes and furniture. A farmer from the village, whose home had been ruined, asked Piet and Anne if he could stay at the Soetendael temporarily along with his wife, four kids, and his livestock. As was their habit, Piet and Anne said yes, and soon the home was again alive with people and its pastures and barns put back to good use.

Nature continued its usual turning. The summer sun stretched the grass long, and the sparrows still played in the rafters of the hayloft. The fruit trees bloomed and budded and grew heavy with apples and pears. Piet restored his lab to working order, and the apples fell ripe as the summer came to its close. The farmer and his family eventually left.

Autumn brought with it the cold winds and the oaks and poplars shed their leaves. Classes began, and the three older children again awoke with their father, shared breakfast together, and left at orderly intervals to their respective schools, returning to the Soetendael to share lunch, and again when classes closed. The snows of winter arrived, and Christmas passed in peace. Yet despite the farm's reconciliation, it was, in fact, still incomplete. Those three seasons passed over the farm without the company of that quiet girl with the long auburn braids. It seemed as though she had simply been forgotten.

* * *

SHORTLY AFTER the tanks had paraded through Wormerveer, both Eline's and Marianne's parents travelled to Bergen aan Zee to fetch their children. In a single day, the village's newly liberated shoreline was transformed from the Nazis' natural buttress against the Allies and their war ships to just another gentle beach. This fact, coupled with the spring weather, beckoned a visit.

The Schoorls and the van der Pols and the van Leeuwens enjoyed their time. Hot tea was served in the van der Pols' garden, and everyone shed their shoes when they walked along the sandy coastal shores. The van Leeuwens took their daughter home to Rotterdam. Anne took Marianne to Wormerveer.

That my mother's friendship with Eline had come to its end was not mentioned. The two girls took the hands of their parents and parted ways just as abruptly as when their time together began on that dark night five years earlier. It seemed that whenever Mom's life found a rhythm, the war plucked her up and discarded her haphazardly. This day would be no different. Though Eline would travel back to Rotterdam with her parents, Marianne would not be so fortunate. Anne and Piet dropped her off at yet another strange home—this one belonging to the van Delft family in Wormerveer.

For Marianne, it did not matter that Mr. van Delft owned the Verkade cookie factory, or that he was as kind as he was wealthy. And it did not matter that he and his wife had also looked forward to caring for this particularly cute refugee. And it also didn't matter that their attic rivaled the one in Vreeland with its treasure of toys and its make-believe store filled with make-believe food, and all of its many dolls and many games. It wasn't home, and these weren't her people. It seemed to Mom that war had not really ended, and she continued inward.

While life at the Soetendael resumed without her, Mom had no choice but to follow her own routine. She would leave the large home in the mornings to walk to school alone. The three-story house had been built next to the canal and in company of several other proud residences, and she ambled through the shadows that the opulent building painted on the sidewalks. At school, Marianne's mind drifted. She didn't do well. It was as though she had finally retreated to the one place that had never forsaken her, the place she had built with grass and flowers of the Soetendael, and then the straw in the Kreugers' barn—that kind landscape in her mind. Mr. van Delft could sense the pigtailed girl drifting, and he tried to spoil her with his attention. He would give Mom a cookie, then offer another for a kiss on his cheek. His intentions were noble, but it did not matter. Marianne was irretrievable and his efforts, hopeless. She did not know why she wasn't able to return to the farm with her family. She did not ask. And, of course, no one explained.

During that winter, the canal next to the home froze, and the small boats tied to their moorings that used to bob and sway with the currents were fixed and fastened in place. Sinterklaas came and went. After the New Year of 1946, someone would finally fetch Marianne and bring her home to her beloved farm. However, she was no longer the girl who had sat in the back of that Red Cross truck, close to her bandaged mother and father as it rolled north and into the uncertainty of war. She had since suffered wounds that would refuse to heal, and they would continue to color her days until that very same war revisited her over four decades later, on a hot summer day while behind the wheel of her Subaru. And my mother would not be the only person it visited during that time.

WHEN THE WAR ended, Carla van Leeuwen remained at the Borst farm. She turned seventeen in 1945, and during the spring of that year she waited patiently for news of her mother and father, Leo and Estella. In her mother's last letter, Estella said that Leo was getting a nice tan from working outside and that the two were healthy.

Detailed news of the death camps slowly reached the soggy farms of Alkmaar. Eventually, Jan and Greet Borst had to help Carla come to terms with fact that her parents would not return. I doubt they waited very long to do so, because it was something the old farmer and his wife had already known for some time. During the war, detailed news of Carla's father's murder had somehow made it through the web that comprised the Dutch Underground and to Jan and Greet Borst. But the couple would never divulged these exact details to the child they had now pledged to raise as their own. And it was at their dairy farm that the orphaned Carla grew into womanhood. She eventually met and married a Jewish man, and the two immigrated to America. In time, they would sponsor my own parents' immigration, and so I became American.

When I interviewed Carla, she had told me that her parents had perished in Sobibor, but she had misspoken. What she had meant to say was that for most of her adult life she thought they both died in the camp. But just moments after the statement, she stood up from her small kitchen table. "A cousin of mine wrote a book," she said, as she walked to the living room to retrieve it. One of the elegant Dutch clocks on her wall rang twelve times. Carla returned. "He wrote a book about . . . would you like some more coffee?" She filled my small cup.

"He wrote a book for his children. Of course it's in Dutch." She opened it and handed it to me. The size and glossy pages resembled an expensive coffee-table book, the kind usually adorned with pictures of National Parks. I flipped the thick pages and looked at the photographs of original documents, letters, and portraits of the many van Leeuwens before, during, and after the holocaust. It was a thorough and enviable work. Her cousin had also unearthed the details of Estella and Leo's last days. The book had come into Carla's possession about the same time that my own mother was writing her war memoir. Her cousin had explained the events.

The Gestapo had indeed waited at the summerhouse for Estella and Leo. When the couple arrived that evening, the two were arrested. As Leo had suspected, someone had been watching the home, and the Germans knew the couple had a daughter. And they knew she was now in hiding. Leo and Estella refused to answer any questions. The police then divided the couple and took Leo to their headquarters where they continued to ask questions while torturing him.

Two years before I interviewed Carla, she had flown from California to Holland to visit. During her time there she visited my great aunt, Cor Borst, with whom she lived for those last years in Alkmaar. Cor was ninety. The two reminisced about their life together on the dairy farm, and they talked about the war. Not aware that anyone had ever explained exactly what happened to Leo, Cor wanted Carla to understand that Leo's love endured until his final moments "You know your father was a hero," she began.

During his last moments, Leo van Leeuwen had not only saved the life of his only child, but also the lives of countless others. Had he allowed the words to slip from his mouth, the Nazis would have found his daughter and also that old farmer who was hiding her at his dairy. And from there, the Germans would have easily connected the dots between this farmer's eldest daughter and that prisoner they already had locked up behind the barbed wire fences of Vught. It's likely everyone would have been lost.

Leo endured at the hands of the Nazis until the life slipped from his body. His wife died in the gas chambers of Sobibor.

Chapter 30

IWOULD INVEST years descending into this story, working to bring the events to life. At times, the heartache stopped all progress and with one elbow pressing down on my oak desk, I'd prop my chin in my palm and stare forward. I'd often weep.

I wrote in the mornings. Photos of my three children rest on my office windowsill. In one, I am in my twenties. My eldest son looks to be around two, naked and snuggled against my chest. My arms wrap around his butt, his around my neck, forehead buried against my thin beard. On some mornings, I would have to stop writing and go for a walk. Green grass or a gentle rain would help.

But as much as this story travels into some of humankind's darkest depravity, it is also a story of a fierce and triumphant love. And it always left me wanting to be a better person. A history professor with whom I shared the story suggested I title it "The Banality of Good," a play upon the phrase "the banality of evil" coined by Hannah Arendt to describe the acts of Adolf Eichmann, a chief facilitator of the Holocaust. She argued the possibility that Eichmann's crimes stemmed not from a single driving darkness, but a combination

of numerous, more benign choices—one selfish choice
followed by another—that culminated in the horrors
of the death camps. Conversely, my grandfather never
set out to be a hero and certainly didn't consider himself one. He did what he expected any good man to
do. One decision led to the next, each pulling Piet and
Anne deeper into the war. Largely, those seeking refuge within the couple's quiet farm survived, and their
very lives would act as a celebration of all the sacri-
fices endured. This was never more apparent to me than
during one of my final trips to Europe, when I rode a
high-speed train from Amsterdam to Paris—the pastures of Belgium and France streaking past at nearly
200 mph—to meet Eline van Leeuwen. She picked me
up at the train station and I was a guest in her home,
a classic Parisian apartment in an exclusive neighborhood of white, six-story stone buildings, each only a
touch different from the next, and all carefully appointed with architectural details reflecting the character of
Paris—ornate, proud, and fashionably precise.

The following morning, Eline opened the tall living room windows, then unfolded the heavy steel shut-
ters. The sounds of the street mixed with those of the
Bois de Boulogne, a wood just south of the Champs-
Élysées. Parisians walked their dogs, and an occasional
bike crossed over the cindered park trails. A refreshing
spring breeze moved through her spacious apartment.
"Can I get you some coffee?" she asked.

I relaxed on her couch. "Herman liked heavy furniture," she tells me. But she doesn't mean heavy in
the literal sense. The couch is full and round and the
smooth leather buttoned taut. The couple bought the
apartment forty years earlier and purchased each piece
of furniture and artwork carefully over time, an eclectic

mix of Paris, Holland, and Herman's eastern European ancestry. The end of one couch is stained dark where Herman used to rest his head. It's been two years since he died. Also a Jew, he had suffered immensely during the war and it haunted him until his last days as Alzheimer's gradually took ownership of his mind. A grand piano sits quietly in the corner of the room. I hadn't asked if anyone played.

After breakfast, we sat side-by-side on that couch looking at black-and-white photographs from the 1930s and '40s. Eline mostly laughs and giggles as she recalls her precocious youth. She is seventy now. "I can hardly believe it," she exclaimed in her bubbly fashion. She is animated and short, and always smiling, and one gets the sense that she is rarely ignored. When she looked at pictures of her father, she seemed to glow. Van Leeuwen means the "the lion," she tells me.

When the war ended, Leo and his family returned to their life in Rotterdam. He got his family settled and resurrected his commodities business. He also worked to locate Frau Broekman, the widow who had saved Leo's son, Carel. Leo provided her with a home and financial support and would continue to do so.

During those post-war years, Leo and Pauline would also make regular trips to Bennekom, visiting Piet and Anne at the Soetendael. When Pauline walked into Mr. Hartman's butcher shop, she would always dash behind the counter and, ignoring the fact that he was usually wrapped in a bloody apron, give him a large hug.

On the top of Eline's dark wood fireplace mantle sit two lion figurines. At first glance they look porcelain. But they are far too heavy. Leo purchased them shortly after his marriage. The male lion stands on all fours, and the female, with her muscled legs and sharp eyes, is lying down. The lioness looks formidable, her mate more so.

I continued to thumb through photos of Eline's past. In a caption underneath one of the family, snapped during a warm summer day in 1940, Pauline had written "Worrisome, but with wise guidance, Leo dragged his family through the war." Leo was not only born to the name of a lion, but he appears the part. He carries his sturdy frame and heavy shoulders in a confident, upright fashion. His thick hair, always with a distinct part down the middle, seems lion-like. "I always loved my father so much," Eline cooed. "I'm like my father. Carel is like my mother."

Eline is easy company and warm. She had left her parents' home at seventeen and lived in seven different countries working in tourism. She was a beautiful young woman—her blonde hair long and often pulled back to reveal the delicate lines of her face and her thin smile. Pauline did not approve of Eline dancing from country to country and implored her to find a husband and settle down. She finally met Herman Koeffler during her early twenties and married. Eline speaks seven languages. Her late husband spoke fourteen.

During my short stay with Eline, I was reminded of a feeling likely familiar to many adults when visiting their parents or older aunts and uncles. Despite my more-than-four decades of life, I was spoiled like a child. Eline had called my mother before I arrived asking what foods I enjoyed. When I needed to take the subway, she reached into her purse for tickets. Her maid washed and then ironed my t-shirts.

We conducted our interviews in the mornings, and then Eline would lead me through the splendors of Paris in the afternoons in her dark green Renault.

Just a few blocks from her home, a side street ended into the roundabout surrounding the Arc de Triomphe, the grand structure commissioned by Napoléon in the beginning of the 19th century, built of the same creamy golden stone that typifies most of the architecture prominent throughout the city. Five layers of thick traffic orbited the arch, and Eline hardly slowed as she veered into the heart of it. I clenched the door handle and pushed my feet into the floorboard. Eline glanced over at me. "Just don't look," she said, noticing my fear. I could not make the slightest sense of the traffic. Eline continued, cutting off every car to her left. Impact seemed imminent until the very last moment when the drivers of the oncoming cars braked for the little Renault.

"How does anyone know when to yield?" I asked almost wincing.

"It's all a matter of guts," she replied in her throaty accent, curling the "r" sound. A hint of satisfaction glimmered in her bright eyes. I took her advice and fixed my eyes on the passing buildings.

Eline knows every back road and shortcut and seemed to relish the role of host. When parallel parking on a narrow cobblestone hill in Montmartre, she bumped the car behind her. "In Paris, we call that a kiss." We walked beneath the white-domed Basilica of the Sacre-Coeur, which looks out on the vast city. When near Notre Dame, Eline pulled in front of the immense cathedral. "Take your time," she said. I'll wait for you by the taxis. And she took her place in a long line of vehicles, hers the only one without a white "TAXI" sign on the roof. This was clearly Eline's city. And as her guest, I had no place struggling through the normal tourist scrum.

We regularly dined throughout the famed city, on the peaceful Ile Saint Louis overlooking the Seine and in the bustling corridors in the heart of downtown, served by veteran Parisian waiters clearly cognizant of Eline's status as fellow senior resident. I made numerous efforts for the bill, but Eline dismissed these with the same iron resolve she used to navigate traffic. There was no chance.

During one of my final days with Eline, we walked close together down the Rue de la Paix toward Paris' premier opera house. It's easy to grow fond of Eline, fond of her gusto, her charm, and her gentle sweetness. "When you play Monopoly, this is the street you want to own," she said. We passed world famous jewelry stores and cafés. I could smell rain in the gusts of wind blowing through the avenue.

The grand opera house faced the street head-on as if the road had been built as its private driveway. Bright golden statues on the shoulders of the palatial building looked down upon the square. The cut stone and columns and carved filigree on the building's outside seemed modest when compared to its inside.

Two days earlier, when we passed the opera house for the first time, I casually mentioned how I would love to see a show there some day, envisioning a future trip with my wife. Eline and I now sat in the third row. The orchestra played Tchaikovsky and the ballet performed John Cranko's Onegin. Eline was somehow able to find last-minute tickets. It was the best of the best, as Eline put it.

It was not lost on me that this regal trip through Paris was in part tribute to my late grandparents. I felt a bit sheepish receiving Eline's generous attention. In a way, the same parts of me that lived so separate from my Dutch roots, made me feel like an imposter—a stranger gaining entrance into a world to which he had no right. But the week seemed to give Eline joy, and it was one I would never forget.

After the curtain fell, we stepped outside and down the stone stairs toward the square. The rain had come and gone and the cobblestones shimmered in the night light. The opera house glowed. Though born in Holland, Eline now has French citizenry. Her children were all raised in France. Two have since moved to Israel. Her daughter, who lives a short drive from Eline's home, followed in Leo's footsteps and trades commodities. Eline has numerous grandchildren.

"Do you feel more patriotic to Holland or to France?" I asked as we made our way to her Renault.

"Holland," She responded with a touch of reverence, speaking slowly. "Holland saved my life."

Marianne and Eline, after the war

Epilogue

A FEW YEARS after the war, the Schoorl family would say goodbye to the Soetendael for the final time. Though the children felt the home belonged to them as much as they to it, Piet had only leased the farm, and its legal owners planned to return. The pathways the children had worn into the pastures would soon grow over, and the kitchen would no longer fill with the aroma of Anne's soups. The family continued to live in Bennekom for several more years, moving into another large home, with its own unique character, but the Soetendael—that Sweet Dell—would remain within all of the Schoorls' children forever; the memories of that gentle farm mixed with images of all who had found sanctuary within its borders.

As the seasons turned, the war grew more distant. Anne would eventually give birth to two more boys, and the couple worked hard to maintain a large family in the lean post-war years. Dr. Schoorl's lab struggled to earn a profit, and Anne rented out rooms to help pay the bills. One of the new tenants was another scientist, Dr. C. J. Briejer, who used the room during business trips to the region. Legend has it that the first time

Dr. Briejer's young son, Martin—my father—met his future wife, he threw a rock at her.

My mom and dad still live in their home, nestled in the woods adjacent to the Hood Canal. They're working through the last of their eighth decade and are slowing. My father still loyally tends his deep rows of dahlias imported from Holland. Mom, her white hair thinning and wispy, is usually found in her garden or sewing room. She is a prolific quilter and an out-of-control gardener. In only the last year, she's accepted that her body cannot always endure her ambitions. For nearly sixty years, her garden provided equal parts refuge and stage. My parents' garden rivals most parks, and Mom's worn her shoulders almost to the bone—literally. She explains that she is learning to garden less, but when I look out from her deck, I regularly see new sections of their seven acres that she has conquered with a streak of wildflowers or a fresh cedar hedge.

Piet and Marianne

My mom is happy, and it's not come to her easily. A survivor, she has always forged forward. It's a family quality. Mom has also always worked to do the right thing. Growing up, she collected people—strays from varying backgrounds, lured into our warm house with home-cooked meals and cheerful company. It was not unusual to see a dozen people squeezed around the dinner table. A few years back, she helped a family raise quintuplets. As of late, she's been more restrained in this regard. Though Mom may not agree, or appreciate the assertion, I see a lot of Anne in Mom, Anne's strengths and weaknesses. Equally, I am my mother's son.

I now make efforts to arrive at Mom and Dad's with a meal in tow, and recently visited with my 13-year-old son and a bag of take-out from my favorite old-school Italian delicatessen. Mom heated her homemade soup to complement the meal.

Lately, she's been scrapbooking, and she showed off her new photo album of our ancestors, dating back to the 1800s. Later, we looked at photos taken during the war.

MY SIBLINGS AND I grew up in the shadow of World War II. I believe we've walked through a good part of life afraid of something that we had no way of understanding, children of parents who regularly sneaked an unconscious peek backwards, with scared eyes. Thusly, it seems we've all found ways to add some flesh and bone to this specter. My eldest sister has worked nearly her entire adult life as a labor and delivery nurse, the first twenty of those years at the University of Washington Hospital, which attracts the hardest cases. I once met a young doctor in residence who had worked with my sister during her OB rotations. She mentioned that my sister could at times be abrasive, as she didn't suffer newly minted doctors easily, but if a delivery turned potentially deadly, she said my sister was the nurse you hoped was in the room. In earlier years, I worked out some of my fears a few thousand feet up on the clean granite walls of Yosemite's El Capitan. My younger brother has a bad habit of crashing hang gliders.

Anne at her spinning wheel

MOM SAT ACROSS from me, turning the pages of her album. Post-war photos of her and her father drew my eye. One in particular looks especially tender—Mom appears to be in her late teens and pretty, her hair in thick braids. The two lean in towards each other. Their smiles look serene. I wonder if, when posing for this photo, my grandfather still believed his children could help change the world. On numerous occasions, Piet's children told me that the war had taken parts of their father that would never entirely return—that he carried wounds that would not mend. However, I have also listened to stories of Piet's vitality and resilience, and he continued into the latter half of his life as a prominent scientist and a good father. I did not know him. I have only dim memories of his few visits to our home in California. Scoliosis had curved his spine and he walked with a cane, his back hunched sharply.

"Eventually, his spine curved so severely, a rib cracked and punctured his heart," my mom said. "Or at least that's my story—the one I remember. Iet and Hans have a different story." Whether or not Mom remembers correctly, the imagery is potent. Piet departed our world on October 25, 1980.

Anne would survive her husband by fifteen years, and she remains in my memory as strong, intelligent, and a bit prickly. But it's necessary to underline that my memories are those of an outsider. I saw Anne through the filter of my mother's eyes, as well as those of the self-absorbed teenager that I was when I spent time with Anne—perhaps only a couple months of my life in total. When one of my cousins read the pages of an early manuscript of this book, she felt it necessary to share her warm and fond memories of her grandmother—the one she visited regularly throughout her childhood—the grandmother who patiently taught her to spin and knit. It's not hard for me to envision this part of Anne. And I like to think that this part lives within these pages. I can see Anne's large heart and the gentler embers of her fiery spirit—that spirit that seemed able to will life to her demands. Anne's death—also as remembered by my mother—appears equally telling. "One day, Mom just decided that she was done with life," Mom said. "She got into bed, refused to drink or eat, and then died."

WEST OF JERUSALEM, on the pined flanks of Mount Herzl, the Jewish nation built the sprawling memorial named Yad Vashem in remembrance of the holocaust. If you wander down the Avenue of the Righteous, you can find a tree planted in memory of my grandparents. On March 1, 1980, only months before Piet's death, the couple was recognized as *Righteous Among the Nations*, the highest honor Yad Vashem bestows on non-Jews.

The coin awarded to Piet and Anne as
"Righteous Among the Nations"

Acknowledgments

To consider the long list of personal accomplishments that would not be possible without the loving support of my wife Kristin is humbling. To write is to partly battle one's frailty, and Kristin—with her unfailing ability to see and nurture the best parts of me—could always be counted on to cheer me forth. And she did so while also gracefully sacrificing that most coveted resource necessary to write a book, time.

This work amply testifies to the contributions of my mother and her siblings, Hanneke, Iet, and Ruud, as well as Eline van Leeuwen, Ruth de Leeuwe, and Carla Polak—without them, there simply is no story. Each was not only exceedingly generous with their time but also placed their memories in my care with few expectations. Though this work captures only a small piece of their experiences, I hope that it allows an enduring window into their past and that each will forgive the limits of my skill.

I am also very thankful for the timely emergence of Judith Jones and her keen and kind editing skill. Without her, these pages would still sit patiently in the corner of my office awaiting a willing suitor.

About the Author

Nicholas Briejer earned a Masters of Fine Arts from Antioch University, focusing on nonfiction. He teaches writing and literature at Pierce College. When not writing or teaching, he can often be found with his youngest son, chasing surf in the cold waters of the Washington coast.

He can be reached at www.thesweetdell.com.

CPSIA information can be obtained
at www.ICGtesting.com
Printed in the USA
FSHW012014240919
62366FS